Charlie Chapli

M000296256

Richard Carr's *Charlie Chaplin* places politics at the centre of the filmmaker's life as it looks beyond Chaplin's role as a comedic figure to his constant political engagement both on and off the screen.

Drawing from a wealth of archival sources from across the globe, Carr provides an in-depth examination of Chaplin's life as he made his way from Lambeth to Los Angeles. From his experiences in the workhouse to his controversial romantic relationships and his connections with some of the leading political figures of his day, this book sheds new light on Chaplin's private life and introduces him as a key social commentator of the time.

Whether interested in Hollywood and Hitler or communism and celebrity, *Charlie Chaplin* is essential reading for all students of twentieth-century history.

Richard Carr is a Senior Lecturer in History and Politics at Anglia Ruskin University, Cambridge, UK. His previous publications include *Veteran MPs and Conservative Politics in the Aftermath of the Great War: The Memory of All That* (2013). He has also co-authored the books *Alice in Westminster: The Political Life of Alice Bacon* (2016) and *The Global 1920s* (2016).

Charlie Chaplin
A Political Biography
from Victorian Britain to
Modern America

Richard Carr

Routledge
Taylor & Francis Group

LONDON AND NEW YORK

First published 2017
by Routledge
2 Park Square, Milton Park, Abingdon, Oxon OX14 4RN

and by Routledge
711 Third Avenue, New York, NY 10017

*Routledge is an imprint of the Taylor & Francis Group,
an informa business*

British Library Cataloguing-in-Publication Data
A catalogue record for this book is available from the
British Library

Library of Congress Cataloging-in-Publication Data
Names: Carr, Richard, 1985– author.
Title: Charlie Chaplin : a political biography from Victorian Britain
    to modern America.
Description: Milton Park, Abingdon, Oxon : New York, NY :
    Routledge, 2017. | Series: Routledge historical biographies |
    Includes bibliographical references and index.
Identifiers: LCCN 2016048529 | ISBN 9781138923256 (hardback :
    alk. paper) | ISBN 9781138923263 (pbk. : alk. paper) |
    ISBN 9781315201672 (ebook)
Subjects: LCSH: Chaplin, Charlie, 1889–1977. | Chaplin, Charlie,
    1889–1977—Political and social views. | Motion picture actors
    and actresses—United States—Biography.
Classification: LCC PN2287.C5 C35 2017 | DDC 791.43092/
    33092 [B]—dc23
LC record available at https://lccn.loc.gov/2016048529

ISBN: 978-1-138-92325-6 (hbk)
ISBN: 978-1-138-92326-3 (pbk)
ISBN: 978-1-315-20167-2 (ebk)

Typeset in Sabon
by Apex CoVantage, LLC

Contents

Figures

Tables

Acknowledgements

This project has almost been as global as Chaplin's life. Along the way its author has racked up innumerable debts. My employers at Anglia Ruskin University (ARU) have been generous with research funding as and where appropriate. Alison Ainley has been a model of support and kindness at the top of the Humanities and Sciences tree at ARU. Teaching history and politics alongside Lucy Bland, Jon Davis, Sean Lang, Rohan McWilliam, Luke Cooper and Susan Flavin remains a pleasure. I've leant on the historical expertise of the first four to read through chapters of this work, and particular gratitude is due for that. My apologies to all students who have had to suffer my crowbarring Chaplin into every subject under the Sun. I should say I'll stop, but I won't.

Many archivists have helped along the way with this project and the following is a no doubt massively incomplete list. Nevertheless, Bill Davis at the National Archives, Washington, D.C answered a rather hasty request for access to HUAC material incredibly swiftly. Allen Packwood and Katharine Thomson at my old stomping ground of the Churchill Archives Centre (CAC), Cambridge, UK have been as helpful as ever. Jennifer Hadley at Wesleyan University, Middletown, Connecticut went above and beyond in chasing down an obscure Social Credit link. Marti Gibbs was very welcoming in allowing this historian to wade through the Strachey papers. To all who digitised material that appears in this book's archival bibliography – many thanks indeed. Permissions to utilise the various photographs that appear here are also gratefully received.

On matters Chaplin, Kate Guyonvarch, Cecilia Cenciarelli and Nicole Meystre-Schaeren were incredibly helpful in many ways as I made my way through the Chaplin trail of Paris–Bologna–Montreux, respectively. Through them, my wider gratitude is expressed to the Chaplin Office, Cineteca di Bologna and Les Archives de Montreux, too.

Although all errors, opinions and anything else remain my responsibility alone, this work has been vastly improved through the help of others. Audiences in Cambridge and Bologna who have heard my various papers and presentations on all things Chaplin have no doubt helped sharpen some of the arguments that appear here. Lord Robert Armstrong is thanked in the bibliography for his recollections on the issue of Charlie's knighthood, but a further such acknowledgement is deserved here. At Routledge, I must thank Catherine Aitken, Bob Pearce and Laura Pilsworth for being unstintingly helpful in the production process for this book. The anonymous reviewers for the initial proposal doubtless whipped some of the more nonsensical claims into shape, as did the reviewer of the manuscript itself. I should also acknowledge the comments of Professor Steven J. Ross who, in an earlier version of the proposal for this book, pointed the author in some very fruitful directions. In terms of other US folks, I first discussed a Chaplin book with David Singerman in a Pepperpot at Churchill College, the University of Cambridge, more than a decade ago, so his views on this manuscript are both gratefully received and only appropriate. Another ex-Churchillian Bradley Hart is at least owed a further pint at Little Woodrow's, Houston for reading through this manuscript and offering valuable suggestions. Our watching huge American flags fly over car lots with pro-Donald Trump shock jocks on the radio while on the drive to Liberty, Texas was certainly an eye opener. Equally, Dominic Rustecki and Tom Shakespeare (DPR) offered useful thoughts on Chaplin's private life and his South London background, too.

I should finally thank those who have lived with this project as it has evolved over the years. The two felines have been lovely company during the writing process. Larry: most cats don't bring in rabbits, take note. Molly: well done for recognising that. To mum thanks for all the support (and Chaplin gifts) over the years. But as ever, I am most grateful to Sarah. I may have been working for the past four years on a historical figure who was often a night mare of a husband, but I am very lucky indeed to have married such a wonderful wife. All my love, as ever.

Chronology

Date	Personal/Filmic events	Political activities	Global context
1889	C[harlie] C[haplin] born in London, UK		
1894	First appearance on stage by CC		
1896, 1898	CC enters the workhouse for a combined total of thirty-two days		
1898	CC joins the Eight Lancashire Lads	CC travels around the UK, seeing poverty throughout the land	
1899–1902		CC finds Boer War patriotism distasteful	Protracted Boer War campaign eventually won by Britain
1901	CC's father dies, aged thirty-seven		
1903	After several trips in/out of infirmaries, asylums and workhouses, Hannah Chaplin committed as a lunatic		
1903–6	CC plays Billy in *Sherlock Holmes* for H.A. Saintsbury		

(continued)

(continued)

Date	Personal/Filmic events	Political activities	Global context
1906			Election of interventionist Liberal government in the UK
1908	CC joins the Fred Karno Company (until 1913); meets/falls in love with Hetty Kelly		
1911, 1912, 1913	In the US with Karno Company tours		
1913	Signs with Keystone Film Company ($150 a week)		
1914	Film career takes off – *Kid Auto Races at Venice* features first appearance of Tramp character; signs contract to join Essanay ($1,250 per week)		Britain enters the First World War
1915	Tramp character matures in films such as *The Bank*; CC meets Mildred Harris for the first time	CC employs Rob Wagner, later to become something of a political mentor	
1916	Signs with Mutual Film Corp. ($10,000 per week)		The Battle of the Somme
1917	CC signs 'Million Dollar a Year' contract with First National	*The Immigrant* seems to criticise the notion of America as 'the land of the free'; CC faces charges of 'shirking' military service by	Russian revolution; the US enters the First World War

1918	Marries Mildred Harris; their son (Norman Spencer) dies after three days (1919)	CC takes active part in Liberty Bond drives for British and American governments; *The Bond* and *Shoulder Arms* released backing the war effort; CC first meets Upton Sinclair	Allied victory in the First World War
1919	United Artists launched by CC, Douglas Fairbanks, Mary Pickford and others	CC hears Max Eastman speak on the subject of 'Hands Off Russia'	
1920	CC employs Lita Grey for the first time	CC extols the virtues of communism over a beer with Buster Keaton	Palmer Raids (1919–20) in the US suggest growing climate of anti-communism; Republicans win the White House (to hold until 1933)
1921	Releases *The Kid*, which contains numerous allusions to his own impoverished childhood	CC praises Henry Ford; returns to Europe to promote *The Kid* where he makes numerous political statements; reads C.H. Douglas's work on Social Credit	Arbuckle case leads to accusations of Hollywood debauchery

(continued)

(continued)

Date	Personal/Filmic events	Political activities	Global context
1922		MPPDA formed to self-regulate the movie industry – CC against; start of FBI surveillance against CC	Benito Mussolini becomes Italian Prime Minister
1924	To circumvent Californian law, CC marries Lita Grey in Mexico (two sons born, 1925/6); works on *The Gold Rush* (1925)		
1927	CC's divorce from Lita Grey becomes headline news and, later, a political weapon; makes *The Circus* (1928)	IRS seeks *c.*$1.35 million of unpaid income tax from CC; his wealth then estimated at $16 million	
1929		Winston Churchill visits CC on the set of *City Lights* (1931)	Wall Street Crash
1930		Ivor Montagu brings Soviet director Sergei Eisenstein to Hollywood to meet CC	Oswald Mosley resigns from British Labour government and begins his journey to fascism
1931–2	CC's world tour to promote *City Lights*; meets Gandhi, Mosley, MacDonald, German Reichstag deputies, Einstein and more	Extensive political chronology in Chapter 5; includes praise for Mussolini's Italy	

1933	Plans for *Modern Times* (1936) begin to take shape; Alistair Cooke brought in to help with the script (removed from this role, 1934)	CC gives radio address in support of FDR	Hitler becomes Chancellor of Germany; Roosevelt inaugurated as US President
1934		Social Credit movement attempt to gain CC's explicit public support; CC described as a 'nerve killing fidgeting Jew', in Nazi propaganda	Upton Sinclair runs his 'End Poverty in California' campaign, endorsed by CC
1935		Soviets claim that *Modern Times* will depict the 'struggle against capitalism'; English leftist John Strachey drafts a script for an unused Napoleon film	
1936	*Modern Times* released; CC marries Paulette Goddard		Hitler invades the de-militarised Rhineland
1938		CC praises Mussolini's Italy and Hitler's Germany before, later in the year, beginning work on *The Great Dictator* (1940)	Munich Agreement between UK, France, Italy and Germany averts war temporarily; Martin Dies assumes control of the House Committee on Un-American Activities (HUAC)

(continued)

(continued)

Date	Personal/Filmic events	Political activities	Global context
1939		British Foreign Office makes enquiries trying to tone down political content of Chaplin's film; CC pledges that all profits from *The Great Dictator* will go to helping European Jewry	Britain and France declare war on Nazi Germany
1940	*The Great Dictator* released; Churchill sees and enjoys the film	White House sources praise *The Great Dictator*	Hitler's Wehrmacht sweeps through most of Western and Northern Europe
1942	CC's affair with Joan Barry occurs, which will later lead to two court cases over the Mann Act and a paternity suit (both 1944)	CC gives several speeches endorsing the Soviet war effort and demanding the Western democracies launch a 'second front' against Hitler	The murder of European Jewry through the Holocaust is sped up after the German invasion of the Soviet Union (1941)
1943	CC marries Oona O'Neill, with whom he will have eight children		
1945			Allied victory in the Second World War; President Truman authorises dropping of atomic bomb

	respectable' end of American cinema industry from the 'Hollywood Ten' of those who refuse to testify before HUAC
	means that CC's loyalty to America is heavily questioned; CC called to testify before HUAC, although eventually does not have to do so
1952	*Limelight* released
	Attorney General James McGranery revokes CC's re-entry permit when he leaves the country to promote *Limelight* on grounds of political affiliation and moral turpitude
1950s	Releases *A King in New York* (1956), which mocks the McCarthyite mood that had gripped America
	Meets Nikita Khrushchev and Nehru; awarded International Peace Prize by the World Council of Peace (1953)
1960s	Last of CC's children born (1962); *My Autobiography* published (1964); releases *A Countess of Hong Kong* (1967)
1972	Awarded temporary visa to visit the US; awarded Special Academy Award in Los Angeles
	The Nixon White House refuses to meet CC
1975	Awarded a Knighthood by Queen Elizabeth II
1977	CC dies on Christmas Day

Introduction: A very political life

To cut a long story short, we need to view Charlie Chaplin's undeniably famous films as a component piece in a much more complex puzzle: Chaplin's real-life politics and what others made of them. In essence, the following thereby invites the reader to take a cinematic comedian seriously almost the entire time – no small feat. Yet the politics-centred approach outlined in this book merely serves to restore the creator of the Little Tramp to the way that many saw him during his lifetime. Indeed, comments along these lines were frequent. For his dining companion and sometime host Winston Churchill, 'the real Chaplin, as revealed to those who, like myself, have had the pleasure of meeting him in private life, is by no means funny. He is a man of character and culture.'[1] For another confidant, the 1934 left-wing Democratic Candidate for Governor of California Upton Sinclair, Chaplin's work – especially those films with 'undercurrent[s] of tragedy' – gave 'tremendous meaning to *everything* we are witnessing' and 'will earn you the gratitude of millions of people whom you have never seen'.[2] Fundamentally, therefore, Chaplin was never viewed as *just* a clown, but as a social commentator whose views could be dangerous or inspirational depending on one's own political leaning. He was, as his great biographer David Robinson describes, *The Mirror of Opinion*.[3]

Partly due to Chaplin's own impoverished background in Victorian South London, his later filmic commentary often meant supporting the dispossessed. His most famous creation of course was a *tramp*: 'a bum with a bum's philosophy' to quote his friend and sometime rival Buster Keaton.[4] Indeed, the very notion that the cane-twirling vagabond had any kind of 'philosophy' speaks to the near endless contemporary speculation on what experience or moment in Chaplin's early life had driven its creation. As no less a luminary than Sigmund Freud pointed out, Chaplin 'cannot get away from those [childhood] impressions and to this day he obtains for himself the compensation for the frustrations and humiliations of that past period of his life'.[5] But the point was that Chaplin was about more than the tramp, and his artistic creations were generally viewed as symptomatic of a far more serious agenda. By way of brief illustration, according to one British Foreign Office memorandum in the late 1930s, Charlie's 'racial and social sympathies are with those groups and classes which have suffered most'.[6] Unlike some of the political aspersions cast on Chaplin, this Whitehall verdict was no doubt true – and indeed more or less summed up the plots of *The Great Dictator* (1940) and *Modern Times* (1936), respectively. Yet whatever the veracity of its content, such a document is arguably odd in that it exists at all. The very fact that British diplomats were exchanging a flurry of correspondence over Chaplin in the fateful summer of 1939 suggests that this is someone whose politics could do with further review. That is the purpose of this book.

To view Chaplin in this new light, this work draws on a whole host of under-utilised archival sources. Chaplin lived a global life and has thus left behind an internationally scattered collection of material that numerous accounts of his work have overlooked.[7] This study corrects that imbalance. Since Chaplin was a British subject his whole life, the Foreign Office and Security Service material held at the National Archives at Kew, London, provides valuable insights into the way those in the corridors of power of his homeland treated him. Likewise, key British archival collections, such as those of Winston Churchill (held in Cambridge), Oswald and Cynthia Mosley (Birmingham), the Society for the Protection of Science and Learning (Oxford) and the Astors (Reading) offer material related to Chaplin's political thoughts at various points, as well as just helping to pinpoint his movements. The British side of Chaplin's archival trail has arguably been particularly overlooked, perhaps understandably, by an American-centric approach to his life to date.

To be fair, living as he did in America from 1914 until 1952, a plethora of archives across the continental United States also help highlight the recollections of Chaplin insiders, such as Harry Crocker (Los Angeles, CA) and Upton Sinclair (Bloomington, IN), as well as the outpourings of direct opponents like Martin Dies (Liberty, TX). These are utilised here. Above and beyond these accounts, the American establishment's views on Chaplin will be outlined through material held not only by various Presidential Libraries, but also by the Federal Bureau of Investigation (FBI), the Library of Congress and National Archives (all Washington, D.C.). And, finally, there is the 'Chaplin trail' of material running from the office of his estate in Paris to the reams of newspaper material in Montreux, Switzerland (near his final residence) to the digitised Chaplin archive currently held in Bologna, Italy. In utilising British, continental European and American archival leads (and more), this study is able to connect political dots that other studies have overlooked. In doing so, it arguably forms a more overtly political companion text to Chuck Maland's wonderful work on Chaplin's *Star Image* and the cult of celebrity that followed him.[8]

And yet for all the new combination of sources presented here, it would be disingenuous to claim that this is the first work to discuss Chaplin's politics. Filmic accounts, including Walter Kerr's *The Silent Clowns*, contain the odd flash of political insight, as does Kyp Harness's work on *The Art of Charlie Chaplin*.[9] The notion of the Little Tramp as a working-class hero bravely resisting the forces of capitalism has been touched on by Eric L. Flom's survey of Chaplin's talkies, while the literature on Hollywood's collaboration with Nazi Germany has swelled over the last decade – with accounts by Thomas Doherty and Ben Urwand igniting a controversial debate that has obvious ramifications for a biography of the creator of *The Great Dictator*, Adenoid Hynkel.[10] On a wider scale, Steven J. Ross's accounts of *Working Class Hollywood* and *Hollywood Left and Right* deserve all the praise they have received for their intertwining of Hollywood and American politics, and the latter includes an insightful chapter on Chaplin.[11] Moreover, Owen Hatherley has recently explored the connections between Chaplin and the USSR to much acclaim, and Libby Murphy has provided an important and rigorous discussion of Chaplin's reception in France, too.[12] No book is an island, and this work undeniably builds on a substantial body of work. The British end could do with some buttressing, but there is little doubt that Chaplin has been a well-studied figure.[13]

For all that, two gaps in the literature emerge. The above works notwithstanding, many accounts of the politics of film still under play both the relatively developed nature of Chaplin's ideology and his overall place in the story. In Larry Ceplair and Steven Englund's studious 1983 work on *The Inquisition in Hollywood* Chaplin is an incidental character mostly reduced to the margins of a broader red-baiting story.[14] More recently, Urwand's study of the late 1930s alludes to *The Great Dictator* but, given its remit naturally extends beyond the Tramp, treating the issue as an episodic debate about Hollywood, rather than exploring its ramifications for Chaplin the man.[15] Chaplin is thus parcelled off as one of Hollywood's nobler lights. In this specific context, this was no doubt true, but things were neither so completely black and white when it came to fascism for Charlie, nor was officialdom completely out of line for being suspicious of him. If academic and commentators have paid attention to, for example, Benjamin Disraeli's literary career or the extra-political writings of a Boris Johnson or a Winston Churchill, then the process deserves to be run in reverse. Culture can bleed into politics, but the opposite is also true.

Second, there is also a tendency among film scholars, understandably enough, to prioritise interpreting possible political 'meanings' of Chaplin's cinematic output at the expense of looking at the people he was definitely meeting and the things he was actually saying. This account is not a shot-by-shot reading of Charlie's films. It would be difficult to write a biography of the man without mentioning his films at all, but in large part they are not the focus here. Instead, this book restores Chaplin to what he was for many – a political operator turned lobbyist who happened to be in the business of making world-class cinema. The volume of FBI files on Chaplin, for example, were almost exclusively concerned with Charlie Chaplin the living, breathing man and the supposed 'radicals' he was associating with – not the meanderings of the Little Tramp or if and when Charlie should move from making silent cinema to the talkies. J. Edgar Hoover had other, and, for him, more important interests. There is a strong literature on such cinematic topics, and other accounts do it better than here.

Instead, this study rather borrows from political science theory and the work of scholars such as John Street. For Street, the very notion of a *celebrity politician* can and must be cut two ways. While scholars have written much on what Street calls 'Celebrity Politician (CP) 1' – elected legislators such as Tony Blair, Barack Obama or Justin Trudeau who use the cult of celebrity to aid their room for political manoeuvre – less attention has been given to 'CP 2' – 'the entertainer who pronounces on politics and claims the right to represent peoples and causes'.[16] Partially as a by-product of celebrity activists such as Russell Brand, George Clooney and Angelina Jolie, and the politicalisation of comedy (including Jon Stewart, John Oliver and Matt Forde), the scholarly CP1–CP2 gap has narrowed of late, but a study that explicitly addresses this with reference to Chaplin has much to add.

There are specific areas of advocacy that can be expanded upon. For example, Kenneth Lynn's *Chaplin and His Times* allows just over a page for discussion of Chaplin's decision not to enlist in the British or American armies during the Great War.[17] David Robinson discusses his belief in the related causes of Social Credit and a version of quantitative easing at a similar length in his classic *Chaplin: His Life and Art*.[18] More recently, Peter Ackroyd gets through his entire trenchant biography without mentioning Henry Ford, Oswald Mosley or John Strachey at all.[19] That is not necessarily a criticism – they are different types of books to this. But it does suggest that a monograph-length consideration of Chaplin's politics may have something to bring to the table. At just over 100,000 words this work constitutes less than half the size of either Robinson's magisterial tome or Lynn's incisive analysis, and the trade-offs with regard to comprehensiveness versus a punchy account are readily acknowledged. There will be more work for scholars to do on his politics in years to come, but this book can certainly help nudge that debate on.

Throughout, we will not adopt a universally linear structure but rather jump back and forth between periods of time. Our goal is to draw out different themes of Chaplin's life, not chronicle his every waking moment. Through nine main chapters the goal of this book is to tease out aspects of the political Chaplin, and this can be best done through a thematic approach. To begin with then, while his impoverished origins provided much of the inspiration for the feel, look and motivations of his Little Tramp character they also, as Chapter 1 makes clear, imbued within him an initial antipathy to the idea of the state as a force for good. Partly due to timing and the broader political climate in which he grew up, these early years also meant that Chaplin's politics were always rather idiosyncratic, and not easily reduced to one particular label. Although he was never a communist, he cannot always be completely pigeon-holed as, for instance, an interventionist European social-democrat either. In many ways Charlie would flip-flop between positions – not unlike many a politician in his or any other day. But this does not diminish his political seriousness. If Britain's Ramsay MacDonald could move from the Labour Party's first ever Prime Minister to leading a de facto Conservative administration in a matter of weeks in the autumn of 1931, we perhaps should not be too harsh if Charlie occasionally jumped from socialist to anarchist sympathies.

The First World War shook Charlie's political kaleidoscope some more, as it did so many. Here, as our second chapter makes clear, the fact that he did not perform active military service during the defining moment of his generation would bring a whole series of political consequences for the man in the coming years. Equally, the fact that this period saw him make a staggering amount of money on the one hand and marry his first 'child bride' on the other set up two further sources of opprobrium for any would-be political opponents. In not fighting from 1914 to 1918, Charlie would thereby pave the way for several fights that would dog his career for decades to come. As Republican Senator Harry Cain put it in 1949, 'Chaplin has sat out in luxurious comfort in two wars in which his native Britain and his hospitable United States were involved, in the defense of those freedoms which he perverts so glibly.'[20] This would be a continual refrain from those who opposed his progressive politics.

Once Allied victory in the war had been secured, however, Chaplin considered the type of world he wished to build. Chapter 4 will make clear how his political reach was already coming under fire due to his controversial relationships with several very young women, but, prior to it, the third chapter shows he was having his world view shaped by interactions with several left-wing thinkers – not least the radical pamphleteer Max Eastman and Chaplin's own employee, Rob Wagner. Together with Upton Sinclair, these figures shaped Chaplin's vague sympathies for the American (and British) working man into a more positive line on the recent communist takeover in Russia. Indeed, according to a letter from the US Department of Justice to J. Edgar Hoover, Director of the FBI, by 1922 Chaplin stood as 'an active part of the Red movement in this country'.[21] Except it was a good deal more complicated than the anti-Chaplin forces in D.C. would have it. At the same time that Charlie was breaking bread with those praising Vladimir Lenin or, over a cold beer, trying to convince Buster Keaton that communism was the future, he was one of the most successful capitalists of his era, and praised other such innovators – most starkly Henry Ford – to the hilt. After all, ultimately, he would form United Artists to make money, not to constitute the cinematic wing of *The Daily Worker*. If in the 1920s the 'business of America was business' – to paraphrase Republican President Calvin Coolidge – than Charlie was not averse to taking advantage of this atmosphere. Precisely because he had grown up with so little money, Charlie was always more about his own capital than he was *Das Kapital*.

We then turn to what Chaplin did in the aftermath of the Wall Street Crash of 1929. In Chapter 5 we look not only at Chaplin's world tour of 1931–2 but how it served important political purposes above and beyond promoting the majesty of *City Lights*. Touring through a Britain on the verge of seeing its Labour government fall from office unable to address the slump, an Italy seemingly revitalised under Mussolini and a Berlin soon to fall to Nazi takeover, Chaplin would not only be a satirist of the major events of the 1930s, but a key witness to them. Along the way he would not only avariciously read economy theorists from John Maynard Keynes to C.H. Douglas, but he sat down and wrote his own concrete schemes to address the world's ills. Chapter 6 then shows how he brought these political ideas home. Looking at the road to what became *Modern Times*, we chart Charlie's support for Roosevelt's New Deal, as well as the Upton Sinclair inspired 'E.P.I.C.' programme that sat well to the left of a very interventionist White House. His political activities would certainly *extend* to the big screen, but this was simply the tip of the iceberg.

The final three chapters then look at Chaplin on the world stage. Beginning with *The Great Dictator* in Chapter 7, we explore Charlie's complicated and changing relationship to fascism. Given his early hatred of state power (a position he would return to in the 1940s) and the hard evidence of *The Great Dictator*, it is understandable why Charlie should have been judged as a total and unwavering anti-fascist. Rather like Churchill, he ended up on the right side of history by 1939–40, and all else is forgotten. And, certainly, the Nazi regime's anti-Semitism was always completely anathema to him, partially due to familial and romantic connections. Yet there are two factors we also need to build into this picture – factors that do not override this ingrained perception, but should nuance it somewhat. On the one hand, once he decided to make the picture, Charlie faced down significant pressure from major governments and his own industry to stop production. It was a brave move to resist it, not least commercially. This remains to his eternal credit. Yet equally, before he decided to make *The Great Dictator*, the man who would go on to play Adenoid Hynkel was not without a kind word for elements of the Italian fascist regime, or indeed other fascists such as Oswald Mosley. In many ways this chapter therefore desanctifies the way that Chaplin is viewed vis-à-vis fascism, but makes him all the more human (and arguably, therefore, all the more impressive).

Having taken on Hitler, Chapter 8 then deals with how Charlie viewed Stalin and the Red Army, and how this stance was received in America. As we will see, words designed to encourage America and Britain's ally the Soviet Union in 1942 would go on to become Exhibit A for those who wanted to rid the country of an allegedly 'un-American' actor. This chapter therefore considers how Chaplin's sex life and his politics intertwined once more. It details how this 'cockney cad' – a double insult, taking in both his refusal to become an American citizen on the one hand and his nefarious activities in the bedroom on the other – faced a trial under the Mann Act (for sexual impropriety) before being hit by the terms of the McCarran Act (for alleged communist sympathy) six years later. Chapter 9 ends our story on Charlie's years in Swiss exile, his final political views, as well as an eventual reconciliation – of sorts – with America.

Before beginning, it must be said that many limitations dog any analysis of Chaplin. The first is that for much of his early life there is scant contemporary source for either his whereabouts or his opinions. Much is retrospectively claimed about his Dickensian childhood – including here – but pinpointing where he even was at various points remains a difficulty. David Robinson commendably includes a chronology of Chaplin's known addresses in the appendix of his *Life and Art* but there remain gaps in Charlie's backstory that inevitably involve a degree of supposition on behalf of any biographer. This is exacerbated by Chaplin's own half-truth and bare-faced lies during interviews in the early years of his career. Such chicanery was partly designed to lend himself greater intrigue, but was no doubt also a product of mere boredom at the regularity of such promotional fluff. Even Chaplin himself spun versions of, for example, the death of his father and his first appearance on stage. His birth is likewise shrouded in mystery. Although later taken in anti-Semitic directions by political opponents in Germany, America and beyond, the confusion as to where Charlie entered the world in part arose from Chaplin's own reluctance to pin down a location. Given the more recent furore over the birthplace of the forty-fourth President of the United States Barack Obama, having the political right jump on such issues is a notion hardly limited to Chaplin's time. But at least Obama was able to eventually, and understandably grudgingly, produce a birth certificate. No such document existed for Charlie. We must rely heavily on his autobiography, and given it was written in Chaplin's early seventies, this brings its own issues of memory and reinvention.

In any event, the adult Charlie was also an utter hypocrite at times. As his friend Harry Crocker noted, 'In this world there were to be two sets of laws: those which controlled all other men, and those with concern to Chaplin.'[22] Therefore, what Charlie said – for example, urging politicians to help the poor – was often at odds with what he did (in this instance, avoiding paying the taxes to fund the social programmes that could do just that). Yet this in a sense again humanises the man. Charlie the liberal political saint who was persecuted by the American right and yet still had the bravery to make *The Great Dictator* is a construction not without foundation, but does not tell the whole story. The man was complex, and his opponents' claims against him may have been caricatures, but they were often broadly true. Charlie was a nightmare to be married to and a person with questionable sexual ethics across the board; thus, those who had a beef with his morality were more or less kicking against an open door. To condemn officialdom as unthinking and unfeeling while being a millionaire sleeping with fifteen-year-old girls was not a particularly tenable pose. Today, he would have been issuing press-gagging injunctions on a weekly basis. Unpicking the world of claim and counter-claim about Chaplin is therefore not easy and, certainly, mud was slung both at him and from him. But in documenting his views 'warts and all', we may at least understand where he was trying to get to, and how worried his political opponents need have been.

Third, on something of a technical note, we must also concede that our task is made more difficult by the fact that Charlie never voted in any election for a British Member of Parliament or an American President. We deal with why this was so in our first chapter – in essence it boiled down to ineligibility rather than abstention. But it meant that Charlie never had to assume any degree of personal responsibility for his political views until the tide of public opinion began to turn against him. He was not grounded in democracy per se and was not aligned to any party (much as the House Un-American Activities Committee (HUAC) would try to pin communist affiliation on him). On the one hand this must have made his life easier – he could hobnob with the Churchills and the Viscount Astors while being able to jovially parry away any uncomfortable discussions with jokes about not being able to vote or vagaries about being a 'citizen of the world'. But it also meant that he would never assume much of a tribal identity, either in Britain or America. This gave him the freedom to say what he wanted, but it also meant that when the heat was on, people whom he had previously enjoyed convivial discussions with could slink back into the mist and leave the lecherous Englishman to take the heat of a morally righteous America.

A final comment must be added. Fundamentally, Charlie was a man of power. Although estimates of cinema audiences in a non-digital age are by nature ballpark, even on a very conservative reading we can say that up to ten million Americans saw the class divide of 1931's *City Lights*, perhaps twelve and a half million 1921's autobiographical *The Kid* and more than twenty million witnessed the pathos and snow of *The Gold Rush*.[23] In an America with a population of about 116 million in 1925 these were significant numbers. It is highly likely therefore that more people saw Charlie perform the famous roll dance of 1925 than voted for any Republican Presidential Candidate up to Dwight D. Eisenhower in 1952. For politicians seeking to tap into the newly democratised masses, film had a particular utility and potentially a very strong effect – positive or negative. Charlie himself would famously lampoon this through the ludicrously stage-managed theatrics seen in Hynkel's Germany of *The Great Dictator*. But as millions of Americans took to the cinemas to stare at screens for hours a week, what was projected on them began to take on greater and greater significance. Figures like Chaplin had the potential to assume a Weberian charismatic authority that could sway the masses for or against a particular political position, and were readily seen in this light.

Academically, this notion of film as a political and ideological weapon was outlined most famously by Theodor Adorno and Max Horkheimer in their *Dialectic of Enlightenment* of the early 1940s. There the two Frankfurt School theorists wrote of a 'culture industry' that was providing 'mass deception' to the masses. Rather than being served an enlightening and wholesome diet of progressive cinema, audiences were being fed bland gruel. In this view, although films may differ in terms of their individual plot, the overall message would always remain the same. As Horkheimer and Adorno wrote in 1944, 'What [movie] connoisseurs discuss as good or bad points serve only to perpetuate the semblance of competition and range of choice [between] . . . Warner Brothers and Metro Goldwyn Mayer productions.'[24] On the one hand, this could result in some pretty turgid structuring. Today's audiences bored of Judd Apatow 'Bromances' or Jason Statham firing a gun at some bad guys may well recognise the contention that 'no independent thinking must be expected from the audience: the product prescribes every reaction . . . any logical connection calling for mental effort is painstakingly avoided'.[25] But the problem was deeper than just a boring product. For Horkheimer and Adorno the overall consequence of all cinema, up to and including 'Donald Duck in the cartoons', was that 'the unfortunate in real life get their thrashing so that the audience can learn to take thei own punishment'.[26] The seeming 'choice' of Warner Brothers ver sus MGM was really just one form of conformity versus another The massification of film after its anarchic early days (more on thi in Chapter 2) had produced a politically anodyne Hollywood: 'I front of the appetite stimulated by all those brilliant names and images there is finally set no more than a commendation of the depressing everyday world [people] sought to escape.'[27]

Chaplin himself was referenced in this regard by Horkheime and Adorno. Having condemned movie writers for seeking to ensure that 'developments must follow from the immediatel preceding situation' (and 'never from the idea of the whole'), the pair lambasted the 'tendency mischievously to fall back on pur nonsense . . . right up to Chaplin and the Marx Brothers'.[28] The tramp kicking a policeman on the backside was not a politica act, or at least an insufficient one. Yet, despite such scepticism, i must be acknowledged the Frankfurt School was not a uniforr set of principles. While Horkheimer and Adorno cast a pessimis tic eye on the movie industry, Frankfurt theorists such as Walte Benjamin could view film's potential much more positively. In hi seminal essay on 'The Work of Art in the Age of Mechanical Pro duction', Benjamin noted that 'so long as the movie-makers' cap ital sets the fashion, as a rule no other revolutionary merit can b accredited to today's film than the promotion of a revolutionar criticism of traditional concepts of art'. So far, so Frankfurt. Ye there was an important caveat. For one, Benjamin placed greate emphasis than his contemporaries on the fact that 'today's film can also promote revolutionary criticism of social conditions even of the distribution of property'. Certainly, this was the cas with Chaplin, whose audience, Benjamin believed, experience a 'progressive reaction . . . characterized by the direct, intimat fusion of visual and emotional enjoyment with the orientatio of the expert'. This idea that film, unlike books, could cultivat an expert's mentality among the masses was an important one For Benjamin, 'it is inherent in the technique of the film as we as that of sports that everybody who witnesses its accomplish ments is somewhat of an expert'. Unlike literature, therefore where 'for centuries a small number of writers were confronte by many thousands of readers' – film was a medium that th audience could not just passively and obediently consume, but that they could understand, critique and potentially help shape the future of themselves. Indeed, writing in the 1930s Benjamin was able to conclude that 'transitions that in literature took centuries have come about in a decade'. Contemporary film may indeed have been Donald Duck taking his beating at the time, but there was no historical inevitability about this. Processing the images of film would allow audiences to comprehend the changing nature of the industrial process, and the ills of capitalism. At the forefront of this alternative agenda, red flag literally in hand, appeared the Chaplin of *Modern Times*.[29] The stakes on which Chaplin made his comedies were therefore high, and increasingly elevated by those both for and against him. This would indeed go on to become a very political life.

Notes

1 'The Future of Charlie Chaplin's Contribution', *Collier's Weekly* [undated 1934/5], Churchill Archives Centre [CAC], Cambridge, UK, Winston Churchill Papers [CHAR] 8/521.

2 Sinclair to Chaplin, 2 May 1941, Lilly Library, Bloomington, Indiana, USA [LLBI], Upton Sinclair Papers [UPS]. My italics.

3 David Robinson, *Chaplin: The Mirror of Opinion* (London, 1983).

4 Buster Keaton, *My Wonderful World of Slapstick* (New York, 1960), 126.

5 Freud to Schiller, undated, within Margaret Herrick Library, Los Angeles [MHL], Harry Crocker Papers [HRC] f.12.

6 Kenney to Brooke-Wilkinson, 16 June 1939, National Archives, Kew, London, UK [TNA], Foreign and Commonwealth Office Papers [FCO] 395/663.

7 For example, Eric L. Flom, *Chaplin in the Sound Era: An Analysis of the Seven Talkies* (London, 1997) and Colin Chambers, *Here We Stand, Politics, Performers and Performance – Paul Robeson, Charlie Chaplin and Isadora Duncan* (London, 2006) utilise no archival material.

8 Charles J. Maland, *Chaplin and American Culture: The Evolution of a Star Image* (London, 1989).

9 Walter Kerr, *The Silent Clowns* (London, 1975), passim and Kyp Harness, *The Art of Charlie Chaplin: A Film-By-Film Analysis* (London, 2007), passim.

10 See, e.g., David Denby's blunt review of Urwand in *The New Yorker*, 23 September 2013.

11 Steven J. Ross, *Working-Class Hollywood: Silent Film and the Shaping of Class in America* (Princeton, 1998) and idem, *Hollywood Left*

and Right: How Movie Stars Shaped American Politics (Oxford, 2011), ch.1.

12 Owen Hatherley, *The Chaplin Revue: Slapstick, Fordism and the Communist Avant-Garde* (London, 2016); Libby Murphy, *The Art of Survival: France and the Great War Picaresque* (New Haven, CT, 2016), ch.8.

13 Indeed, emphasising Chaplin's Britishness somewhat extends Hatherley's analytical axes of Berlin–Moscow and America to further embed a new geographic framework.

14 Larry Ceplair and Steven Englund, *The Inquisition in Hollywood: Politics in the Film Community, 1930–1960* (Berkeley, 1983).

15 Ben Urwand, *The Collaboration: Hollywood's Pact with Hitler* (Cambridge, MA, 2013).

16 John Street, 'Celebrity Politicians: Popular Culture and Political Representation', *British Journal of Politics and International Relations*, 6 (2004), 435–52.

17 Kenneth S. Lynn, *Charlie Chaplin and His Times* (London, 1998), 175–6.

18 David Robinson, *Chaplin: His Life and Art* (London, 1992), 456, 458.

19 Peter Ackroyd, *Charlie Chaplin* (London, 2014).

20 A speech clipped by supportive voices in the press, e.g., Hoover Institute, Stanford University, California, USA [HOOV], Elizabeth Churchill Brown Papers [ECB] Box 18 Folder 13.

21 Burns to Hoover, 28 August 1922, Federal Bureau of Investigation, Washington, D.C., USA [FBI], FBI Chaplin Online file 7.

22 Harry Crocker's unpublished memoir, 'Charlie Chaplin: Man and Mime', MHL/HRC, X–12.

23 Assuming gross receipts of $2.5m, $6m and $5m respectively, with cost of entry at 20c, 25c and 50c. As mentioned, this is likely an understatement given discounted 5c or 10c entry fees towards the end of such runs or at matinee showings.

24 Theodor W. Adorno and Max Horkheimer, *Dialectic of Enlightenment* (London, 2010), 123.

25 Ibid., 137.

26 Ibid., 138.

27 Ibid., 139.

28 Ibid., 137.

29 All Benjamin quotes readily available online via www.marxists.org/reference/subject/philosophy/works/ge/benjamin.htm (accessed 7 November 2016).

1 Chaplin's England

In the mid-1930s a globally known figure began to pen an account for the American magazine, *Collier's Weekly*. This author was a regular contributor to the serial, writing on issues including press freedom and the future of publicity. Yet on this occasion our narrator turned his hand to the undeniably trau-matic events of 9 May 1901:

> In a room in St Thomas's Hospital, London, a man lay dying. He had had a good life – a full life. He had been a favourite of the music halls. He had tasted the triumphs of legitimate stage. He had won a measure of fame as a singer. His home life had been happy. And now Death had come for him. While he was yet in the prime of manhood, with success still sweet in his mouth, the curtain was falling – and forever. The other windows of the hospital were dark. In this one alone a light burned. And below it, outside in the darkness, shivering with cold and numbed with fear, a child stood sobbing . . . The dying man and the child outside the window both bore the same name – Charles Chaplin.[1]

Despite the dramatic, almost cinematic tone here, the author of this retrospective was not Charlie Chaplin himself. Nor was it Alistair Cooke, Thomas Burke, Upton Sinclair or any of the other prominent literary and cultural commentators who often reflected on the 'meaning' of Chaplin. Instead, this piece of jour-nalism was written by Winston Churchill (see Figure 1.1) – at the time of publication marooned in the political wilderness before

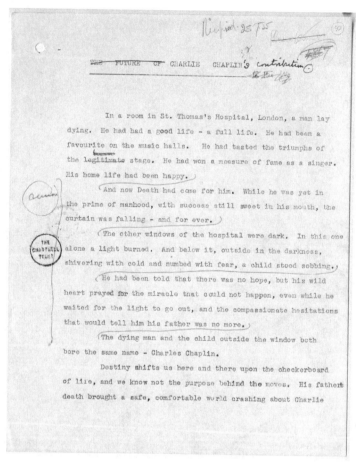

THE FUTURE OF CHARLIE CHAPLIN's contribution to the arts

In a room in St. Thomas's Hospital, London, a man lay dying. He had had a good life - a full life. He had been a favourite on the music halls. He had tasted the triumphs of the legitimate stage. He had won a measure of fame as a singer. His home life had been happy.

And now Death had come for him. While he was yet in the prime of manhood, with success still sweet in his mouth, the curtain was falling - and for ever.

The other windows of the hospital were dark. In this one alone a light burned. And below it, outside in the darkness, shivering with cold and numbed with fear, a child stood sobbing.

He had been told that there was no hope, but his wild heart prayed for the miracle that could not happen, even while he waited for the light to go out, and the compassionate hesitations that would tell him his father was no more.

The dying man and the child outside the window both bore the same name - Charles Chaplin.

Destiny shifts us here and there upon the checkerboard of life, and we know not the purpose behind the moves. His father's death brought a safe, comfortable world crashing about Charlie

Figure 1.1 Numerous global politicians speculated on Chaplin's background, including, here, Winston Churchill.

Courtesy of the Churchill Archives Centre, Churchill College, UK

his stridently anti-Nazi oratory, and the actions of Hitler himself, brought this maverick hurtling back into favour in the eyes of his fellow countrymen.

Although they were politically dissimilar as we will see, Chaplin and Churchill always got on rather well. Winston visited Charlie on the set of what would become the 1931 film *City Lights*, while

Charlie stayed at Chartwell when back in Britain promoting the same product. Highlighting this connection from the outset is not merely to begin with some interesting trivia. Instead the Chaplin–Churchill friendship suggests three important issues that will run throughout this book. The first is Chaplin's political malleability. Although broadly of the left, Chaplin was terribly interested in political ideas generally, and rather impressed by aristocratic figures of the right. The Astors – Lady Nancy and Viscount Waldorf (both Conservative MPs) – got on famously with Charlie, and were indicative of a series of relationships where Charlie provided the frisson of fame and glamour, and such well-to-do couples the political table talk. Certainly, politicians of whatever tribe were keen to glad hand this modern icon. For example, presaging the modern obsession with the 'selfie', Waldorf recorded in his 1926 diary that during a trip to Hollywood he was 'photoed with [Charlie] of course'.[2] Perhaps this was no big deal. But what was more intriguing – for a man of the left – was that during his 1931 promotional tour of the UK Charlie missed several engagements, including visiting the children then studying at his old school because, as the left-leaning *Daily Herald* newspaper sardonically noted, he was 'detained at the Astors'.[3] In February or March 1931 you were far more likely to find Chaplin at the Prime Ministerial residence of Chequers, or dining at the House of Commons, than in a leftist discussion group, or dolling out the produce to real-life Little Tramps in a soup kitchen. Throughout the book, as we will see, Charlie's politics could be slippery. His deeds did not always match his words.

The second issue that the Churchill article suggests was the regularity in which politics intersected with Charlie's life, particularly from those wishing to project a particular 'meaning' onto his childhood. This occurred for good and ill. When, in 1933, Chaplin was reported as saying he would make his next picture without his famous moustache for fear of invoking comparisons with Hitler (a stance that would clearly be reversed by *The Great Dictator* in 1940), the Nazi press in Berlin responded that 'the creator and leader of the new Germany stands much too high to even hear the barking of a dog from London's ghetto'.[4] Chaplin's origins were both mythologised by the man himself and by those desiring to talk him up or down. But his entire life – involving as it did such extraordinary highs and lows – was innately political, experiencing capitalism at both ends of the income scale from being reliant on the charity of Victorian Londoners to becoming one of the wealthiest men in America. As such, it is impossible to do Chaplin's life justice by reference to the film studio or the antics in his bedroom alone. The man lived a very political experience.

The third theme, by no means a point limited to Churchill's slightly overly dramatic prose, was just how ambiguous and shrouded in mystery Chaplin's life actually was. The later sex scandals, flirtations with communism and manic personality we will get to, but public understanding of his origins – given how important they were to the man who would become the world's most famous filmmaker – was perhaps the haziest of a rather hazy lot. We may not expect a cheque-chasing piece of journalism from a cash-strapped Winston Churchill to be strictly accurate in all the dotting of the i's and crossing of the t's, but the fact that his excerpt described Chaplin's father's 'home life' as 'happy', and that Churchill would go on to state that 'his death brought a safe, comfortable world crashing about Charlie' was certainly stretching credulity, as this chapter will set out.

Yet, if misleading, Churchill's intentions were at least benign enough – something that could not always be said for those who speculated on Chaplin's past. Nazi references to Chaplin's 'ghetto' background were just the tip of the iceberg. Guesses as to Charlie's allegedly 'real' name competed with one another to be the most stereotypically Jewish, while speculation on the location of his birth was an equally enjoyable parlour game for many in the press. One 1935 article claimed that Charlie was the son of a Chaim Kaplan, a tailor from Whitechapel in London's East End – then known for its significant Jewish population.[5] On the back of such tall tales both the FBI and British Special Branch would later investigate allegations that he had been born Israel Thornstein, with either a German or Franco-Jewish background. Another press account (from which both intelligence agencies seemed to have gathered much of their interest in Chaplin) accurately asserted that 'accounts of his birth are as vague as those concerned with the nativity of divinities', yet went on to report the second-hand gossip that 'Charlie's father was a French pantomimic clown, his mother an English Jewess'.[6] In Canada *The Toronto Standard* even carried a completely fabricated quote from Charlie that upon returning to London at the height of his fame, 'I set out immediately to find the house in which I was born, and when I reached the ghetto I saw the frightful loneliness and need of my brother Jews'.[7] This was wrong on many levels. With *The Great Dictator* in pre-production in the late 1930s this would reach something of a crescendo when pro-Nazi elements in the American press published a list of 'Big Money Jewish Names' that labelled Chaplin as a Jew originally named Tonstein.[8] The story did not go away.

All this was simply made up. His father Charles Senior's roots lay in Protestant Suffolk, England and, although stories of a maternal gypsy connection lingered, Charlie's mother Hannah could trace her family tree through South London. Yet, interestingly, the notion of a more 'exotic' heritage was a lie occasionally peddled by Charlie himself in early interviews. There are a variety of possible explanations of this – Charlie may have done so either to embellish or deflect from the very real and tragic nature of his childhood. His half-brother Sydney also had a Jewish father, and there was no doubt an element of solidarity with someone he cared deeply about. Charlie may just have been bored at the relentless grind of publicity. But it was also a legend able to gain some currency because, as one Special Branch letter put it, 'although his claim to have been born in London on 16th April 1889 has been accepted by the Passport Office since at least 1920 . . . we cannot find particulars of his birth at [record keeping facility] Somerset House'.[9] Whoever Special Branch's 'source[,] which is usually considered fairly reliable', actually was, it subsequently transpired that there was not a shred of evidence to back up his claim that Chaplin had been born in Fontainebleau or Melun in France either.[10] Perhaps this informant had just read the papers and passed on the gossip to the authorities.

For all its mystery, this was far from an unusual state of affairs, however. When his son entered the world Charles Senior had been on stage in Hull in the north of England and thus missed Charlie's birth. As David Robinson notes, it was easy for 'music hall artists, constantly moving from one town to another' to 'put off and eventually forget' formalities such as registering births.[11] In May 1889 an edition of the music periodical *The Magnet* recorded that 'on the 15th ultimo, the wife of Mr. Charles Chaplin, [was delivered] of a beautiful boy'. This may (or may not) have been a day out, but it certainly stands as at least as powerful an argument for Chaplin's British birth as anything waged against this.[12] Charlie himself later placed his birth as taking place at eight o'clock on 16 April 1889 East Lane, Walworth, South London.[13] In a neat coincidence, his future nemesis Adolf Hitler entered the world in Brannau-am-Inn, Austria only four days later.

The descent

Before we get to the difficulties of Chaplin's childhood, a further contextual point needs to be added. As his son entered the world in 1889, the twenty-six-year-old Charles Senior was undoubtedly a professional success. Kenneth Lynn records that, after the start of his career in 1887, his 'pleasing baritone voice and sophisticated manner soon brought him top billings . . . He became sought after as well by music publishers, who realized that having his name and photograph on their sheet strengthened sales.'[14] Having progressed artistically from mimic to storytelling singer (often about staple topics such as mothers-in-law or nagging wives) between 1890 and 1896 several of Charles Snr's recordings were released to commercial success. Like his son, this would provide a platform to work in America, and in August 1890 Charles Snr appeared at Union Theatre, New York for several weeks. At least initially, his father's career was something of a triumph.

Certainly the music hall in which mother, father and Charlie himself would make their names held a special place in Victorian life. In the 1880s there were about 500 music halls in London, and by the 1890s it was estimated that the biggest 35 were catering to a combined audience of more than 45,000 people an evening. This was not welcomed by all it must be said. As Gareth Stedman Jones notes, while middle-class religious communities tried to foster a similar devotion among the worker class, late Victorian England's 'dominant cultural institutions were not the school, the evening class, the library, the friendly society, the church or the chapel, but the pub, the sporting paper, the race course and the music hall'.[15] The fare provided by the latter sought to highlight 'the peculiarities of the working-class situation in London', which could often be precarious. Few music hall performers could therefore progress without at least one of 'fatalism, political scepticism, the evasion of tragedy or anger, or a stance of comic stoicism' within their armoury.[16] A certain world-weariness, no doubt partially imbued by the free-flowing alcohol around such premises (despite, again, middle-class disproval), was a natural product of anyone raised in such an environment.[17] So it would be with Charlie.

The younger Charlie's geographic hinterland would be South London, and much of this would indeed appear, as in Churchill's account, rather Dickensian. But it did not start this way. Due to his father's artistic success Charlie Chaplin began his life in a relatively well-to-do environment. As Charlie recorded in *My Autobiography*, in his early years 'our circumstances were moderately comfortable; we lived in three tastefully furnished rooms'.[18] The Chaplins could even afford a housemaid at this stage, and the reminiscences of the early 1890s in his autobiography are relatively misty-eyed and nostalgic. As he recorded: 'London was sedate on those days. The tempo was sedate; even the horse drawn tram-cars along Westminster Bridge Road went at a sedate pace and turned sedately on a revolving table at the terminal near the bridge.'[19] Charlie remembered everything from the 'rubicund flower-girls at the corner of Westminster Bridge, making gay boutonniere' from fern and tinsel to the 'galaxy of colour' afforded by a nearby fruit shop offering 'pyramids of oranges, apples, pears and bananas . . . in contrast to the solemn grey Houses of Parliament directly across the river'.[20] With his father's theatrical career bringing in forty pounds a week – far higher than the then average British weekly salary of just over one pound – the Chaplins were doing well. His father may have been distant, but he certainly was not poor.

Yet, as Charlie later noted, problems could be seen from the outset: 'The trouble was that [father] drank too much, which Mother said was the cause of their separation.'[21] For all its (temporary) financial security their marriage was clearly volatile and occasionally violent. On one occasion when Charles Snr became physically violent towards Hannah she fled to Brighton with some friends. To his frantic telegram of 'What are you up to? Answer at once!' she managed the gay reply of 'Balls, parties and picnics, darling!' The madcap violence of the Little Tramp may have been mostly comedic, but at times young Charlie must have seemed like the boxing referee in *City Lights* – marooned between two pugilists, and not a clue of what to do. Charles Snr's lengthy absences at least saved him from this fate most of the time.

In the absence of this alcoholic father the young Charlie's attachment to his mother grew ever stronger. Aside from Hannah's obvious love for her children – which included Charlie's half-brothers Sydney (four years older than he) and George (the younger sibling snatched from Hannah aged just six months by his father Leo in a particularly Dickensian episode) – she and young Charlie also shared a love of the music hall. Like her estranged husband, Hannah enjoyed sporadic success in this area, and when the Chaplins separated in 1890 her wage of twenty-five pounds a week was sufficient to convince Hannah not to seek any alimony from Charlie's father. As her career began to experience peaks and troughs, up until 1893 Hannah kept the wolf from the door through a combination of Charles Snr's patchy payments of support for his son (about 10 shillings a week when they did arrive), her own theatrical career and performing odd jobs such as sewing. Up to this point the Chaplins got by. Through 1894 and 1895, however, two varieties of ill-health rocked the foundations of Hannah and young Charlie's world, and gave the future film star his first taste of what 'the state' as a political concept could look like.

The first dose of ill health was actually comparatively minor, if debilitating for a performer: laryngitis. Hannah's voice – 'never strong' by her son's account – was virtually useless should she be hit with any cold or more debilitating malady. As Charlie noted, 'The slightest cold brought on laryngitis which lasted for weeks; but she was obliged to keep working, so that her voice grew progressively worse . . . In the middle of singing it would crack or suddenly disappear into a whisper.' Contemporary crowds were not kind: 'The audience would laugh and start booing. The worry of it impaired her health and made her a nervous wreck.'[22] For mother this meant lost bookings, but for son it helped launch a career. When playing the Canteen at Aldershot – 'at the time a grubby, mean theatre catering mostly to soldiers' – Hannah lost her voice and fled the stage.[23] After a brief discussion with the floor manager, young Charlie was led by hand on to the boards where he performed the then well-known song *Jack Jones* (ironically, given his later life, about a working-class man who loses touch with his roots upon gaining great fortune). A shower of coins was thrown onto the stage in appreciation at his performance. At the time Charlie was only five years old. His first appearance on the stage had occurred the same night as his mother's career took a nose-dive.

Hannah's misfortune saw a significant slide in the Chaplins' circumstances. From their initial three rooms, they moved into a house with two rooms, and then into a single-room garret: 'our belongings dwindling and the neighbourhoods growing progressively drabber'.[24] Poignantly, the last item Hannah sold as she sought to make what money she could was her old trunk of theatrical costumes – she long clung to a return to the stage that would never come. Even with this slide down the social spectrum, however, Hannah retained several middle-class airs – one was a belief in the church, and another was to ensure that her children spoke with a middle-class diction (which Charlie maintained all his life). Sitting by the window, she continued to indulge in amateur dramatics by mimicking people who passed by their garret, much to her young son's amusement.

For a while they made do, and blind luck intervened at one point when Sydney returned home with a purse he had found on the bus containing seven golden sovereigns (£7). But it could not last. Hannah's needlework dried up and she and her family were forced to 'live on parochial charity, soup tickets and relief parcels'.[25] Sydney's newspaper selling around his few hours at school was not enough to sustain them. At several points in the late 1890s, Hannah, lacking any alternative, took herself and her two children to the last resort of Victorian London: the workhouse.

Chaplin's Dickensian period

From the comfort of 1930s Chartwell, Winston Churchill wrote of Chaplin that 'poverty is not a life sentence. It is a challenge. To some it is more – it is an opportunity. It was so to this child of the theatre.'[26] This is a profoundly Conservative reading of Charlie's childhood – talent had elevated Chaplin out of poverty and thus, ipso facto, the system worked. Churchill's verdict was certainly not a prospect the seven-year-old Charlie could have envisaged with any degree of certainty as he considered the gates of a workhouse for the first time (for the accompanying Sydney this was actually a second trip, with a previous three-day spell in 1895 during a period of ill health for Hannah). Perhaps most jarringly, Churchill even claimed to identify with Chaplin's difficult childhood:

> Genius is essentially a hardy plant. It thrives in the east wind. It withers in a hot house. That is, I believe, true in every walk of life. The reason why the historic English families have produced so many men of distinction is that, on the whole, they have borne great responsibilities rather than enjoyed great wealth . . . I am glad I had to earn my living from the time that I was a young man. Had I been born heir to millions I should probably have had a less interesting life.[27]

There were elements of being a self-made man to Churchill's career it is true. But it is fair to point out that Churchill's background of being born in Blenheim Palace, going to the prestigious Harrow School and having a father who served as Chancellor of the Exchequer was not entirely replicated by Chaplin's own youth. And yet in later life Chaplin would himself take something of the Churchill line. Commenting on the seemingly instant celebrity status of two 1960s icons, the then seventy-something Charlie spoke of

> Marilyn Monroe, you see, that whole story is fairy tale. My God, The Beatles – a fairy tale – little boys from Liverpool, came along – well whatever they had. They do something and suddenly they're shot up and the whole thing has an unreality to it. I'm telling you, people in my day, people like [the actor Herbert] Tree, had to put in servitude – years and years – until eventually they became prominent.[28]

These years of servitude have something of the David Copperfield about them, and the Dickens comparison has often been made. In his recent book on Chaplin, Peter Ackroyd – former biographer of the Victorian novelist – has argued that with their similar affinity for the minor theatres of nineteenth-century London, their 'military manner in relationship to their families', their 'driven, relentless, overwhelming' personalities and, crucially, their lower-middle-class ambition, 'it might even be suggested that Chaplin was Dickens' true successor'.[29] There is much in that. In 1935 Churchill noted that 'the alchemy of genius transmuted bitterness and suffering into the gold of great literature and gave us the novels of Charles Dickens. Between [Chaplin and Dickens] there is, I think, an essential similarity. Both knew hardness in childhood . . . [B]oth quarried in the same rich mine of common life.'[30] Twenty years later, from across the political spectrum, the former Labour Lord Chancellor William Jowitt began his oration to the February 1955 Dickens dinner by welcoming Charlie as its guest of honour. He noted that

> a great artist . . . must possess, as Dickens did, enormous vitality. He must suffer, as Dickens suffered, from an extreme sensitiveness . . . We ordinary people are apt to think our own age is good and be complacent about the misfortunes of others just because we have not got the imagination or the sensitiveness to know what those misfortunes mean. Where could I find someone who resembled Dickens in these characteristics . . . who cares about the fortunes of others? As I cast about in my mind to find such one, I thought of Charles Chaplin.[31]

There is something of a sting in the tale to all this mutual appreciation, however. As the actress Louise Brooks noted of one such analysis of Charlie, 'this was [Alistair] Cooke's most glaring omission when he compared Chaplin with Dickens – their mutual passion for little girls'.[32] In many ways, as we will see, it was sex that undermined Chaplin, not just the politics of this book.

In the 1890s, however, you would have gotten long odds on Chaplin reaching any such pedestal from which to fall. The poverty of Chaplin's youth was real, sustained and eventually overcome by the force of his own talent. As discussed, as Hannah's illness took hold and Charles Snr's maintenance payments proved erratic, the Chaplins began a steady decline through the London property ladder.

In Charles Booth's landmark, multi-volume sociological study *Life and Labour of the People in London* he produced a map detailing the conditions he had observed in each of London's streets during Chaplin's youth. Booth was a social reformer who had originally set out to ascertain the precise levels of poverty in the late-Victorian East End (which he later extended to all of the capital). Whereas previous estimates had put the level of abject poverty at one family in four, Booth's work placed the figure at an even higher 35 per cent. Producing a colour-coded map to support his findings, Booth's work provides a useful measure through which we can gain a handle on some of the Chaplins' dwellings. The first property Charlie can remember was West Square, near the present site of the Imperial War Museum in Lambeth, where they lived up to about 1892. According to Booth, this address was mostly for the comfortable working class ('22s to 30s per week for regular work') and even included elements of the 'lower middle class. Shopkeepers and small employers, clerks and subordinate professional men.' This latter group of lower-middle Britain, Booth noted, was 'a hardworking sober, energetic class'. Charlie's later dwellings, including Methley Street, mostly conformed to the 'respectable' working class who were not well off but kept the wolf from the door. Farmers Road just off Kennington Park – where many working-class Londoners were 'the victims of competition and on them falls with particular severity the recurrent depressions of trade' – was an exception. These were generally 'labourers, poorer artisans and street sellers'. Certainly Booth provides a great service to the historian trying to understand the period, but what strikes one from a twenty-first-century perspective is the rampant moralisation in his descriptions. The worse off in Booth's classifications could be 'loafers, criminals and semi criminals', adding 'their life is the life of savages'. Those higher up the ladder were 'paid for [their] responsibility and are men of good character and much intelligence'. This was a much-divided age indeed.[33]

Hanwell and the workhouse

The most obvious instance of this societal division came on 30 May 1896, when Charlie and Sydney were admitted to Newington Workhouse. Initially Charlie thought that it would be 'adventurous and a change from living in one stuff room. But on that doleful day I didn't realise what was happening until we actually entered the workhouse gate.' The 'poignant sadness' of the separation of mother into the women's ward and her sons into the children's equivalent remained with Charlie all his life.[34] Like all residents, his clothes were steamed and replaced with the workhouse uniform upon entry while his hair was shorn in case of lice. Such actions were of course largely medical and intended to disinfect the new arrival, but there was a symbolic importance, too: to cleanse the child of the sins of Victorian London, and to mould a new, 'better' individual from scratch.

We deal below with the moralism that informed the workhouse, but it is worth outlining what these institutions conjured up to many. In January 1866 Lambeth's Princes Road Workhouse had been the subject of a piece of populist investigative journalism from a man named James Greenwood. This was not the exact institution that Charlie would enter, but it does give something of a geographically similar flavour. Greenwood had voluntarily entered the workhouse in disguise to write about its conditions, and his articles appeared in the *Pall Mall Gazette* from 12 January. He told an enthralled readership (his articles were eventually republished as a stand-alone pamphlet due to popular demand) that 'no language with which I am acquainted is capable of conveying an adequate conception of the spectacle I . . . encountered'. Entering a makeshift shed thirty feet square in diameter, 'my appalled vision took in thirty of them – thirty men and boys stretched upon shallow pallets with but only six inches of comfortable hay between them and the stony floor'. Attempting to bed down for the night, Greenwood noticed that 'in the middle of the bed I had selected was a stain of blood bigger than a man's hand! I did not know what to do now. To lie on such a horrid thing seemed impossible; yet to carry back the bed and exchange it for another might betray a degree of fastidiousness repugnant to the feelings of my fellow lodgers.' For Greenwood, 'from the moral point of view . . . the wakeful ones were . . . dreadful. Towzled, dirty, villainous, they squatted up in their beds, and smoked foul pipes, and sang snatches of horrible songs, and bandied jokes so obscene as to be absolutely appalling.' At points, he reserved some sympathy for his fellow shed dwellers, but Greenwood ended his description of the night's events with two riders. First, he wrote that he had 'avoided the detail of horrors infinitely more revolting than anything that appears in this pamphlet'. It is likely that this meant sodomy. And, more pointedly, he concluded that 'the moral of all this I leave to the world'.[35]

Partly in response to the shock that the Greenwood articles had engendered, the state deemed further action necessary. Yet this was not necessarily along the lines one may expect. For those who could, the state encouraged outdoor paupers to fall back on support from relatives, and in the case that they still needed to claim outdoor relief, the relevant tests to gain access to such funds were made more stringent. This 'crusade against outrelief' went hand in hand with the desire to reduce total welfare spending. Yet this could be something of a false economy. In making outdoor relief more difficult to acquire, many paupers were forced into indoor relief – the workhouse. And, thus, between 1870 and 1910 the proportion of the English population in receipt of some form (indoor or outdoor) of pauper relief fell by almost half. In one sense this was an arguable success. At the same time, however, by 1910 30 per cent of all paupers were relieved in workhouses compared to only 15 per cent forty years earlier.[36] The workhouse had become even more residualised by consequence – only the absolutely desperate would contemplate entry through its gates.

We tend to view the late Victorian period rather optimistically. Yet the *general* gains in real income seen across the board in England from 1870 thus require further clarification. Certainly the 1890s workhouse that Charlie encountered was therefore something of a cross-class coalition. On the one hand, it contained the poorest of the poor who were in a sense prisoners. Added to this mix was the 'Chaplinite' Londoner forced into such a world by the cumulative effect of the global 'Long Depression' that marked the latter quarter of the nineteenth century on the one hand, and the tightening up of outdoor relief on the other. Chaplin was ultimately institutionalised by both a laissez-faire global economy that could not sustain levels of income for 'casual' professions from labouring to the music hall, and a state that pulled up the drawbridge for those afflicted by such maelstroms.[37]

If Charlie had encountered any dramatic visions along the James Greenwood model while in the workhouse, he did not directly refer to them in later years. After three weeks during which Charlie remembered 'little of incident' the Chaplin brothers were transferred to the Hanwell School for Orphans and Destitute Children in Ealing, West London on 18 June 1896. For all the drudgery of the workhouse in some ways this was arguably a worse fate for the young Charlie. At the workhouse 'I always felt that mother was near . . . but at Hanwell we seemed miles apart'.[38] Sydney was also put into the older classes while Charlie remained with the infants. In despair, Charlie recalled looking out of the oblong windows, mournfully taking in the sunset while singing the hymn 'Abide with Me'. In part, Chaplin's retrospective descriptions of this period seem slightly cinematic, but there can be little doubt that it was a traumatic time in his life.

During his trip to London in 1931 when he returned as all-conquering hero, Chaplin paid a visit to Hanwell. Greeted by a friendly school headmaster, he was shown a record that stated 'Sydney Chaplin handed back to mother March 10, 1896. Charles, ditto.'[39] Whatever the confusion about dates (possibly due to poor record-keeping, or Chaplin's own faulty memory), the forty-something Chaplin was 'anxious to see the interior of the school'. Walking through the school yard, he noted that 'contrary to some ideas about objects or locations appearing smaller after one grows up, it looks just as big as it ever did'. He saw 'the tailor's shop, the school steps; the punishment room; the blacking hole where we would shine our boots on a frosty morning; the dormitories and the depressing slate wash sinks'. Walking up the aforementioned school steps, he 'felt myself going up them with the same sensation of oppression and confinement that I had then'.[40] In 1931, after observing an altogether more humane Hanwell, Charlie could make his excuses and leave. In 1896 there was no such luxury.

Briefly, however, it had all seemed to be mercifully over when, in August 1896, Hannah applied for a discharge and her boys were returned to her. Meeting their mother at the gate of the workhouse, they all took a leisurely stroll through Kennington Park, bought half a pound of black cherries and later enjoyed a two-penny teacake. It was all a temporary ruse to allow them to spend some time together, however: 'In the afternoon we made our way back to the workhouse. As mother said with levity: "We'll be back in time for tea."'[41] A poignant moment, emblematic of the type of pathos that Chaplin would later inject into his movies. Meanwhile, it was back to Hanwell for the young boys.

This was hardly all Hannah's doing, however. Where, for one, was Charlie's father during this slide? There were occasional glimpses of potential light in this regard. Some respite seemed possible when, in the summer of 1896, Charles Snr was compelled by the local board of Guardians to pay 15s a week towards the support of Charlie and Sydney, although by this stage liquor had taken hold and this was irregular at best. In September 1897, the Lambeth Board of Guardians offered £1 for information leading to Charles Snr's arrest for non-payment of child support, although his brother Spencer would eventually cover the £44.8s then due.[42] In 1898 Charlie would briefly (albeit through the means of court order) live with his father, but, if his recollections are true, he can rarely have experienced him not either drunk or hungover. Certainly their last meeting was far from Churchill's Hollywoodesque hokum with which we began this chapter. Instead, in April 1901 Charlie happened to be walking past the Three Stags pub on Kennington Road. Peeking inside, his saw his father who beckoned him over. Charlie 'was surprised at such a welcome, for he was never demonstrative'. But this was not a pleasant sight: 'He was very ill; his eyes were sunken, and his body had swollen to an enormous size. He rested one hand, Napoleon like, in his waistcoat as if to ease his difficult breathing.' Undoubtedly drunk, Charlie did, however, receive the first and only kiss his father would ever give him on this occasion. It would prove the last time they saw each other; three weeks later he was dead from dropsy – a product of years of drinking. Far from the tranquil scene painted by Churchill, however, Charles Snr had to be plied with booze before he drunkenly consented to go to St Thomas's Hospital. There his healthy declined further. Even in this moment of sorrow the Reverend who came to comfort the dying man did not sugar-coat matters: 'Well Charlie, when I look at you, I can only think of the old proverb: "Whatsoever a man soweth; that he shall also reap."'[43]

Back in 1896 Hanwell became worse when, at the age of eleven, Sydney elected to join the Royal Navy in the form of the *Exmouth* training ship that November. This left Charlie alone and scared in a school he would, all told, spend eighteen months in. With his combined stays at Newington (1896: twenty days) and Lambeth (1898: eight days, three days and one-day stints) workhouses totalling just over a month, Hanwell would form the state institution where the young Charlie would personally spend the most amount of time. There he recalled he was 'well looked after' but 'it was a forlorn existence'. Feeling the local villagers' eyes staring at him as he trudged with the other boys into the school, Charlie heard them refer to his friends as inmates of the 'booby hatch' – the workhouse. He must have felt like the bottom of the pile. In actual fact, this was not quite true: Hanwell tended to take the children of the 'striving poor' rather than Charles Booth's 'savages'. But self-perception mattered.

Punishment was very much the order of the day at Hanwell, and it was administered by an intimidating figure, a former naval officer Captain Hindrum. Every Friday afternoon 300 boys marched into the school's imposing gymnasium, where they stood in line forming the sides of a square. At the fourth end, behind a large desk, stood Hindrum, addressing those waiting for trial and punishment. This was imposing stuff: 'In front of the desk was an easel with wrist-straps dangling, and from the frame a birch hung ominously.'[44] For 'minor offences' a boy would be laid across the desk, and then 'slowly and dramatically' Hindrum would lift a 'cane as thick as a man's thumb and about four feet long' before bringing it down with a terrifying swish on the boy's backside. 'Invariably,' Chaplin shuddered, 'a boy would fall out of rank in a faint.' The punishment varied between three and six strokes – naturally judged relatively arbitrarily by Hindrum himself. The victim then had to be carried to one side and laid on a gym mattress, 'where he was left to writhe and wriggle for at least ten minutes before the pain subsided'. And this was the minor punishment. For maximum offenders, there was the birch, where, after that ordeal, boys would have to be carried away to the infirmary for treatment.[45]

In late 1896 the list of affected boys included Master Charles Chaplin. On Thursdays, ever the theatrical, Hindrum would sound a bugle before reading through a megaphone the list of boys who would report for punishment the next day. Charlie was astonished to hear his name – 'yet for some unaccountable reason I was thrilled – perhaps because I was the centre of the drama'.[46] Charged with setting fire to the school lavatory, Charlie was not guilty of this offence. Yet, as he recalled, 'boys would advise you not to deny a charge, even if innocent, because, if proved guilty, you would get the maximum [of six lashes]'.[47] Here again the young Charlie encountered the notion of a repressive, unfeeling state. He took his three lashes – 'the pain was so excruciating that it took away my breath' – but felt 'valiantly triumphant'.[48] In his later films, albeit in a more jovial sense, he would get to kick the backsides of a good few authority figures himself by small way of revenge.

Hanwell was the institution through which Chaplin most directly felt the oppressive reach of government. It also imbued a sense of class consciousness within the young boy – all were against the 'system' as represented by Hindrum, and therefore against a particular vision of England. Later, he would tell the author Thomas Burke, who had also been sent to Hanwell, that, unlike Britain, 'in America the questions are "What do you know?" and "What can you do?" not "Where do you come from?" [and] "Are you public school?"' Hanwell undoubtedly had a long reach in Charlie's life – cinematically and politically.[49] Equally, however, this development could never *only* be reduced to economics. Chaplin in many ways forms an exemplar of the nineteenth-century world of the historian Patrick Joyce – where class conflict did not just mean monetary or social division, but also imbued an anti-aristocratic populism and scepticism towards the state, and could attune minds to injustice and oppression from whatever source.[50] Money mattered, but such protest was never just about economic envy.

Even after the horrors of Hanwell, Charlie was not done with the workhouse either. As such, two factors lend the workhouse real significance in his political development. The first was its high death rate – and, thus, for a man who would not fight in the First World War, it was his most dramatic exposure to human casualty and trauma. To give some context, Lambeth's Renfrew Road Workhouse in which Chaplin spent a combined twelve days in the summer and autumn of 1898 (after his time at Hanwell) was intended to cater for in the region of 820 people. Held within the London Metropolitan Archives, its surviving register records thirty-two deaths in 1898, fifty in 1899 and seventy-three in 1900.[51] In early 1900 the death rate in the Borough of Lambeth for the previous year was recorded at 29 people per 1,000.[52] Depending what year a person was admitted, the death rate in the workhouse could be up to two or three times worse than the local average, and certainly more geographically concentrated. The workhouse was the bottom rung of an already dangerous ladder.

Perhaps more significantly, if Charlie's own exposure to the workhouse was mercifully relatively brief (if still shocking), his mother's was far more significant and sustained. It was *this* experience of the workhouse, albeit second-hand, that combined with Hanwell influenced his early life more than any other. To truly understand this, it is worth turning to the experts – and there can be few more qualified exponents of the link between child and mother, and indeed childhood trauma and later life, than Sigmund Freud. Intriguingly, in 1931 Freud chose to dwell on the early life of Chaplin. Commenting on the Tramp, Freud noted that 'he always portrays one and the same figure; only the weakly poor, helpless, clumsy youngster for whom, however, things turn out well in the end'. 'Now,' the Viennese doctor continued, 'do you think that for this role he has to forget about his own ego? On the contrary, he always plays himself as he was in his early dismal youth. He cannot get away from those impressions and to this day he obtains for himself the compensation for the frustrations and humiliations of that past period of his life.' For Freud, Chaplin was 'an exceptionally and transparent case', and, this study contends, his mother's spell in the workhouse provided the most visceral early trauma.[53]

Hannah's own spell in the workhouse from July 1898 had exacerbated her physical frailty and she had severe dermatitis. But after her physical slide from accomplished songstress to workhouse waif, matters became worse when she began to exhibit signs of madness. After a short spell in the infirmary to treat her physical ailments (which included bruising, likely the consequence of fights with fellow workhouse residents) she was admitted to Cane Hill Asylum in September 1898. This began a series of trips in and out of the asylum for Hannah. She was in Cane Hill until November 1898 for her first stay, from May 1903 to January 1904 for her second, and from March 1905 to September 1912 for the final time. Prior to Hannah's committal, Charlie admitted to spending much time at his new neighbours', an Irish family called the McCarthys who often looked out for him – 'anything to stay away from our awful garret'. Returning home after a lunch with them, a little girl told him that 'your mother's gone insane . . . She's been knocking at all our doors giving away pieces of coal, saying they were birthday presents for the children.'[54] A doctor was summoned who made a perfunctory summary: 'insane: send her to the infirmary'. For all the heartbreak, logistically this was easier said than done. Charlie was forced to support his malnourished mother in the one-mile walk to the infirmary, while 'mother staggered like a drunken woman from weakness'. Lying to the infirmary doctors that an aunt would take him in, Charlie spent the walk to his now empty home contemplating the 'heart-breaking look as they led her away'. Hannah was transferred to Cane Hill the next day and her young son spent the next few days as a hermit – refusing to speak or see anyone out of shame and sorrow: 'Like a fugitive I kept out of everyone's way.'[55] In order to stop his landlady seeing him and reporting him to the parish authorities, this included sleeping rough on occasion. Only Sydney's surprising return from travel overseas a week or so later helped brighten his mood.

Charlie would forever be dogged by the feeling that one day he may experience the same degree of diminished mental capacity that had befallen his mother. Indeed, to speculate somewhat, it is possible that Charlie hinted at a potentially Jewish background in order to throw reporters off the scent of what he considered a more shameful and very real family history. Mary Ann, Hannah's mother, had herself been committed to Banstead Asylum for the last two years of her life. After the effect that years of drinking had wrought (mostly due to gin consumption), the doctors recorded her as 'incoherent' and as thinking the medical staff were trying to poison her.[56] She was dead by her mid-fifties. Hannah's father Charles Hill (described by Charlie, possibly erroneously, as 'an Irish cobbler' from Cork) did not suffer such problems, but he too, required the refuge of the workhouse, with two (1904) and six (1912) month spells in Renfrew Road following an earlier spell in 1899. Alcoholism, poverty and madness constituted the collective genetic material Chaplin most feared to be buried within himself. As *Limelight* collaborator Jerry Epstein recalled, even in old age 'Charlie had a persistent fear he would go insane'.[57] Visits to Cane Hill, some twenty miles away from the garret in Pownall Terrace, only exacerbated this feeling. When Charlie and Sydney went there for the first time, they encountered a frail, blue-lipped

Hannah who 'sat listening and nodding, looking vague and pre-occupied'.[58] This would be the case for many years.

As his wealth increased, Charlie made sure that his mother's institutional surroundings became more salubrious. In 1921 he arranged for her to move to California to be closer to himself and Syd (although she was officially denied permanent residence on the grounds of her mental instability). She died in Glendale in August 1928 at the age of sixty-one, with Charlie at her bedside. Intriguingly, obituaries to her would often cite some variation of her having been 'the victim of a mental illness induced by horror of air raids on London during the Great War'.[59] This may well have been another false impression given off by Charlie, if perhaps an understandable one given attitudes of the time towards mental health issues.

Boer War

Hannah was undoubtedly Charlie's overriding concern in the years that her instability took hold, but he was not myopic to the changing world around him. Talking to Harry Cocker, co-star of 1928's *The Circus*, Chaplin reminisced about his youth that 'being poor, the children in my neighbourhood were forced to make up most of our games. I liked to play soldier best.' Crocker was surprised: 'That's odd, because now you're a decided pacifist.' But, as Chaplin told him,

> at the time of the Boer War we naturally played at being Boers and British soldiers. When we played the surrender of Kronjen (the children must have invented the name, as I can find no mention of a prominent Boer leader by that name. Perhaps it is a corruption of Oom Paul Kruger). I never wanted to play the part of a British general, upright and stiffly military, who received the surrender: I asked for the role of . . . the defeated Boer leader, because his harrowed face and bent figure gave more ample scope for characterization.[60]

It was difficult to avoid such news. As Chaplin recalled in the 1960s, '1899 was an epoch of whiskers: bewhiskered kings, statesmen, soldiers and sailors, Krugers, Salisburys, Kitcheners,

Kaisers and cricketers – incredible years of pomp and absurdity of extreme wealth and poverty, of inane political bigotry of both cartoon and press.'[61]

The Boer War – formally the *Second* Boer War after a previous conflict (1880–1) – began in October 1899. While a war of imperial plunder – gold having been discovered near the city of Pretoria – the British were able to claim a fig-leaf of 'legitimate' concern for the plight of the so-called *uitlanders* (white, non-Boer immigrant labour) who had come, mostly from Britain, to capitalise on the new gold rush. With *uitlanders* outnumbering the longer-settled Dutch ancestral Boers by the mid-1890s, the British pressed the Transvaal government under Paul Kruger for concessions to safeguard their economic and political standing. When no such agreement was reached, those pressing for war, such as the colonial secretary Joseph Chamberlain, were able to lever Kruger into attacking British garrisons in the region, thus precipitating a conflict. With approaching half a million imperial troops put into the field by the British in the course of the war and less than a fifth of that number of defending Boers, the conflict looked, on paper, to be an easy one. Utilising mobility and guerrilla warfare against the British, however, the Boers proved effective warriors. Several British garrisons experienced sustained sieges during the three years of battle.

For its part, the *South London Chronicle* carried regular articles on the local regiments of Chaplin's youthful abodes – particularly the 3rd Middlesex Artillery – and their heroism was described in detail. Concerts were given – including one at the Horns Tavern and Assembly Rooms opposite Kennington Park where 'staircase and lobby [were] draped with royal standards, union jacks, garlands of artificial flowers . . . the effect being exceedingly pleasing'.[62] Even for the most politically disinterested, there would have been few ways to avoid encountering the glorification of empire in 1900. The stakes were high and emotions ran deep.

As the war ebbed and flowed the 'pomp and absurdity' that Charlie would later refer to only intensified. The relief of one British garrison, Mafeking, was met on 26 May 1900 with scenes of unrestrained jubilation in Charlie's hinterland:

> South London put all other occupations on one side, and started at once to compete with the rest of the Empire in

testifying its joy and delight. To put it comprehensively, the place at once went mad. In ten minutes ten thousand people lined London-Road and the fronts of the Alfred's Head, Elephant and Rockingham, and cheered themselves hoarse. Everyone had apparently a flag up his sleeve, for thousands were in evidence immediately. Every 'bus and 'tram that passed had a yelling crowd on top, whose demonstration was responded to by those on the pavement and on the road.[63]

At one theatre, the appropriately named Mr Bull (there was no mention whether his first name was John) stopped the performance of a play to joyfully announce, 'Mafeking is relieved!' His Elephant Theatre stage was then 'full of performers hand shaking and laughing while the band played the national anthem and Rule Britannia'. According to the *South London Press*, 'every house and every club' soon had bunting over it. Chaplin himself recalled the swing from 'dolorous news about the Boers surrounding Ladysmith' to 'England [going] mad with hysterical joy at the relief of Mafeking . . . Then we won. All this I heard from everyone but Mother. She never mentioned the war. She had her own battle to fight.'[64]

To the eleven-year-old Charlie, patriotism would always be the last refuge of a scoundrel. The dichotomy between the drab reality in which he lived and the grandiose 'Rule Britannia' nationalism then sweeping the nation was stark. If Britain truly was so 'Great' then how had it condemned generations of his family to the workhouse, madness or both? The relief of Mafeking was one vision of the British Empire, the mental asylums of South London another. The spectre of poverty during the Boer War – when up to four in ten men attempting to enlist to fight were deemed unfit for military service – launched a high-profile debate in British politics surrounding the efficacy and righteousness of the Poor Laws. Eventually, after a split between so-called 'Minority' and 'Majority' report factions (advocating increased state intervention versus increased charitable endeavour), the big state argument won out in British public life. If the most important institution of the state – the army – could not be relied on in times of war, there would need to be greater state intervention elsewhere in times of peace. If such paradoxes were not always resolved by Charlie's own later political philosophy, English statesmen had scarcely an easier time of it.

The state Charlie was in

Because of Charlie's constant movement as a child much of his location we must pin down by his formal registration in institutions of the state: schools or the workhouse. Identifying his precise location is often a challenge. His spell at Hanwell aside, he ranged across the hinterland of South London around Kennington Road. As such, late Victorian and Edwardian Camberwell, Clapham, Lambeth, Newington, Norwood, Tooting, Vauxhall and Walworth were all familiar to the future screen icon.

My Autobiography includes several vignettes concerning these places. In the week after his mother's transfer to the Cane Hill Asylum, for instance, the nine-year-old Charlie would wander the streets of South London. Passing by a mews at the back of Kennington Road, he encountered a collective of 'derelict-looking men who worked hard in a darkened shed and spoke softly in undertones, sawing and chopping wood all day, making it into halfpenny bundles'. Young Charlie was fascinated by the sight, and would hang about the shed's open door, watching them. Eventually he joined in, seeing the lumber brought in from contractors during the week, chopped by the men, and sold over the weekend: 'but the selling of it did not interest me; it was more the clubby working together in the shed'. Bonding with the older men – particularly since they provided funds to buy 'a pennyworth of cheese rinds and a pennyworth of bread' to make Welsh rarebit – Chaplin received an indirect connection to a future world when the men treated them all to a trip to see Fred Karno's comedy *Early Birds*. For the theatrical vehicle that would eventually lead him to the Little Tramp, it is no small irony that Charlie first encountered Karno through the benevolence of actual transients. Indeed, when Winston Churchill wrote 'how characteristically American are these homeless wanderers', he cannot have known of Charlie's early experiences.[65]

Likewise, when living in the unwelcome surroundings of his father and temporary step-mother Louise's abode on Kennington Road, Charlie would often walk around the streets simply to avoid having to deal with either an empty house, or Louise herself. Finding no food in the larder one day, Charlie walked to Lambeth Walk and then the Cut, 'looking hungrily into cook-shop windows at the tantalizing streaming roast joints of beef and pork, and the golden-brown potatoes soaked in gravy'. There he watched 'for hours . . . the quacks selling their wares. The distraction soothed me and for a while I forgot my hunger and plight.'[66] After night fell he returned home, only to be met by a drunken Louise who promptly threw him out. Remembering that his father drank at the Queen's Head pub on Prince's Road about half a mile away, Charlie promptly tracked him down, whimpering, 'She won't let me in and I think she's been drinking.' His father, no doubt honestly, replied, 'I'm not sober myself' as the two staggered home. The evening ended with Charlie safely in bed, but not before his father had thrown a heavy clothes brush at Louise's head, knocking her unconscious. This was Charlie's South London: insecure housing at best, institutionalisation at worst.

It is therefore worth providing a brief outline of the political landscape of such areas because as well as imbuing a negative impression of broad notions of 'the state' and 'government', his childhood was presided over by local politicians who were, to say the very least, not to Charlie's later way of thinking. For example, elected as Liberal Unionist member for Lambeth North in 1895, Henry Morton Stanley had previously been a prominent explorer of central Africa on behalf of the British Empire. On one such expedition he encountered the missionary David Livingstone, and uttered the famous greeting, 'Dr Livingstone, I presume?' Stanley argued that might was right and believed that 'the savage only respects force, power, boldness, and decision'.[67] Stanley's own actions apart, his association with the even crueller regime in the Belgian Congo did not mark him out as representative of the young Charlie, nor the man he would become. On such issues of race, in later life Chaplin stated that 'speaking of Negroes, I never laugh at their humour. They have suffered too much ever to be funny to me.'[68] Very few black characters would appear in his films. Indeed, in December 1925 his friend Upton Sinclair would write to Charlie telling him he had 'a find for you. A man turned up to repair our roof, with a negro helper who is the living image of you . . . If you were to bring him on screen with you, dressed in the same costume, it would raise a howl.'[69] This offer, like so many others that Sinclair would make Charlie, was batted away. Charlie's generally positive line towards the black experience was expressed in the fourth-wall-breaking final speech of 1940's *The Great Dictator*: 'I should like to help everyone if possible: Jew, Gentile, black man, white.' In expressing equivalence between the races, this certainly marked him out from Henry Stanley.

Stanley's successor as MP was the Conservative Frederick Horner – a man who had less blood on his hands than Stanley but was hardly a model of propriety either. Horner had been elected during the Khaki election of 1900 – when the Conservatives won a strong parliamentary majority on the back of the type of Boer War jingoism that Chaplin himself had seen after the relief of Mafeking. Although his political career was modest, he soon came to public attention. In 1902, Horner was accused of falsely obtaining cash and credit from a series of European hotels using cheques from his publishing business that usually bounced. In 1905, a series of new accusations came to light, detailing five more dishonoured cheques cashed across Monaco, France and Switzerland – totalling in excess of £500 pounds (more than £50,000 in modern money). After losing the seat in 1906, Horner was later imprisoned for forging a telegram sent to the *Daily Mail* that libelled the then Chancellor David Lloyd George. Not every late Victorian or early Edwardian British politician was such a rum character. Sir Frederick Cook as member for nearby Kennington and Sir Ernest Tritton in Norwood were less overtly controversial Conservative MPs in Chaplin's hinterland, but once again there were few models for positive governmental action at the national level for the young boy to latch on to.

All told, in Chaplin's youth the reach of government was rather limited, and deliberately so. As Michael Ball and David Sunderland note, the welfare system under which Victorian Britain was governed – the New Poor Law of 1834 – 'set out the rather unpleasant consequences of relying on state benevolence to ensure personal survival, and most other aspects of welfare had to be found somehow by individual family endeavour or not at all'.[70] The new legislation discouraged the provision of so-called 'outdoor relief' in favour of 'indoor relief' – targeting help, in other words, for those willing to enter the workhouse. As noted, this policy emphasis only increased as the century progressed. The workhouse was intended to be a harsh, fear-inducing place where only the truly desperate would enter. In the 1890s this, of course, included the Chaplins – with Charlie therefore marked out by the state as undeserving, feckless and beyond the pale from an early age.

More broadly, throughout the nineteenth century the 'mass of voluntary organisations, friendly societies and non-profit institutions grew substantially'. On the one hand, there was undoubtedly a large degree of philanthropy that occurred during this period – in the 1880s *The Times* even boasted that the £5 million annual income of the various charities around London was 'twice that of the Swiss confederation'. Yet this system, so far as it worked at all, was reliant on the rich continuing to pay a largesse for which they were under no compulsion. And equally, to be effective, those administering such voluntary donations had to be sympathetic to those in most need of the funds. This clearly was not always the case. To many within bodies such as the Charity Organisation Society – formed to disperse the various voluntary donations across England – the poor were essentially undeserving and were confined to their fate by bad morals, not mere bad luck. For a family such as the Chaplins – alcoholic absentee father and mentally unstable mother – this did not bode well. By the late 1890s Charles Booth recorded about 1.3 million Londoners living in primary ('struggling . . . to make both ends meet') or secondary ('in chronic want') poverty, with only 122,000 of these receiving any form of welfare relief.

There were exceptions that proved the general anti-state rule, however. The spectre of a mass cholera outbreak in 1849 mandated the creation of the Metropolitan Board of Works (MBW) in London six years later. Although initially set up to tackle the growing problem of the capital's sewers, the MBW later assumed a more overarching role concerning wider infrastructure matters, such as building regulations and street improvements. Indeed, part of Chaplin's later political oddity was that for all he feared the big state he often admired the type of public works schemes enacted by 'big government' – particularly the New Deal in 1930s America. When journeying back to London in 1954 he recalled that 'naturally I was shocked when I saw [the new] Waterloo Bridge – that beautiful, slick, modern, very fine utility'.[71] Charlie could often be impressed by the power of the state, even when he would simultaneously fear its reach.

Much of this may have emerged from his early experiences in London. Joseph Bazalgette's role as chief engineer at the MBW saw a tripartite project of embankments spring up alongside the River Thames at Westminster, Chelsea and Vauxhall Bridge Road. These huge undertakings of new infrastructure, built in the 1860s and 1870s, were a significant reference point for Chaplin – not least because his first date with his first love Hetty Kelly would end on the embankment, with Charlie so ecstatic with the way that it had gone that he donated £3 to the tramps lining the riverside. Indeed, it was originally intended that *City Lights* would commence on the Thames embankment, with the Tramp awaking and the story segueing into the business with the statue that eventually would begin that work. Back in the real world, as Londoners generally clamoured for greater democracy and transparency, however, the MBW that had produced these embankments gave way in 1889 to the London County Council (LCC). The early LCC was dominated by the so-called 'Progressive' block of would-be Labour and left-leaning Liberal politicians. The Progressive era was built on a modest reform platform including the taxation of ground rents, a municipal death duty and trying to increase London's share of Treasury (that is, national government) support. As work took Charlie out of the capital his experience of this more active example of local government was, however, limited. The day-to-day nuts and bolts of municipal rates would be less his experience of the MBW and LCC than the imposing architectural achievement that they left behind.

What Chaplin almost certainly did not take from this time – and he certainly did not mention doing so – was any innate affinity with socialism or the various left-wing parties inhabiting the late-Victorian/early Edwardian British political spectrum. For one, as Stedham Jones notes, the Social Democratic Federation (or its successor from 1911, the British Socialist Party) never possessed more than 3,000 London members in a population of approximately 6.5 million (1901). Moreover, any 'strength it did possess was mainly concentrated in the new outlying working-class areas like West Hammersmith and Poplar [in East London]'. Equally 'areas where trade union or labour candidates could win elections – Deptford, Battersea and Woolwich – were similarly situated on the outskirts'. Conversely, 'the inner working-class area, the old home of radical working-class activity, remained largely unresponsive to socialist influence'.[72] At this stage it is very likely that such apathy included the young Charlie Chaplin.

Charlie finds his career, and his country

In any case, politics could wait for now because his performing career was about to take off. Charlie's initial theatrical break came through the troupe of William Jackson, the Eight Lancashire Lads. Jackson was known to Chaplin's father, and Charles Snr had convinced Hannah that it would be good for their son to make a career on the stage. The economics of the matter were certainly beneficial: Charlie would be given free board and lodging, while his mother would receive half a crown (2s 6d, or one-eighth of a pound) a week. The Jacksons were staunchly Catholic, leading to everyone initially attending mass save Charlie. Even so, 'I was lonely, so occasionally I went with them. Had it not been for deference to Mother's religious scruples, I could easily have been won over to Catholicism, for I liked the mysticism of it.'[73] After six weeks training Charlie began dancing with the troupe, enjoying such activities but all the while hoping to be able to explore more comedic avenues. One night, playing a cat, Charlie let his instincts roam. Only supposed to act as an arch for the main character, a clown, to tumble over his back, Charlie instead decided to embellish his role, including going up to the rear end of a dog also included in the scene and beginning to sniff. In however crude a form, a comedian was born.

The mobile nature of Chaplin's new profession meant that he saw rather more of his homeland than the average citizen. When touring with the Eight Lancashire Lads, he spent more than two months in Manchester in late 1898 and early 1899. The year 1899 saw visits to Cardiff and Swansea in Wales, and 1900 to the North-East of England (Newcastle and South Shields), Scotland (Glasgow and Edinburgh), the industrial West Midlands (Birmingham), Yorkshire (Sheffield, Leeds and Bradford) and Ireland (Belfast and Dublin). Since numerous cities – Belfast and Edinburgh included – experienced higher costs of living and lower wages in several professions than London, seeing life outside the capital was an important development.[74] Certainly Charlie played to grandiose settings, such as the London Hippodrome, but the spectre and geography was varied. In April 1901, his run with Jackson's troupe finally ended.

Before relaunching his theatrical career, and wishing to be close to his mother, Charlie then undertook various odd-jobs to make ends meet. As he later recalled, 'I had been newsvendor, printer, toy-maker, glass-blower, doctor's boy etc, but during these professional digressions, like Sydney, I never lost sight of my ultimate aim to become an actor.'[75] It was something akin to entrepreneurialism that sustained young Charlie through his mother's ill health and his father's waywardness: 'There was a strong element of the merchant in me.' 'Continuously preoccupied with business schemes', the young Charlie decided that 'all I needed was capital'.[76] A conversation with his mother later, he left school and embarked on his professional career. Charlie may or may not have been a shirker during the Great War – and we will get to that controversy in the next chapter – but one could hardly describe his career, all told, as shirking. If we take his scoring the music for the 1975 re-issue of *A Woman of Paris* as the end of his career and take his debut at Aldershot in 1894 as the start, we are talking about a career that lasted more than eight decades (and at least seventy-five years, even if we date his debut as occurring with the Eight Lancashire Lads). Just as the Tramp was usually on the lookout for gainful employment, so, too, was this the case with his young creator.

Returning to the stage, he also once again saw British life outside the capital. When playing Billy in Sherlock Holmes for H.A. Saintsbury between 1903 and 1906, he had week-long stretches everywhere from Perth in the East of Scotland to the South Wales coal-mining area of Tonypandy. These experiences were undeniably formative – not least in confirming to the young Charlie that the harshness of his own upbringing was not unique to him. If the sociologist Karl Mannheim is right and people are defined for the rest of their lives by the person they were at the age of seventeen, then Charlie spent most of that supposedly crucial summer (1906) in England's industrial north, not South London.

London was obviously crucial in a number of ways for Charlie, but his concept of Britain was perhaps wider than is always acknowledged. For instance, Charlie had a particularly long memory for an encounter in Ebbw Vale, Wales. Only there for three nights, Charlie was 'thankful it was not longer, for Ebbw Vale was a dank, ugly town in those days, with row upon row of hideous, uniform houses, each house consisting of four rooms lit by oil-lamps.'[77] Put up in a local hostel, Charlie became curious that he was never allowed to enter the kitchen. Then, one evening, the landlady's husband who had been to see Charlie perform told him, 'I've got something that might fit your kind of business.' He continued: 'Ever seen a human frog?' The man led Charlie into the locked kitchen where he rested a lamp on top of a dresser and said, 'Hey Gilbert, come on out of there!' Charlie recalled that 'a half a man with no legs, an oversized, blond, flat-shaped head, a sickening white face, a sunken nose, a large mouth and powerful muscular shoulders and arms, crawled from underneath the dresser . . . the grisly creature could have either been twenty or forty.' After the landlord encouraged him to jump, Gilbert launched himself upwards by the power of his arms, almost to the height of the young Charlie's head. 'How do you think he'd fit in with a circus? The human frog!' exclaimed the man. Young Charlie was 'so horrified I could hardly answer'. Although he made sure his bedroom door was locked overnight, Charlie would later, 'with an effort to be casual, shake [Gilbert's] large calloused hand' before he left.[78]

Karno and Kelly

Saintsbury established Charlie as a professional actor, but he did not make him a star. As such, even in a book concerning Chaplin's politics it would be remiss to leave out two decisive personal connections: Fred Karno and Hetty Kelly. After all, Fred Karno helped shape the career that gave Chaplin the political platform of this volume while Hetty Kelly proved vital, albeit unknowingly, in influencing Charlie's relationships with women.

Fred Karno was born in Exeter in 1866 before his parents settled in the East Midlands city of Nottingham where he spent his youth. Like Charlie himself, the young Karno scratched a living in various odd jobs, including being a barber's boy, a costermonger, a bricklayer and a chemist's shop boy. Discovering he had an ability as a gymnast, he formed the Three Karnos troupe with two acrobats, Bob Sewell and Ted Tysall, which met with moderate success. Karno had a natural flair for business, however – and from 1894 began to put on his own shows that included the high-flying exploits of his background but soon moved in a more comedic direction. A brash self-promoter, he used stunts such as faking police chases to draw attention to his various touring acts. Quite apart from Hetty Kelly, there are many links between Chaplin and Karno. Billy Reeves, the brother of Charlie's future studio manager Alf, invented the character of the inebriate that Charlie later took over to stunning reviews. From 1906 Charlie's brother Sydney had worked for Karno on a contract of £3 a week and soon set about trying to convince his boss to bring his younger brother on board. Karno was initially sceptical, feeling Charlie was 'much too shy to do any good in the theatre, particularly in the knockabout comedies that were my speciality'.[79]

After a successful trial in February 1908 Charlie overcame such reticence, however. With Charlie on a contract that was 10s a week better than Sydney's, the Chaplins were now doing rather well. They jointly rented a flat at Glenshaw Mansions, Brixton Road, which put them according to Charles Booth solidly in the 'lower middle class' of 'hardworking, sober, [and] energetic' individuals. If the legacy of Charles Snr and Hannah must have acted as something of a corrective for any cocksureness, this did not always translate to personal attitudes on tour. Sydney was always a welcome companion, but Karno recalled that Charlie was at this time 'not very likeable. I've known him go whole weeks without saying anything to anyone in the company.'[80] One exception to this could, however, soon be seen: for Charlie had fallen in love.

By all accounts Hetty Kelly was a pretty fifteen-year-old understandably overwhelmed with the degree of sudden affection the then nineteen-year-old Charlie showed her in the summer of 1908. This relationship – such as it was – seems to have knocked Charlie for six, and was something he arguably did not get over for decades. As David Robinson notes, 'for anyone else it would have been an adolescent infatuation, a temporary heartbreak forgotten in a week. But Chaplin was not like anyone else, and something in his sensibilities or rooted in the deprivations of his childhood caused this encounter to leave a deep and ineradicable impression upon him.'[81] All told, Charlie's courting of Hetty lasted a week and a half and saw the two alone for no more than twenty minutes at a time.

The two had first met at the Streatham Empire, where Hetty was performing in a song and dance troupe that was the opening act before Karno's *Mumming Birds* headlined the bill. Standing in the wings watching the show, Charlie noticed 'two large brown eyes sparkling mischievously, belonging to a slim gazelle with a shapely oval face, a bewitching mouth, and beautiful teeth'. The effect of Hetty Kelly Charlie found 'electric', and the two soon arranged a date for the Sunday. Meeting Hetty at Kennington Gate, Charlie recalled that 'her presence so overwhelmed me that I could hardly talk'. Taking a taxi into the West End, the date itself would prove a disaster. Dining at the Trocadero, Hetty said she was not hungry and so ordered a sandwich to keep Charlie company. Since 'we were occupying a whole table in a very posh restaurant', Charlie remembered, 'I felt it incumbent to order an elaborate meal which I really did not want'. Nerves getting the better of him, Charlie thought 'we were both happy to leave the restaurant and relax'.[82]

After he had walked her home to Camberwell Road, the two agreed to meet at seven the following morning where Charlie could walk her to the nearest tube station to get her to rehearsals. This continued on the Tuesday and the Wednesday – the two walking hand in hand to the station, enjoying each other's company. Yet on the Thursday Hetty became cold towards Charlie. She refused to take his hand, followed by Charlie reproaching her for not being in love with him. 'You expect too much,' she replied. 'After all, I am only fifteen and you are four years older than I am.' Recalling this in his autobiography, Chaplin follows it with the very pointed remark: 'I would not assimilate the sense of her remark.'[83] Indeed, a four-year age gap was about as good as it was going to get for Charlie's love life from this point forward. He would get older, the women would remain youthfully Hettyesque.

When Hetty declared that she did not know if she loved him, Chaplin began interrogating the young girl. He asked her: 'Would you marry me?' 'I'm too young,' she replied. This was actually technically inaccurate – as minors (under twenty-one years old) both Charlie and Hetty would have required parental consent, but

the minimum age possible for marriage at this time was the fourteen years for boys and twelve years for girls that it had been for
centuries. It would, however, have been unusual (the average age
for one's first marriage in late Edwardian England was in the mid-
twenties), and certainly pre-marital sex would have been illegal –
since the Criminal Law Amendment Act of 1885 sixteen years
had been the legal age of sexual consent, with heavier punish-
ments for sex with those under the age of thirteen. Nevertheless,
Charlie continued: 'Well, if you were compelled to marry, would
it be me or someone else?' 'I don't know . . . I like you . . . but . . .'
'But, you don't love me.' Reaching the entrance to the Underground, Chaplin remarked that he had 'let this thing go too far'
and that the two should never see each other again. Undaunted, the
next morning Chaplin did pop around to see the Kellys, eventually
persuading Hetty's mother to let him see her daughter. 'Well,' he
remarked, attempting to be humorous, 'I've come to say goodbye
again.' Hetty appeared 'anxious to be rid of me', and with a simple
'goodbye' she slowly closed the door on Chaplin. The sixth chapter
of Chaplin's autobiography ends rather poignantly: 'Although I
had met her but five times . . . that brief encounter affected me for
a long time.'[84] Indeed so.

Still, at least Charlie's career was taking off. In 1909, the Karno
Company had been engaged for a month in Paris where Charlie
played at the Folies Bergère. Other than artistic merit, this was
a trip where Chaplin let himself go. Getting drunk on absinthe,
Charlie spent several nights – together with other members of the
Karno troupe – in Parisian brothels. Attempting to procure a high-
class prostitute at one of his shows, he had an interpreter who
worked at the theatre 'write down a few *phrases d'amour*' on the
back of a postcard. Armed with several gems – including *'Je vous
ai aimée la première fois que je vous ai vue'* – this proved unsuccessful since it turned out that the proposed 'vingt francs' transaction fee was indeed only 'pour le moment' and not the 'toute la
nuit' marathon session Charlie had planned. Sensing poor value,
he backed out. The man was careful with his money.

More foreign travel was to soon follow. In September 1910, the
Karno Company was engaged for a North American tour – thus
forming the first time that Charlie would set foot in the land he
would reside in for more than forty years. An improved contract

of £6 a week for 1911/12 (£8 for 1912/13 and £10 for 1913/14)
suggested this career was going places. Initially that place was
Quebec, followed by a train to New York where the Karno Company played a three-month engagement. Following this, a twenty-
week tour saw Charlie travel across America, from Chicago to
Los Angeles, via such less glamorous locations as Butte, Montana
and Tacoma, Washington. After twenty-one months in the States
Charlie briefly returned home in June 1912. Discovering that Sydney had become engaged and had left Glenshaw Mansions behind,
Charlie found England increasingly dull by comparison with the
land of the free. He had seen the world, and now wanted more of
it. When the Karno Company was re-engaged for another American tour he leapt at the chance to go. On 9 October 1912, he went
to Southampton to set sail for America, this time for good.

First sights of America

In 1931 Charlie branded the British 'the World's Greatest hypo-
crites'. Chaplin remarked that 'they say I have a duty to England,
I wonder just what that duty is. No one wanted me or cared for
me in England seventeen years ago. I had to go to America for my
chance and I got it there. Only then did England show the slightest bit of interest in me.'[85] This idea that America could prove a
salvation to immigrants from Britain was of course hardly Chaplin's alone. From 1876 to 1900, almost two million adult males
left Britain for North America all told, with the vast majority (five
in six) settling in the US itself. In 1890, about 5 per cent of the US
population had been born in Britain, and the theatre – as proven
by Charlie's own father – had long been a boom export.[86] In any
event, for mostly better, sometimes worse, America was about to
show *a lot* of interest in Charlie. But, while the Karno company
was doing decent business in the States, Chaplin was hardly a
household name at this point. He needed a wider platform.

The troupe began its tour by playing the smaller theatres around
the Midwest and North Eastern United States, before they were
scheduled to depart for the Pacific Coast. After five months 'working the sticks' six days a week, Charlie was 'discouraged' and
determined to enjoy a week's lay-off, mostly by living the high
life on a vacation to New York. Returning to Philadelphia where

the troupe was based, he passed by the theatre where Alf Reeves showed him a telegram he had just received. 'Is there a man named Chaffin in your company or something like that STOP If so will he communicate with Kessel and Bauman 24 Longacre Building Broadway.'[87] Kessel was one of the owners of the Keystone Film Company, and had seen Charlie perform his inebriate character at the American Music Hall on 42nd Street. Keystone was looking for a replacement for their main star Ford Sterling who was leaving to form his own production company with Universal. After some negotiation, an agreement was signed. Charlie the movie star was born, and set off to Los Angeles to meet his future boss Mack Sennett (who ran the Californian end of Keystone) and co-star/ director Mabel Normand.

By this stage he had certainly come a long way, not least geographically. Yet so much of Charlie's life would be determined by what he had experienced in these formative years. Later he would comment, 'I am not in politics because I am not particularly impressed with systems of politics, but I do think I am a humanitarian, as everyone who follows the artistic profession believes himself to be.' He retained a lifelong antipathy for 'the idea of an individual or a system kicking around a lot of small helpless people'.[88] This was doubtless a product of some all too memorable experiences in his youth, and a Patrick Joyce-esque populism was buried within him. Marrying his art, these early impressions and a significant dose of politics would mark the rest of his life. His pathological fear of losing money and returning to his childlike poverty would manifest in a number of ways – stinginess when it came to picking up a tab, refusal to pay an appropriate level of taxation until threatened with jail and, perhaps, the refusal to donate meaningful sums of money to his preferred political causes. The spectre of his youth haunted him all his life.

Yet perhaps we may end this summary of these early days on two things that he had *not* experienced, or at least fully imbibed. As several historians have contended, the English theatrical stage in the Victorian and Edwardian eras could be a place for radical political engagement. As Marc Brodie has noted, 'theatre performances could act as one of a range of influences on how the poorest of the London working class saw the political conflicts of the day'. He continues, outlining that while such lessons 'gained could be quite different from the "reality" of politics, [they could] provide a much more rational explanation for the political responses of the poor than the purely "mob mentality" usually ascribed to them'.[89] This was a legacy that Chaplin certainly took from his early years, but that had not fully emerged from its ideological chrysalis. As yet, he had not worked out how to transmute his still developing political views – anti-establishment, anti-patriotism and a desire to curb poverty – into an artistic form; but there was that latent experience within him.

Second, more directly, by the time he left the UK, Charlie had never actually voted in a national election. He was off on tour during the election of the new interventionist Liberal government in 1906. Even as his career took off, he still did not fulfil the property qualifications to vote at the next election in January 1910. And when a snap election was again called in December 1910 he was off touring the States. As someone who would never take American citizenship, he cannot have voted in any later American federal election either. When Charlie later spoke in such grandiose terms about fighting for democracy, therefore, he was speaking something that was, for him, an abstract notion. Not only would he not join any political party, he would never take part in that most basic affirmation of the social contract between citizen and their elected representatives: an election. His difficult upbringing had given him good reason to distrust a political elite he would never have the option of having to sully his own ideological purity by voting for. The next sixty years would see this play out in several ways.

Notes

1 'The Future of Charlie Chaplin's Contribution', *Collier's Weekly* [undated 1934/5], Churchill Archives Centre, Cambridge, UK [CAC], Winston Churchill Papers [CHAR] 8/521.
2 Astor diary, 26 July 1926, University of Reading, UK [UOR], Nancy and Waldorf Astor Papers [AST], MS 1,066/1/36.
3 *Daily Herald*, 26 February 1931, clipped in Municipal Archives, Montreux, Switzerland [MAM], Charlie Chaplin Clipping [CCP] Book 31.
4 Reported in *New York Mirror*, 28 September 1933.
5 Clipping from Chaplin Office, Paris, France [COP], CCP file 50.
6 *Footlights*, November 1929.

52   Chaplin's England

7 *Toronto Standard*, 22 May 1931.
8 Late 1930s typescript, Hoover Institute, Stanford University, California [HOOV], News Research Service [NRS] 791.
9 See Clapham letter, 19 February 1953, National Archives, Kew, London [TNA]. Security Service Papers [KV]/23/700.
10 See Clapham letter, 30 April 1953, TNA/KV/23/700.
11 David Robinson, *Chaplin: His Life and Art* (London, 1992), 10.
12 Kenneth S. Lynn, *Charlie Chaplin and His Times* (London, 1998), 39.
13 Charlie Chaplin, *My Autobiography* (London, 2003), 13.
14 Lynn, *His Times*, 37.
15 Gareth Stedman Jones, 'Working-Class Culture and Working-Class Politics in London, 1870–1900; Notes on the Remaking of a Working Class', *Journal of Social History*, 7/4 (Summer, 1974), 460–508, 477, 479.
16 Ibid., 498.
17 On such 'principal motifs' such as 'booze, romantic adventure, marriage and mothers-in-law' see Peter Bailey, 'Conspiracies of Meaning: Music-Hall and the Knowingness of Popular Culture', *Past and Present*, 144 (1994), 138–70.
18 Chaplin, *My Autobiography*, 13.
19 Ibid., 14; although in the 1920s, flush with the freedoms of America, he would complain of England being 'so set and solid and arranged' See the Burke interview within London Metropolitan Archives [LMA]/Greater London Council [GLC]/DG/AE/ROL/34/5(i).
20 Chaplin, *My Autobiography*, 14.
21 Ibid., 15.
22 Ibid., 17.
23 Ibid., 17.
24 Ibid., 19.
25 Ibid., 23.
26 Churchill, 'Chaplin's Contribution', CAC/CHAR/8/521.
27 Ibid.
28 Margaret Herrick Library, Academy of Motion Pictures Library, Los Angeles, California, USA [MHL], Charlie Chaplin Interview Transcript [CCI]/33.f-302.
29 Peter Ackroyd, *Charlie Chaplin* (London, 2014), 124.
30 Churchill, 'Chaplin's Contribution', CAC/CHAR/8/521.
31 Jowitt speech to Dickens dinner, 7 February 1955, Parliamentary Archives, House of Lords, London, UK [HOL], William Jowitt Papers, JOW/2/40.
32 Brooks letter, 14 November 1977, within MHL/Louise Brooks Papers, Collection 874.
33 All via Charles Booth, *Life and Labour of the People in London* Volume 1 (London, 1902), 33–62.
34 Chaplin, *My Autobiography*, 26.
35 All via James Greenwood, *A Night in the Workhouse* (London, 1866) passim.

36 Mary McKinnon, 'Poverty and Policy: The English Poor Law, 1860–1910', *Journal of Economic History*, 46/2 (1986), 500–2.

37 The cumulative effect of the nineteenth-century reform acts was also to exclude many recipients of poor relief from the franchise, too.

38 Chaplin, *My Autobiography*, 27.

39 Charlie Chaplin (Lisa Stein Haven ed.), *A Comedian Sees the World* (Missouri, 2014), 47.

40 Chaplin, *A Comedian Sees the World*, 47–8.

41 Chaplin, *My Autobiography*, 28.

42 'Correspondence concerning Charlie Chaplin', within LMA/GLC/DG/AE/ROL/34/5(i).

43 Chaplin, *My Autobiography*, 58–9.

44 Chaplin, *My Autobiography*, 29–30.

45 Harsh treatment was not atypical. One former workhouse boy, H.A. Webb, would write to *The Times* on 20 September 1964 recalling that 'I was given six lashes just for feeding the hungry sparrows who hopped in the hallway while we dined!'

46 Chaplin, *My Autobiography*, 31.

47 Ibid., 30.

48 Ibid., 31.

49 'The Tragic Comedian' by Thomas Burke, *Pearson's Magazine*, vol. 53, via LMA/GLC/DG/AE/ROL/34/5(ii).

50 See, e.g., Patrick Joyce, *Visions of the People: Industrial England and the Question of Class 1848–1914* (Cambridge, 1990).

51 Register of deaths, 1890–1915, LMA/Microfilm related to Lambeth Workhouses [X113]/018.

52 *South London Chronicle*, 17 February 1900.

53 Freud to Schiller, undated, within MHL/Harry Crocker Papers [HRC] f.12.

54 Chaplin, *My Autobiography*, 68.

55 Ibid., 70–1.

56 Robinson, *Life and Art*, 16.

57 Jerry Epstein, *Remembering Charlie: The Story of a Friendship* (London, 1988), 13.

58 Chaplin, *My Autobiography*, 74.

59 *Reading Eagle*, 29 August 1928.

60 Harry Crocker's unpublished memoir, 'Charlie Chaplin: Man and Mime', MHL/HRC, 1–23.

61 Chaplin, *My Autobiography*, 54.

62 *South London Chronicle*, 6 January 1900 via Minet Library, Lambeth Archives [MLA]/South London Press [FPP3].

63 *South London Chronicle*, 26 May 1900 via MLA/FPP3.

64 Chaplin, *My Autobiography*, 54.

65 Churchill, 'Chaplin's Contribution', CAC/CHAR/8/521.

66 Chaplin, *My Autobiography*, 37.

67 Henry M. Stanley, *Through the Dark Continent* (Dover, 1988), 31.

68 Cited in Theodore Huff, *Charlie Chaplin: A Biography* (London, 1952), 261.

69 Sinclair to Chaplin, 29 December 1925, LLBI/UPS Box 6.

70 Michael Ball and David Sunderland, *An Economic History of London, 1800–1914* (London, 2001), 365.

71 BBC Radio Interview, 8 December 1954.

72 Stedman Jones, 'Working-Class Culture', 481.

73 Chaplin, *My Autobiography*, 44.

74 Ian Gazeley and Andrew Newell, 'Poverty in Edwardian Britain', *Economic History Review*, 64/1 (2011), 52–71, 62.

75 Chaplin, *My Autobiography*, 76.

76 Ibid., 57.

77 Ibid., 84.

78 Ibid., 84–5.

79 Robinson, *Life and Art*, 76.

80 Ibid., 77.

81 Ibid., 80.

82 Chaplin, *My Autobiography*, 104–5.

83 Ibid., 106.

84 Ibid., 107.

85 *Springfield News*, 11 May 1931 via COP/CCP.

86 Statistics via Alan G. Green, Mary Mackinnon and Chris Minns, 'Dominion or Republic? Migrants to North America from the United Kingdom, 1870–1910', *Economic History Review*, 55/4 (2002), 666–96.

87 Chaplin, *My Autobiography*, 138.

88 Christian Delage, *Chaplin: Facing History* (Paris, 2005), 28.

89 Marc Brodie, 'Free Trade and Cheap Theatre: Sources of Politics for the Nineteenth-Century London Poor', *Social History*, 28 (2003), 346–60, 346.

2 To shoulder arms? Charlie and the First World War

In the summer of 1933 the English writer Alistair Cooke sat on the deck of a yacht that was gently sailing some twenty miles south-west of Los Angeles Harbour. Cooke was on a two-year fellowship to Yale and had networked his way through J.L. Garvin – editor of the British *Observer* newspaper – on to a boat owned by Charlie Chaplin. Later to be known on both sides of the Atlantic for *Masterpiece Theatre* on PBS, and BBC Radio 4's *Letter from America*, at the time he encountered Chaplin Cooke was just a young journalist trying to make his way in the world. The scene was tranquil enough – Paulette Goddard, Chaplin's then romantic and cinematic partner, Cooke remembered as 'enchanting'. The other two guests, Chaplin's chef and the boat's skipper, were both unobtrusive enough. All in all, the fare was good. Eggs, bacon and pancakes were soon served, and Chaplin beckoned Cooke over to the food by tossing a napkin over his forearm, cocking his head expectantly, and placing 'his right hand . . . in a kindly step-this-way freeze'.[1] As surviving home-movie footage of Charlie clowning around showed, he was often 'on' even when not formally at the studios. Certainly, on that morning off Catalina Island, all seemed convivial enough.

Perhaps triggered by the presence of a fellow Englishman, Charlie suddenly became very serious, however. Cooke recalled this was often the way – 'he was always reciting [his political sermons] in snatches, at the unlikeliest of times, and in the end they led to his banishment from the United States'.[2] We will deal with that later. In 1933, still hoping for a job out of Charlie, the young Cooke listened intently as he consumed his breakfast. The two discussed the old music hall stars Marie Lloyd and Vesta Tilley before Cooke, without thinking, remarked that his father had kept a copy of a record called 'Oh, the Moon Shines Bright on Charlie Chaplin'. Charlie looked shocked: 'That,' he muttered slowly, 'scared the hell out of me.'[3]

It was the First World War – and others' reactions to his actions during it – that would ultimately politicise Chaplin. To understand his sensitivity in recalling the subject, we only have to look at the lyrics of this wartime sensation:

> Oh, the moon shines bright on Charlie Chaplin
> He's going barmy to join the army
> But his old baggy trousers they'll need mending
> Before they send him to the Dardanelles
>
> Charlie Chaplin meek and mild
> Stole a sausage from a child
> But when the child began to cry
> Charlie socked him in the eye
> Charlie Chaplin had no sense
> He bought a flute for 18 pence
> But the only tune that he could play
> Was ta-ra-ra-boom-de-ay
>
> Oh, the moon shines bright on Charlie Chaplin
> His shoes are cracking, for want of blacking
> And his baggy khaki trousers still need mending
> Before they send him to the Dardanelles
>
> Charlie Chaplin went to France
> To teach the ladies how to dance
> First you heel, and then you toe
> Lift your skirts and up you go
> Charlie Chaplin Chuck-Chuck-Chuck
> Went to bed with three white ducks
> One died and Charlie cried
> Charlie Chaplin Chuck-Chuck-Chuck
>
> Oh, the moon shines bright on Charlie Chaplin
> His shoes are cracking, for want of blacking
> And his old fusty coat will need a mending
> Before they send him to the Dardanelles.

As Cooke's cringing reaction to his own faux pas shows, Chaplin's fear was very real. A coward, much more a feminised coward, was not the best review to have for any filmmaker between 1914 and 1918. Shirking war service, being 'meek and mild' and indulging in comedic japes while heroic British and American boys died overseas could look none-too-good to those who wished him ill, and even for those who had only previously understood him as a cinematic comedian. As Cooke well knew, this was all part of 'the insensate jingoism of wartime Britain' that had been stoked by 'the holy indignation of comfortable editorial writers against any famous Englishman abroad who had not dashed home to join Our Boys Out There in Flanders Field'.[4] Brave service or cowardly shirking during the First World War became, for many of this generation, the ultimate test of one's courage, manliness, and loyalty to the crown. Chaplin had not fought, had not joined either American or British armies and to some degree paid the public relations price. He was not of course the only person of fighting age to be uncomfortable with the conflict, or indeed to decide not to serve. In April 1916, about 200,000 British people gathered in Trafalgar Square, London to protest against the introduction of conscription, and more than two million British men of fighting age did not perform active service at any point during the conflict (for various reasons ranging from physical disability to conscientious objection to being employed in a protected occupation). Chaplin was therefore hardly unique in not donning uniform. But his monumental fame set him apart. And to trace the gripe many on the political right had with Chaplin, we must therefore go back to the origins of that fame: the early days of Hollywood.

Hollywood and the evolution of film

For a world for whom Hollywood now means big stars, big trailers and big business it is difficult to recapture the atmosphere of the early cinematic world in which Charlie dipped his toes. The most obvious difference was that, in the first decade of the twentieth century, there *was no Hollywood*, at least not in the modern interpretation of the global capital of film-making. In 1910, 36 per cent of the films shown in London, for example, were French-made compared to only 25 per cent coming out of

America.[5] The world of early film was plural, anarchic and international, not capitalist, plutocratic and always Americanised.

This had particular ramifications in the country Chaplin had now moved to. As Steven J. Ross has observed, 'during the first three decades of the twentieth century, when the movie industry was still in its formative stages, movies and movie theatres were battlegrounds for the control of the consciousness and class loyalties of millions of Americans'.[6] By 1910, about twenty-six million Americans – close to three in every ten – were attending the movies on a weekly basis. Most of these were working class – indeed, as late as 1924 the Motion Picture Theater Owner's Association proclaimed that '80 percent of the movie patrons were either working class or [only] moderately well off'.[7] The early world of movies was not designed for the chattering intelligentsia, but for the working man on his way home from a hard day's toil and seeking twenty minutes of amusement. Indeed, early cinemas were often located in parts of town that the affluent found less than safe, and thus the film industry was a rather ghettoised affair. That was part of its charm.

After an economic Depression that had straddled the mid-1890s, the new Progressive era of policy making in Washington, D.C., therefore, had to try to dovetail with a new medium that was reaching millions of the economically dispossessed. Things were changing, and cinema was depicting this, and thus it needed to be watched carefully. Throughout the late nineteenth century collective bargaining and industrial militancy shortened the usual American working week from a seventy-two-hour, six-day week often seen before the Civil War to a sixty-hour week by 1890 and a fifty-one-hour week by 1920. Real wages for non-farm employees rose more than a third from 1890 to 1920. All this was no doubt positive, but it was another form of upheaval being experienced by a country that had gone through so much in the latter half of the nineteenth century. Combined with significant levels of urbanisation and immigration, America was being irreparably altered. Many American elites were not happy about these changes, much less about their being publicised or potentially praised through the new cinema.

And yet this is precisely what was happening. From the 1905 emergence of the nickelodeon – the early cinema where patrons were charged a 'nickel' (five cents) for entry – until America entered the First World War in April 1917, Ross estimates that there were at least 274 films released that demonstrated so-called 'labor–capital' themes. Far from brushing change under the carpet, these movies highlighted the struggle, explicit or implicit, between workers and their bosses.[8] To be sure, in a climate where up to 5,000 films were released a year this was numerically not the be-all and end-all – most films therefore 'conformed' – but the themes exhibited in such labour–capital plots remained worrisome to many. For one, there was the simple notion that 'if leftist works or personnel could please audiences and make money for producers, then companies were willing to chance their oppositional politics'.[9] What would happen, in short, if these roots took hold and a liberal or radical message proved significantly profitable? A working-class audience watching profoundly leftist cinema was therefore no small concern.

In determining the political perspective of the aforementioned 274 early labour–capital films, Ross utilises five distinct categories (the percentage of those that fit each description is included in brackets): liberal (46 per cent), conservative (34 per cent), anti-authoritarian (9 per cent), populist (7 per cent) and radical (4 per cent).[10] Discounting the conservative category – 'those that presented worker . . . activity in the worst possible light' – for obvious reasons, it is worth considering these other labels when we consider Chaplin's future work.[11] First, Ross himself includes Chaplin as a sometimes 'radical' filmmaker – someone willing to 'advance positive depictions of socialists, their struggles and their goals'.[12] He also rightly notes that the cinematic adaption of a later friend of Chaplin's, Upton Sinclair's *The Jungle* (1914), highlighted the radical theme of 'the devastation that industrial capitalism inflicts upon workers through the exploration of the American meatpacking industry.[13] Thinking forward to *Modern Times* it is difficult to deny this strand to Chaplin's career, although it was arguably more clear in his real-life intellectual leanings. Here we should acknowledge that in many ways Chaplin was breaking free from his music hall roots where, as Peter Bailey has noted, 'the conflict lines of class were elided the site of its most direct struggles, the workplace'.[14]

Such 'radicalism' aside, however, Chaplin could also embody Ross's description of the 'liberal' filmmaker – someone who 'called for co-operation between employers and employees, and advanced reform (not radicalism) as the best method of solving the industrial ills that beset the nation'.[15] Chaplin's 1920s views on Henry Ford, for example, would match this label. In fact, a running theme of this work is that while Chaplin was not a communist, he most certainly was a liberal. As such, and with the earlier referenced comparisons in mind, Chaplin almost precisely mirrors George Orwell's 1940 description of Charles Dickens:

> a man . . . who fights in the open and is not frightened, . . a man who is GENEROUSLY ANGRY – in other words, a nineteenth-century liberal, a free intelligence, a type hated with equal hatred by all the smelly little orthodoxies which are now contending for our souls.[16]

Charlie would face antipathy for such a stance on both sides of the Atlantic, and his 'liberalism' rather neatly straddles the differing American and British interpretations of the term. Just as he supported the liberal domestic interventionism of Henry A. Wallace in the 1948 US Presidential election, so too did he share the nineteenth-century British liberal fears regarding the encroachment of the 'big state'. Sympathetic small businessmen or entrepreneurs – from the prospector in *The Gold Rush* to the barber in *The Great Dictator* – appear with some regularity in Chaplin's work. Charlie's view was that it was possible to fix the world's problems by co-operation between public and private spheres within a democratic system, but that the balance should not tip too far in favour of either.

Ross's third category of so-called 'populist' films – the 'Yellow Press of the screen' that adopted a 'gut-level class hatred' – was, however, rarely Chaplin's style. *The Idle Class* (the one Chaplin film title to include the word 'class') would be gentle enough in its mocking of the 1920s elites – the pomposity of golf rather than the purposelessness of greed was more its target. *A Woman of Paris* would capture something of the 'populist' spirit whereby 'capitalists committed crimes and unspeakable acts that drove honest working people to suicide but went unpunished', but again pulled some punches.[17] Even by *Modern Times*, politicised jokes such as the Tramp unwittingly acquiring a Red Flag that results in a beating down from the police could be seen to be as much about clever execution as they are trying to hammer home the 'class division' point. Perhaps.

Lastly, however, Ross's description of the anti-authoritarian filmmaker – those who 'did not directly challenge capitalism, [but] mocked the authority of those who often gave workers the hardest time: foremen, judges, police and employers' – fit the early Chaplin like a glove. Charlie was, notes Ross, 'the greatest anti-authoritarian comic of his age'.[18] Yet mocking those in charge did not of course denote a precise platform for what should replace them. In a sense, that is where Chaplin's political statements again augment his cinematic work. His writings and his speeches expressed sentiments it was difficult (due to the censors) or inadvisable (he still wanted to make money) to put on screen. In the 1930s and 1940s the line between his cinematic and personal output certainly began to blur, but we need to consider both to truly understand the man. Hence, in essence, the rationale for this book.

Ross's demarcations of genre matter not least because such anarchic, politically challenging cinema soon received some push back. For example, in 1915 the Mutual Film Company (which Charlie would begin working for the following year) had challenged the right of the state of Ohio to operate a motion-picture censorship board. This board was charged with reviewing all films to be released in the state, and had the power of arrest for anyone producing movies it judged of ill repute. The Supreme Court eventually ruled in the state's favour by nine to zero – judging that First Amendment guarantees of freedom of speech did not apply to the film industry, and operating a censorship board was therefore entirely within the legal confines of state or national government. There *were* such things that were off-limits, therefore, a process that would play out over the next couple of decades through the imposition of various codes to guide producers in what they could and could not show. In such light, creative independence would come to matter more and more.

The overall point then was that as Charlie arrived in Hollywood, and as he began to change audience perceptions of what they expected from film, he was stirring a cauldron that contained a more controversial brew than he realised. Even had the First World War not happened, and even had he managed to keep his sexual exploits out of the papers, he would *still* have been a political filmmaker, because film itself was fast becoming a battleground for the soul of America. America's pastime had become the movies, and thus making any type of cinema that did not reinforce the economic status quo was inherently challenging. Being English born and raised, the fact that he had no grounding in that status quo made a confrontation all the more likely.

Charlie changes film

However he brokered his appeal to the American people, Charlie (or rather his agent, brother Sydney) proved a consummate negotiator with his employers. Beginning at Keystone at the tail end of 1913, Charlie would jump to Essanay (November 1914), Mutual (February 1916) and First National (June 1917) film production companies during the First World War – all of which increased his salary exponentially but, just as crucially, his level of artistic control. As his friend Ivor Montagu later noted of Charlie, 'money [was] pleasant – certainly for one whose formative years were so hard-pressed – but the essential [thing] was the growing independence it secured in the creative field'.[19] Early on, the boundaries for creativity were rather limited. Mack Sennett's production company was known for its high-paced and cartoonish Keystone Cops, and while Charlie's early output had the odd flicker of pathos that would mark his later work, these were films pumped out at a rate that precluded much seriousness. Indeed, when Charles Kessel had asked him what he thought of Keystone in his initial interview, Chaplin 'did not tell him that I thought they were a crude melange of rough and tumble'.[20] After initially struggling to impress Sennett, in the forty-four-week stretch that Charlie appeared for Keystone he managed to act in thirty-six features – mostly single-reel skits.

During the first half of 1914 Charlie was very much second fiddle to Mabel Normand – reflected in titles such as *Mabel's Strange Predicament*, *Mabel at the Wheel* and *Her Friend the Bandit*. Although Charlie found the 'dark-eyed . . . pretty' Mabel attractive, personally the two never got on and Charlie found her direction 'incompetent'.[21] Still, as the year went on it is clear that Chaplin was becoming a star in his own right – November saw titles such as *His Musical Career*, *His Trysting Place* and the last film he would make for Keystone the next month, *His Prehistoric*

Past. In fact, perhaps ironically, it was capitalism that saved Chaplin's career from being ended before it had begun. After one too many quarrels on set with Mabel, Sennett had been determined to fire Chaplin, but had received 'a telegram from the New York office telling him to hurry up with more Chaplin pictures as there was a terrific demand for them'.[22]

From this point on, the relationship with Sennett was always personally close, but it remained artistically limiting. Sennett's view was to begin a film with 'no scenario. We get an idea, then follow the natural sequence of events.'[23] In many ways this infuriating method would remain with Charlie his entire life, but the point was that he wanted to portray 'ideas' of his own. With his move to the Essanay company therefore (which occurred after Sennett pushed his contractual brinkmanship on for too long), Charlie very much became James L. Neibaur's description of an 'artist in transition'.[24] Scenes that previously would have been played with an 'aggressive' air – such as a woman bending over – were 'presented as an accident . . . [helping Charlie become] less of an aggressive knockabout clown and more of a substantial screen character'.[25] This emerged because at Essanay Chaplin was now assured he would no longer have to work for other directors. From April 1914 Charlie had begun to direct some of his pictures at Keystone, but several films were still either co-directed or co-written with Mack Sennett or Mabel Normand. With complete creative control came control over casting, and in February 1915 he would cast a young secretary, Edna Purviance, in *A Night Out* – the first of thirty-three films that Edna would experience under Charlie's directorship. For eight years Edna would serve as Charlie's muse – helping launch her own career no doubt, although also serving to soften the image of the Tramp away from a mere cartoonish scamp to a living, breathing human with real feelings and emotions.

Two Essanay films typify this. First, April 1915's *The Tramp* is often held up, not least for its title, as the moment that Charlie's character became the lonely little man he would go on to be so famous for portraying. The film is fairly knockabout stuff, but it concludes with a trope later often repeated (most famously in *The Circus*) – the Tramp bowing out of a love triangle in the knowledge that his sweetheart and his love rival are better suited.

Likewise, four months later *The Bank* saw Charlie's janitor character attempt to woo Edna's pretty bank secretary, but only to see she has her heart set for another. That film saw Charlie recycle bits from Keystone (the plot is essentially borrowed from *The New Janitor* in which he had appeared the previous year) and Karno (a dream sequence in which he wins Edna over through saving her in a bank robbery). But the ending of both would launch a trend within Chaplin's films of the Tramp striving for a better life, but not quite gaining it. In such fare, as Libby Murphy notes, 'Charlot['s] . . . position is not one of outright revolt or rebellion. Instead it is one of dogged refusal – refusal to accept defeat or give in to dismay.'[26]

Feeling that Essanay were both underpaying and overworking him, Charlie again asked Sydney to look around for alternatives and eventually settled on the Mutual Film Company. At Mutual, Charlie would deliver twelve two-reelers, all of which he would produce, direct and star in. These included several important works and interesting elements of storytelling. For example, in *Easy Street* (January 1917) the Tramp answers a job advert for a local policeman and proves a spectacular success. With a local thug terrorising the poor people of *Easy Street* and the existing police too afraid to deal with him, Charlie goes on to use unconventional methods to bring him down. After gassing the bully in a conveniently placed gas lamp and arresting him, the Tramp later encounters the same, even more enraged adversary upon his escape from the police station. For all the slapstick violence, this was a remarkably brutal picture. At one point a junkie is shown injecting himself with a drug that causes him to attack a defenceless woman. By inadvertently sitting on the self-same needle the Tramp – rather foreshadowing a darker version of Popeye – becomes supercharged and able to defeat the various miscreants of the town. A title card reads 'Love backed by force, forgiveness sweet. Brings hope and peace to Easy Street' before an epilogue scene shows the Tramp as now a pillar of the community, having brought safety and stability to a once chaotic neighbourhood. In many senses, it is an oddly conservative parable about law and order prevailing.

Perhaps the most famous of the Mutuals would, however, prove to be June 1917's *The Immigrant*. The film concerns Charlie and Edna on a boat arriving into Ellis Island, and the welcome – or lack thereof – they receive in America. In 1949, *The Daily Worker* reflected on the meaning of *The Immigrant*, as did so many of Charlie's films. The film had 'appeared during the year of America's entry into the first imperialist war' and in it 'Chaplin dared to show men and women going hungry in a land of plenty at a time when the bugles were blowing'. The maltreatment of second-class immigrants being 'herded like cattle' was, for those communist-leaning Americans, a profound cinematic moment.[27] This article would be later dutifully clipped by some Washington functionary and added to the case the House Un-American Activities Committee was building against Chaplin in the 1940s.

The Immigrant has been compared to Franz Kafka's novel *Amerika* (written between 1911 and 1914, published 1927) that deals with the travails of a German immigrant to the United States. As Parker Tyler argued, in this posthumously published work Kafka took 'his epic hero to the shores of this country and subject[ed] him, in deliberately Dickensian manner, to the hazards of a young modern civilization, ending, as customarily, on an ambiguous note, but this time of hope rather than of despair'.[28] Going further, Tyler argued that Kafka's character 'Karl and Charlie the Tramp are heroes of the identical international myth: the great adventure of the young foreigner coming head-on to the United States to start a new life and hoping to rise to a level beyond any available to him in his native land'. Of course, 'in the real-life dimension, this was literally Chaplin's career'.[29] Like Thomas Paine, William Cobbett and, in later years, Christopher Hitchens, Chaplin brought a contrarian English radicalism to America.

In the work of both Chaplin and Kafka there would be a puncturing of the image of the American dream. In Kafka's *Amerika* the Statue of Liberty is portrayed holding a sword rather than a torch: less 'give me . . . your huddled masses' and more 'might is right'. In Chaplin's *The Immigrant* no such reinvention is proffered, but the very use of the Statue of Liberty in his film was controversial. The Statue made clear that Charlie's film did not take place in the 'never-never' world of Chaplinesque fiction – somewhere non-specific between Lambeth and Los Angeles – but was clearly in the modern-day, real-life America that had just entered a world war to fight for 'liberty' and 'democracy' and had just passed a 1917 Immigration Act that precluded the immigration of anyone from the so-called 'Asiatic Barred Zone'. Although it ends on the happy sight of Charlie and Edna getting married, the poverty depicted throughout the film was also shocking for many middle-class audiences in the American heartland. An extension of themes explored in Upton Sinclair's novel *The Jungle*, the two artists doubtless expressed their mutual appreciation in their first meeting the following year.

Moving on again to the First National Company, Charlie would go on to flesh out the Tramp character further, but this period was also marked by some of his more slapdash works. Having formed United Artists in February 1919, Charlie was eager to work out his contract as soon as possible. As such, the audience was occasionally treated to uneven comedies such as May 1919's *Sunnyside* that barely seemed to be coherent films at all. In that particular work, disjointed scenes are met with the type of title cards that suggest that even Chaplin could not be bothered to create a coherent plot beyond walking his audience through the usual tropes: 'And now "the romance".'

Other than *Shoulder Arms*, which we consider below, there was the odd chink of light, however. For one, 1921's *The Kid* has been remarked upon by many historians as intensely autobiographical, and certainly very poignant. Detailing the horrors associated with the potential separation of (de facto) parent and son by the state, the film lends the Tramp a paternal and altruistic streak that would have been out of place in the early Keystone days. In the film, the Tramp unwittingly becomes the guardian of a baby boy left by his impoverished mother in a rich man's car. The car is stolen by thieves who, discovering the baby, leave him on the street where he is picked up by Charlie. After being initially reluctant to look after John, the Tramp develops a deep bond over several years with the child, reinforced by their scheme involving the child throwing a stone through neighbourhood glass windows and Charlie conveniently walking by offering to affix glass panes to some suddenly needy tenants. When the authorities learn that Charlie is not the father of John, however, two men are sent to take him to an orphanage. The scenes that follow – a weeping child, a desperate Tramp determined to stop John being taken from him – mix melodrama and slapstick comedy to a degree Chaplin was fast becoming a past master at.

The Idle Class of 1922 would also contain some of Chaplin's most inventive comedic asides. A scene where the wealthy husband (played by Chaplin) who unwittingly leaves his bedroom without any trousers – masked by a series of beautifully timed choreography from his servants – and then has to make his way back again is superbly executed. A later scene, shot from behind, where the husband seems to be shaking in fits of tears at his wife having moved out of the marital bedroom (on account of his drunkenness) only for Chaplin to reveal he is mixing a cocktail is also a brilliant moment. But for the only one of Chaplin's film titles to include the word 'class' in it, it was not bitingly political. *The Idle Class* includes a portrayal of the wealthy characters as mostly drunk and/or decadent, and takes much from the absurdities of golf, but the chief romantic plot – which rests on a proto-*City Lights* mistaken belief that the Tramp is a rich man – would not quite deliver. It is a film as much about pure idleness as it is class. Interestingly, it does, however, assert a conventional married life as the Tramp's dream – a flash of sometime artistic conservatism from Charlie at this stage.

Such correctives matter because of how the Tramp was viewed by his contemporaries. For one, Buster Keaton recalled an essential difference between his own silent persona and that of the Little Tramp. He was 'always puzzled when people spoke of the similarities in the characters Charlie and I played in the movies'. For Keaton, his creation was a member of the virtuous working class: 'My little fellow was a workingman and honest.' But 'Charlie's tramp was a bum with a bum's philosophy. Loveable as he was he would steal if he got the chance.'[30] Fundamentally, if either creation wanted to buy a suit he saw in a shop window, Keaton's character would 'start to figure out how he could earn extra money to pay for it' whereas Charlie's would either 'steal the money . . . [or] forget all about the suit'.[31] The Tramp was, in other words, a pauper condemned to perpetual poverty. This may have been true in the early silents, but through the 1920s in *The Kid* or, later, *The Gold Rush* his efforts would increasingly be rewarded in an America that seemed to be growing more at ease with itself. The 1920s, and Chaplin's growing attempts to be taken more seriously, we will address in the next chapter.

Fame

Artistic evolution aside, Charlie's level of fame during the First World War was truly astonishing. Advertising his films for showing in Britain from June 1914, Keystone proclaimed that 'there has never been so instantaneous a hit as that of Chas. Chaplin . . . Most first rank-exhibitors have booked every film in which he appears, and after the first releases there is certain to be a big rush for copies.' This certainly proved to be the case and in this regard Britain was merely mirroring America. From Los Angeles Charlie wrote in August that year to his brother that

> I have made good. All the theatres feature my name in big letters i.e. "Chas. Chaplin hear [*sic*] today". I tell you in this country I am a big box office attraction. All the managers tell me that I have 50 letters a week from men and women from all parts of the world. It is wonderfull [*sic*] how popular I am in such a short time and next year I hope to make a bunch of dough.[32]

He certainly delivered in that regard.

As he later recalled, by 1915 'my popularity kept increasing with each succeeding comedy'. Sydney promptly all but gave up his own acting career to manage Charlie's affairs, and there was much to manage. Although Charlie knew of his popularity in Los Angeles 'by the long lines at the box-office, I did not realize to what magnitude it had grown elsewhere'. In New York 'toys and statuettes of my character were being sold in all the department stores and drugstores'. The Chaplins were also inundated with 'all manner of business propositions involving books, clothes, candles, toys, cigarettes and toothpaste'.[33] Rob Wagner, more of whom later, was taken on at this point to help deal with the sheer volumes of fan mail coming into Chaplin's office.

By way of continuing illustration (and a less positive one), *The Times* of London ran a series of articles entitled 'Notes of a Neutral' that commented on the general climate of the war then engulfing Europe. In August 1915, this anonymous columnist reflected on 'the chief popular indoor amusement in England . . . the cinematograph theatre'. Out of curiosity, its correspondent went to one such attraction where they saw 'not one film shown to give any idea of the work of the British Army or the British Navy'. Instead, 'the whole audience looked forward to the antics of one Charlie Chaplin'. He was, noted a bemused writer, 'the idol of millions of your people'.[34]

A few days later, having read this article, an anonymous letter from the pen-name of 'Action' arrived to the same newspaper demanding that 'someone take the nation in hand'.[35] All hands should have been to the pumps of winning the war, not relaxing at the cinema – and this would be a recurring theme. In December 1915 a letter was published in *The Times* from a wounded soldier stating that

> sometimes a feeling of intense depression would settle on one, and of black despair of England ever facing facts or even words . . . We were, indeed depressed at the strikes, at the failure of recruiting in spite, or perhaps because of, the contemptible methods employed, at the demand for war bonuses and unprecedented waste of them . . . and, at the general rottenness of taste and feeling in a country which can amuse itself with "Charlie Chaplin" in days like these.[36]

By mid-1915, certainly, the Tramp was increasingly used as a metaphor to make political points. In July 1915, the *Evening Times* would portray a man with a globe for a face smiling at Charlie while Kaiser Wilhelm II – portrayed with a rat-like face – looked on rather upset. The caption read that 'the Crown Prince protests to the world he is being superseded by Charlie Chaplin as the universal laughter-maker'.[37] Two months later *Punch* would run a cartoon of the British wartime Minister of Munitions (and soon to be Prime Minister) David Lloyd George in a derby hat and cane with a man labelled 'Trade Union Congress' at his feet. The caption read: 'The Charlie Chaplin of Politics: The Little Champion (Lloydie George) after bringing certain people (at Bristol) down with a run and giving them a nasty jar, toddles off with a spasmodic raising of the hat to seek other adventures.'[38] Evidently, the image of Charlie could now serve as a catch-all for propaganda against the enemy, or as a descriptive means to portray domestic unrest between government and trade unions. This would continue virtually throughout his lifetime, not always for the better.

A shirker?

For all his later controversial statements, Chaplin's biggest early political move was actually a form of inaction. Charlie did not fight in the war while millions of his countrymen (and adopted country of America) did. This matter haunted him for decades and, as Jerry Epstein recalled, 'hurt him deeply'.[39] As one-time Chaplin actor Adolphe Menjou put it during the anti-communist HUAC hearings of the 1940s, 'the only gun Mr Chaplin had ever heard go off was a pop-gun in his studio'.[40] By not fighting in the war, Charlie's reputation would be tarnished for decades, including among those actors – such as Menjou – who had served in the conflict. Yet on the issue of his lack of uniformed service during the Great War Chaplin had no formal case to answer. The British Embassy – the only country, after all, Chaplin was ever a citizen of – issued a statement in 1917 noting that

> we would not consider Chaplin a slacker unless we received instructions to put the compulsory service law into effect in the United States and unless after that he refused to join the colo[u]rs. Chaplin could volunteer any day he wanted to, but he is of as much use to Great Britain now making big money and subscribing to war loans as he would be in the trenches especially when the need for individual men is not extremely pressing. There are various ways for one to do one's bit.[41]

Informally, however, Chaplin was a man of fighting age (that is, from eighteen to forty-one) who was seemingly having a 'good war' while others of his generation fought and died for his liberty to do so. As the Republican-supporting Menjou illustrated, his lack of military service would long be a sore point with the American right.

Part of this emerged from the fact the acting profession per se had stepped up to the plate during the war. By December 1914, 800 actors had signed up for the British Army, a trend exacerbated by the fact that theatres, even more than football grounds, were often major recruiting centres. After conscription was introduced from 1916 pressures became even greater. As Adrian Gregory notes, one magistrate at a North London court 'even threatened to invoke the Vagrancy Act, not used against actors since 1824, to punish an Irish actor who had failed to report to the military authorities'. This magistrate was only sorry for 'the passing of the sterner Puritan days when those who fooled about the country with parties of players would be placed in stocks as vagabonds'.[42] By the time that the dust had settled on the conflict, Hollywood icons present and future, such as Menjou, Buster Keaton and Humphrey Bogart, had been seen to do their patriotic duty for the American war effort, too.

Chaplin's reticence to physically take part at the front was hardly unique. Keaton, who would briefly serve 'as a thirty-dollar-a-month private' in the American Army – far less than the $250 weekly salary he was then on for his films – also expressed reservations about fighting. Keaton later noted that 'it was not always possible to take that war seriously'. He could not understand why 'we, the French and the English were fighting the Germans and the Austrians'. Keaton believed 'people from everywhere in the world were about the same. Not as individuals, of course, but taken as a group.' He also 'resented the uniform which made me look and feel ridiculous . . . The size eight shoes handed me were far too big for my size six and one-half feet.'[43] Spending seven months in France, he slept every night but one in the ground or on the floor of mills, barns and stables. With such buildings often having a strong draught, Keaton developed a cold that impaired his hearing, later leaving him deaf in one ear.

The most famous example of the informal pressure exerted on Chaplin at the time, however, came from the very British Lord Northcliffe, formerly Alfred Harmsworth, the proprietor of the *Daily Mail*. To his allies such as Max Pemberton, whom we will curiously encounter defending Chaplin shortly, Northcliffe was 'a very remarkable personality and a very great patriot – who rendered imperishable services to his country and who never by his countrymen [must be] forgotten'.[44] This was one view. As Winston Churchill commented, however, armed with the 'solemn prestige of *The Times* on the one hand and the ubiquity of the *Daily Mail* on the other' Northcliffe was capable of holding politicians to virtual ransom as and where he felt the urge.[45] By 1915 his latest bugbear had become the prosecution of the First World War where 'in his view, unless Britain demonstrated her determination to France and Russia by instituting compulsion, one or both might make a separate peace with Germany'.[46] In a pattern ably laid out by the historian J. Lee Thompson, through 1915 and early 1916 North-cliffe therefore ratcheted up his campaign for universal conscription.

Judging the 1915 creation of a National Register that listed all men between the ages of 15 and 65 (presumably therefore including himself) who were not members of the armed forces as insufficient since it lacked any element of compulsion to get these 'slackers' to join the army, Northcliffe turned his papers into an all-out demand for conscription. On 16 August 1915, the *Daily Mail* published a manifesto in support of national service that included a pro-conscription form for the reader to fill out and post to the government. By October 1915 the so-called Derby scheme was launched that required all men aged 41 and under to make a public declaration as to whether they were enlisting at once, or to 'attest' to join a list of reserve soldiers who would be called up as and when necessary (and to wear an armband testifying to their declaration in the meantime). Aiming at attracting half a million new recruits to the British Army, it fell short at about 340,000 by the time the scheme ended in December. Part of the shortfall was undoubtedly married men, who were placed at the back of the queue to be called-up, and so-called 'volunteerism' was not going to cut it. By January 1916, partly due to the pressure of North-cliffe, a bill for universal conscription (including married men) was therefore brought before parliament – to take effect from April.[47]

Before we deal with the ramifications for Chaplin it is important to contextualise the Northcliffe affair. Most British newspapers did not take the same stance as this populist maverick. The use North-cliffe made of his tabloidesque *Weekly Dispatch* to claim that 'if Charlie joined up, as is his duty, at least thirty other British cinema performers of military age would have no [similar] excuse' was not a tactic replicated by all.[48] For one, the conservative-leaning *Spectator* magazine did not mention Chaplin's lack of active service during the war, nor did Northcliffe's own more establishment and 'newspaper of record' *The Times*. Local British newspapers were rarely explicitly critical of Chaplin's lack of service. For sure, the dichotomy of horrific (and/or heroic) stories of local regiments appearing alongside an advert for Charlie's latest film did not likely help his reputation, although it is difficult to read into people's views. Was Charlie a slacker or Charlie the man who, for a moment, could help them forget about the horrors of war?

We may deal with the facts first. Charlie's 1916 Mutual contract explicitly specified that as a British subject 'he shall not leave the United States and run the risk of compulsion in Britain within the life of the contract without the permission of the corporation'.[49] It is difficult to ascertain who demanded this clause – the studio not wanting to lose their cash cow, or the cash cow who wanted a plausible excuse not to serve at the front. Certainly, from the moment the ink was dry on this contract Charlie was using it as his formal 'line' to explain why he was not in a uniform. Denying in March 1916 that he was 'hiding behind my player's coat', Charlie did, however, note that 'my professional demands do not permit my presence in the Mother Country'.[50]

This type of activity was certainly ammunition for the anti-Chaplin Northcliffes, but not all publications toed this line. In April 1916, one month after the implementation of conscription for all British men of fighting age, *The Economist* weighed in to *support* Chaplin on the issue. This august publication objected to the 'policy of commandeering the residue of a population which has already been far more depleted of men than that of Russia'. And this was best illustrated 'by a popular case, the case of Mr Charlie Chaplin'. According to *The Economist*, 'that gentleman is said to be earning £2,500 a week in the United States, yet some Fleet Street luminaries cry out for his recall, to be drilled'. The economics of the Northcliffe case simply did not add up:

> If Mr Chaplin, after supplying himself with the necessaries, and perhaps some of the conveniences of life, is remitting £1,000 a week home for investment in the War Loan, he is not only assisting the American exchanges, but he is also paying for some 200 new recruits.

As they noted, 'the alternative is to force him into one soldier. [And so] we would ask every public man who has a moment of leisure to reflect upon the case of "Charlie Chaplin," and to reconsider the policy of draining our industries and commerce dry just when their activity and efficiency are most needed.'[51] Quite aside from Chaplin's own travails, it is worth noting that he was being used here as a means of defending free enterprise and productive capitalism. And possibly also as a tool of resistance against Northcliffe's domination of the British press.

Nevertheless, on 5 June 1917 Charlie Chaplin finally appeared to bow to pressure and formally registered for the American military draft in Los Angeles. Of 'slender' and 'medium' build, this self-declared 'alien' reported for duty while listing one financial dependent, his mother. On 22 June Northcliffe's *Weekly Dispatch* claimed that 'nobody would want [Chaplin] to join up if the army doctors pronounced him unfit, but until he has undergone medical examination he is under the suspicion of regarding himself as specially privileged to escape the common responsibilities of human citizenship'.[52] Here we encounter something of a grey area. In short, Chaplin very possibly was unfit to fight. A history of asthma, chronic nervousness and a malnourished childhood may well have stood him in poor stead to serve the allied effort in the trenches. He also would probably not have made a great soldier. As Harry Crocker stated, 'Charlie was a pacifist. He not only realized the fatality of war, but the futility of his attempting anything which smacked of action.'[53] Indeed, years later, when commenting on the prospect of a war between Russia and America in the 1950s, Charlie stated, 'I know what I'd do if my son was in that. I guess I'd do everything to stop it. I don't want him to go there to fight for democracy or for anything. I mean when you think of the horror of some of their deaths, [or] they come back basket cases.'[54]

But he does seem to have evaded the draft through simple skulduggery. Charlie Chaplin was widely thought to be at least 165 centimetres tall, or 5 feet 5 inches (sometimes he even claimed 5 feet 6 inches). Mysteriously, when it came to his physical examination by the American Army, he had dropped an inch. At an alleged 5 feet 4 inches and 129 pounds, Chaplin was deemed to be too small to don an American military uniform by the doctor at his army physical. Alf Reeves, Chaplin's manager, later released the statement that 'no one could expect Charlie to join up, as he only weighs 8st, and no army doctor would accept him'.[55] With the British minimum height requirements at 5 feet 4 inches from October 1914 (lowered to 5 feet 2 inches from July 1915) even this fiction did not preclude his service in the British Army, but London did not pursue the matter. In December 1917 Chaplin released a statement saying that he was ready and willing to answer my country's call to serve in any branch of military service at whatever post national authority may consider I might do most good, but I am waiting for word from the British Embassy at Washington. Meanwhile, I have invested a quarter of a million dollars (£50,000) in the war activities of America and England, contributing to both loans. I registered for the draft here, and have not asked for exemption. Had I been drawn I would have gone to the front like any patriotic citizen.[56]

A flurry of later reports in April 1918 suggested that he had renounced his British citizenship and would join the American Army, but neither proved to be true.[57]

Charlie's defence at not serving was twofold – he was entertaining the troops (and their loved ones) through his on-screen performances, and these performances were generating a revenue stream that greatly aided the Allied war effort. In March 1916, he remarked in an open letter to the British people that 'if, in my modest sort of way, in occasional bits of cheery nonsense as "Charlie Chaplin" of the films, I can instil a moment of brief relief from the brunt of the fray, this is my contribution to the men at the front'. Although Chaplin's aversion to jingoism has already been noted, in an age of global conflict he was careful to buttress such excuses with statements such as the fact that 'the days of Wellington and Nelson were not lived in vain, for the spirit that underlies present England is no less strong in courage and in absolute fearlessness'.[58]

Contrary to *Blackadder Goes Forth*, the troops do seem to have enjoyed Charlie's work.[59] In November 1916 a gathering of 400 wounded soldiers from across the Allied nations was held in the ballroom of the Savoy Hotel, London. Before an afternoon of tea, food and smoking, there was held 'an exhibition of cinematograph films, with Charlie Chaplin as the *pièce de resistance*'.[60] Moreover, the Imperial War Museum in London retains images of a tank named 'Charlie Chaplin' (lost on 9 April 1917 during the First Battle of the Scarpe), of several soldiers dressed in Little Tramp costumes when off duty, and of a Charlie Chaplin scarecrow built in tribute by Tommies to guard a road (see Figure 2.1).[61] American sources also defended Chaplin's comedic

Figure 2.1 Charlie remained immensely popular with soldiers at the front. Here men of the British Army Service Corps, Mechanical Transport, have placed a model labelled 'Our Charlie' to guard the road against German advance.

Courtesy of the Imperial War Museum, London, UK

value for the front line, too. In August 1917, the *Portland Oak Journal* noted that

> there is one argument . . . which will strike one as absurdly illogical. It suggests that Charlie might amuse the troops in billets if his condition did not warrant him going into the trenches, [but] in billets Charlie would be able to amuse a select few of his comrades at any one time. At the present time he is, on the film, affording entertainment to millions, not least among them being the boys in khaki and blue.[62]

For all the Northcliffes, Charlie clearly had his defenders in the press all told. While *The Economist* laid bare the financial case for

Charlie continuing to make movies as British soldiers lost their lives, the author Max Pemberton put forward the comedic case, too. As noted, Pemberton was a friend and golfing partner of Northcliffe – not innately liable to defend Charlie, therefore. Yet in a September 1915 *Sunday Pictorial* article he posed the question as to whether 'the Charlie Chaplin Craze' was a 'sign of national indifference?' 'Ought we who remain at home to enjoy ourselves,' he asked, 'while our soldiers are sacrificing their lives?' Pemberton's view was emphatically yes: 'Wars are not won by brooding, nor victories achieved by gloom.' Indeed, for the many to whom 'the dawn beings anew the terrible question of yesterday: "Is my son still among the living?"' they were quite entitled to 'turn gladly to those who will break the spell of the doubt even for a little while'. Since many 'owe precious hours to Charlie Chaplin . . . who would rob them of his gifts?'[63]

Comedic utility aside, Chaplin's activities on the Liberty Bonds tours were undeniably significant, too. From April 1917 to September 1918 four separate wartime bond drives (known as Liberty Bonds) were launched by the US government. All told, these raised in the region of $17 billion for the American war effort, and investors garnered returns ranging from 3.5 per cent to 4.5 per cent. Yet the first drive did not prove universally popular, and the tax incentives had to be tweaked to encourage full take-up. In April 1918, Chaplin, Douglas Fairbanks, Mary Pickford and other film stars were therefore persuaded by Treasury Secretary William McAdoo to tour the country 'hawking bonds to movie mad citizens'.[64] In a single afternoon, on the back of crowds of up to 100,000 people, these stars were able to persuade ordinary Americans to part with up to $17 million worth of funds for the war effort. This tour was important above and beyond what it did for the prospect of victory over the Central Powers (see Figure 2.1). As Steven J. Ross notes, 'The war bond tour gave Chaplin his first insight into the political uses of stardom. He discovered that people were more interested in hearing what he . . . had to say than any congressmen, senator or even President.'[65] At the time, this was the usual patriotic stuff about 'the Germans' being 'at your door' and 'we will stop them, if you buy Liberty Bonds', but being given such a platform – and, for a silent comedian, a voice – must have been intoxicating. People listened and, in 1918, agreed with Charlie wholeheartedly. But this in turn worried many in the corridors of power: 'If stars could sell war bonds with such effectiveness, why not political ideas that challenged official policy?'[66]

Such efforts aside, Charlie dealt with the war in two ways on-screen (excluding the later portrayal at the beginning of *The Great Dictator* in 1940). The first was a naked piece of propaganda for the Liberty Loan entitled *The Bond*, released in September 1918. *The Bond* walks the viewer through the three successive 'bonds' of friendship (Charlie and Albert Austin), love, and marriage (Charlie and Edna) before turning to 'the most important: THE LIBERTY BOND'. In the latter skit, the Kaiser (played by Charlie's brother Sydney) attempts to manhandle Edna's Statue of Liberty before an American soldier appears to save the day. The point is then hammered home when the Tramp (portraying 'The People') gives a bag of money to Uncle Sam in return for a Liberty Bond and a hearty handshake, and Uncle Sam then hands the money to a man representing 'Industry' who in turn then provides a gun to both an army soldier and naval warrior. The screen dissolves to black before we again see the Kaiser who is promptly knocked to the floor by the Tramp holding a hammer saying, 'Liberty Bonds'. An arrestingly shot production with a totally black background and stark lighting, *The Bond* would be produced by Charlie for free to help aid the war effort.

More significantly, in October 1918 he released the comedy *Shoulder Arms* – predominantly set in the trenches of France. Having made *A Dog's Life* Charlie was 'worried about getting an idea for my second picture [for First National]. Then the thought came to me: why not a comedy about the war?' Friends warned Charlie off the project, with Cecil B. De Mille telling him, 'It's dangerous at this time to make fun of the war.' Still, 'dangerous or not, the idea excited' Charlie. Initially planned as a five-reeler taking in the Tramp's home life before the war, his service during it and a celebratory banquet at the end, Charlie eventually 'thought it better to keep Charlot a nondescript with no background and to discover him already in the army'. Initially dissatisfied with the film, it was only when Doug Fairbanks saw the film and laughed hysterically that Charlie was persuaded to go ahead with its release. 'Sweet Douglas,' recalled Charlie in the 1960s, 'he was my greatest audience.'[67]

For all its clowning, *Shoulder Arms* remains an intensely patriotic film. There are some nice slapstick gags: Charlie applying a gasmask to eat some Limburger cheese, the Tramp finding it difficult to learn the straight-legged march of the American Army with his natural inclination to bow his feet and the remark, when asked how he single-handedly captured thirteen German soldiers, that he 'surrounded them'. But beneath the comedy, the Tramp is essentially a patriotic soldier who serves bravely for a noble cause (French liberty being portrayed through Edna's role as a makeshift Marianne). Trench life is not idealised – the Tramp is shown sleeping in a trench full of water and as scared to go over the top – but the overall effect is of a brave man doing his bit. Even the end, when Charlie captures the Kaiser only for it to be revealed that the film has been a dream all along, reinforces the righteousness of American participation in the conflict. *Shoulder Arms* suggests that it *should* be the dream of all Americans to do this, and that getting the pretty girl and the acclaim from previously sceptical soldiers as a result of serving in the war is a potential outcome of this war. That this was so at odds with the real life of Charlie's own war experience was rarely referenced in the reviews, with *The New York Times* simply noting that 'the fool's funny'.[68]

Mildred

As British and American soldiers were engaged in the final push to defeat the Kaiser's Army, Charlie was getting married to his first wife, Mildred Harris. Chapter 4 of this study will give much attention to his second 'child bride' Lita Grey, but Chaplin's first union bore much of the same hallmarks. Here we bump up against two conflicting accounts from the respective parties in the marriage – although neither appear terribly flattering to Chaplin. First, for all the talk of youthful beauty and innocence, it is possible that Chaplin liked his wives to be so young simply to avoid any form of intellectual competition. To his friend Douglas Fairbanks, Charlie remarked that 'Mildred was no intellectual heavyweight'. This, however, did not matter: 'I had no desire to marry an encyclopaedia – I could get all my stimulus from a library.'[69] In Charlie's account the affair began after his chauffeur Kono had remarked to Charlie's valet Tom Harrington that Mildred was 'the most beautiful girl he had ever seen'. Charlie later recalled that 'this absurd remark appealed to my vanity – and that was the beginning'.[70] Egged on by the comments of his employees, 'the only possible interest [Mildred] had for me was sex; and to make a romantic approach to it, which I felt would be expected of me, was too much of an effort'.[71] In the belief that he had gotten Mildred pregnant, Chaplin dispatched Harrington to buy a ring and to book a wedding venue for that Friday. 'Perhaps,' recalled a Charlie hardly overflowing with the love of a new husband, 'it would all work out all right.'[72] He barely seems to have paid attention during the matrimonials, even having to be reminded to kiss his new bride at the end of the ceremony.

Chaplin later described meeting Mildred for the first time in late 1917, and placed their marriage as taking place when she was 'almost nineteen'.[73] It is possible that these were tricks of memory, but deliberate sleight of hand seems equally likely. According to Mildred's account, the two first met when she was a much younger fourteen years of age in April 1915. D.W. Griffith, for whom Mildred had previously acted, introduced the two by telling Charlie that 'there is a little girl who is dying to meet you'. Given Charlie's youthful taste in his women, such encounters often seem to have begun with such uncomfortable phrasing. During this first encounter Mildred was delighted to meet her hero and hear him compliment her golden curls, but 'I could not help noticing that he treated me as if I were a little child.' After this, she made every effort to style her hair like Lillian and later Dorothy Gish, and adopt a more adult disposition. Frequenting cocktail parties at the Hotel Alexandria, glamorously dressed and on the lookout for Charlie, Mildred received a disappointment when 'I saw him – but he was not alone. He had with him a beautiful woman whom I knew well by sight . . . Edna Purviance.' This hit her hard: 'I was, after all, but a child and the heart of a 14 year old girl is a strange and tremulous thing.'

A few months later, still aged fourteen, she attended a party thrown by the actress Blanche Sweet. In a rather similar line to that he later used on the also young Lita Grey, Charlie saw her and remarked, 'My, but you have grown up.' The two danced together and Charlie did not leave her side all evening. Asking if he could see her home, Mildred said that she would have to ask Blanche who 'smiled roguishly when I asked her if she minded if "Mr Chaplin" took me home, and readily gave her permission, at the same time admonishing Charlie to take me "straight home".' Charlie ignored this, driving Mildred to the beach at Santa Monica where he talked her through the beauty of the ocean and the moonlight bouncing off it. The twenty-six-year-old Chaplin soon gained the trust of Mildred's mother (oddly over a mutual love of curry), and the romance was set.[74]

To give some sense of the unusual nature of the Chaplin–Harris romance, the following table (Table 2.1) lists the fourteen

Table 2.1 Most successful films released 1918–31, and the age of marriage of their star

	Film	Main star	Age at first marriage	Age of spouse at first marriage	Age gap
1918	Mickey	Mabel Normand	34	42	−8
1919	The Miracle Man	Lon Chaney	22	16	6
1920	Way Down East	Lilian Gish	N/A	N/A	N/A
1921	The Four Horsemen of the Apocalypse	Rudolph Valentino	24	26	−2
1922	Robin Hood	Douglas Fairbanks	24	19	5
1923	The Ten Commandments	Theodore Roberts	44	27	17
1924	The Sea Hawk	Milton Sills	28	28	0
1925	The Big Parade	John Gilbert	21	20	1
1926	Aloma of the South Seas	Gilda Gray	14	20	−6
1927	The Jazz Singer	Al Jolson	21	18	3
1928	The Road to Ruin	Helen Foster	24	28	−4
1929	The Broadway Melody	Charles King	22	16	6
1930	All Quiet on the Western Front	Lew Ayres	22	24	−2
1931	City Lights	Charlie Chaplin	29	16	13

Calculated from *Variety*, 21 June 1932

films that were most successful at the box office from 1918 to 1931, their main star and the age at which they (and their spouse) embarked on their first marriage. It is a crude measure, but does provide something of an insight. Other than Theodore Roberts (who at least married a clear adult), Charlie's first, second and fourth marriages (not to say various exploits in between) would all involve an age gap out of kilter with his contemporaries.

When Charlie and Mildred married on 23 October 1918 she was sixteen years old (hardly 'almost nineteen' as in Charlie's story) and, although it proved to be a false alarm, believed that she was pregnant. Even if we accept Chaplin's claim that they first met in the 'latter part of 1917' as accurate, his view that 'the only possible interest she had for me was sex' was still referring to a then fifteen-year-old: 'a very silly young girl', in Charlie's own words.[75] This was seedy stuff, and would not be an isolated incident. The Chaplin–Harris marriage eventually produced a child, Norman Spencer, who was poorly from birth and died after only three days in July 1919. The next month the couple separated.

During a divorce case that, by Chaplin's later standards, was settled amicably enough, Charlie got wind that Louis B. Mayer had signed up Mildred to star in future productions. Charlie was furious and said that if he ever met Mayer he would punch him on the nose. One day he happened across Mayer in the lobby of the Hotel Alexandria: 'Are you Louis B. Mayer? he demanded 'I don't know you, but I am certain that you are! Take off your glasses.' 'What for?' spluttered the M.G.M. mogul. 'Take them off,' bellowed Charlie. When Mayer obliged, Charlie swung at him. Later he recalled that he did not know 'to this day whether or not I carried out my intention of hitting him on the nose'. Mayer started swinging back, at which point Charlie slipped and fell to the ground. A nearby *Los Angeles Times* reporter saw the incident and asked, 'What's this all about Mr Chaplin?' 'Nothing,' cried a sheepish Charlie, who promptly fled the scene.[76]

Such indignities aside, Charlie had had a good war and immediate aftermath. He had survived. He was rich to a point that would have been unfathomable five years earlier. And he now had full creative control over his art. Yet the war had marked him out as a divisive figure, and someone who could no longer be viewed as just a comedian. Even at the height of his fame, Charlie now had to watch his back. The Little Tramp was now, for some, a big coward. Indeed, during Charlie's 1921 visit to London Harry Crocker recalled that some letters received during this trip contained a white feather – the symbol of cowardice, of not doing 'one's bit' during the conflict. Others included 'an ironic German cross for his war effort'. Even if one British soldier would send Charlie four of the medals he had won on the battlefield because 'you have never been properly recognized', the recipient of this generosity would now be a marked man.[77] Once sexual controversy was matched with its political equivalent his enemies would be ready to pounce.

Notes

1 Alistair Cooke, *Six Men* (London, 2008), 31.
2 Ibid., 34.
3 Ibid.
4 Ibid.
5 Michael Ball and David Sunderland, *An Economic History of London, 1800–1914* (London, 2001), 162.
6 Steven J. Ross, *Working-Class Hollywood: Silent Film and the Shaping of Class in America* (Princeton, 1998), 3.
7 Ibid., 32.
8 Ibid., 57.
9 Ibid., 69.
10 Ibid., 57.
11 That is not to say that Chaplin's work could not be conservative in other ways. See later comments on *Easy Street* and *A Dog's Life*. The dream sequence of *Modern Times* could also be included in this bracket.
12 Ross, *Working-Class Hollywood*, 69.
13 Ibid., 70.
14 Peter Bailey, 'Conspiracies of Meaning: Music-Hall and the Knowingness of Popular Culture', *Past and Present*, 144 (1994), 141.
15 Ross, *Working-Class Hollywood*, 73.
16 Orwell's work is readily available for free online, including via the Project Gutenberg site: http://gutenberg.net.au/ebooks03/0300011h.html#part10 (accessed 7 November 2016).
17 Ross, *Working-Class Hollywood*, 77.
18 Ibid., 81.
19 *Marxism Today*, March 1978, 96.
20 Charlie Chaplin, *My Autobiography* (London, 2003), 138.
21 Ibid., 138, 149.
22 Ibid., 153.

23 Ibid., 154.
24 James L. Neibaur, 'Chaplin at Essanay: Artist in Transition', *Film Quarterly*, 54/1 (2000), 23–5.
25 Ibid., 23.
26 Libby Murphy, *The Art of Survival: France and the Great War Picaresque* (New Haven, CT, 2016), 213–14.
27 *Daily Worker*, 15 May 1949.
28 Parker Tyler, 'Kafka's and Chaplin's "Amerika"', *The Sewanee Review*, 58/2 (1950), 299–311, 299.
29 Ibid., 301.
30 Buster Keaton, *My Wonderful World of Slapstick* (New York, 1960), 126.
31 Ibid.
32 All quotes in this paragraph via David Robinson, *Chaplin: His Life and Art* (London, 1992), 131–2.
33 Chaplin, *My Autobiography*, 172.
34 *The Times*, 28 August 1915.
35 *The Times*, 31 August 1915.
36 *The Times*, 6 December 1915.
37 *Evening Times*, 8 July 1915.
38 *Punch*, 25 September 1915.
39 Jerry Epstein, *Remembering Charlie: The Story of a Friendship* (London, 1988), 17.
40 *Aberdeen Journal*, 22 October 1947.
41 *Washington Post* report via COP/CCP/5.1.
42 Adrian Gregory, *The Last Great War* (Cambridge, 2008), 72–3.
43 Keaton, *Wonderful World*, 98.
44 Max Pemberton, *Lord Northcliffe: A Memoir*, (London, 1922), vii.
45 Cited in J. Lee Thompson, *Politicians, the Press and Propaganda: Lord Northcliffe and the Great War* (Kent, OH, 1999), 66.
46 Ibid., 67.
47 All via Ibid., chs 4 and 5.
48 Cited in Suzanne W. Collins, *Calling All Stars: Emerging Political Authority and Cultural Policy in the Propaganda Campaign of World War I* (PhD thesis, New York University, 2008), 303–4.
49 As per the *Cornishman*, 30 March 1916.
50 *Liverpool Echo*, 29 March 1916.
51 *The Economist*, 29 April 1916.
52 Collins, *Calling All Stars*, 303–4.
53 Harry Crocker's unpublished memoir, 'Charlie Chaplin: Man and Mime', MHL/HRC, VII–11.
54 Chaplin Interview Transcript, MHL/Charlie Chaplin Interview [CCI] 33.f–302.
55 Reported in *Aberdeen Evening Express*, 17 April 1918.
56 *New York Sun*, 7 December 1917.
57 For example, *Sheffield Evening Telegraph*, 16 April 1918.

58 Printed (among others) in *Liverpool Echo*, 29 March 1916.
59 Also true of the French Army. For a persuasive account, see Murphy, *The Art of Survival*, ch.8.
60 *The Times*, 22 November 1916.
61 See, e.g., Q3237, Q5524 and Q8904 within the Ministry of Information First World War Official Collection, Imperial War Museum, London.
62 *Portland Oak Journal*, 5 August 1917.
63 *Sunday Pictorial*, 5 September 1915.
64 Steven J. Ross, *Hollywood Left and Right: How Movie Stars Shaped American Politics* (Oxford, 2011), 20.
65 Ibid.
66 Ibid., 22.
67 Chaplin, *My Autobiography*, 218–19.
68 *The New York Times*, 21 October 1918.
69 Chaplin, *My Autobiography*, 229.
70 Ibid., 227.
71 Ibid.
72 Ibid., 228.
73 Ibid.
74 All via *Ottawa Citizen*, 14 March 1936.
75 Chaplin, *My Autobiography*, 226.
76 Crocker, 'Man and Mime', MHL/HRC, VII–32.
77 Crocker, 'Man and Mime', MHL/HRC, VIII–4.

3 Moscow or Manchester? Chaplin's views on capitalism before the Depression took hold

Whatever else had befallen him, by the end of the First World War Charlie Chaplin had proved an astonishingly successful capitalist. Here was a man from a humble background, possessive of a comedic skill that people wished to pay money to witness, who had combined both these elements to accrue a virtually unprecedented level of wealth. The bluntest measure we have of this rise is his weekly salary. From £10 (~$50) a week working for Fred Karno, Chaplin's film contracts successively brought him $150 each week from December 1913 at Keystone, $1,250 from November 1914 at Essanay, $10,000 from February 1916 at Mutual and more than $20,000 in his June 1917 'Million Dollar a Year' contract at First National. Just counting the returns from his movie-studio contracts, his wage had increased 137-fold in under four years in the United States. This was the American Dream personified. An immigrant, ironically partly through *The Immigrant*, made good.

This level of wealth was the subject of much discussion – as it would be again in the aftermath of the Wall Street Crash. When Chaplin visited London to promote *The Kid* in 1921, the British press welcomed back their now rich prodigal son. *The Star* noted that

> Charlie Chaplin's wealth is strange in our eyes because he had nothing solid with which to secure it. No silver mines, no merchandise, no cunning wares, not even a tin box full of wild-cat mine stock. He has done it all with a pair of bad boots, a pair of very awkward feet, a pair of very baggy trousers, a toy moustache, a toy cane, and a shocking bad hat.

This seems a very inadequate stock in trade to produce a salary of a million dollars a year, but it is a great fact.[1]

That publication did not blame the filmmaker, however: 'It may reveal an unfortunate kink in human nature, but it does not reveal an injustice to anybody that Charlie should not be rich, while we are all, alas! Poor.' Instead, they mused on the extraordinary expansion of film that had made it possible:

> We already hear the cold voice of the 'highbrows' inquiring why it is that Charlie's old boots should give him a salary of 1,000,000 dollars while doctors and saints have to live on £300 a year and less . . . If he were acting his comedies on a theatrical stage he would not receive 1,000,000 dollars a year or anything like it, simply because no theatres would hold enough people in a year to pay him so much for seeing him.

Chaplin was a pioneer – someone who had taken a new medium, and created a product that millions of Americans were prepared to buy into. So it is worth stressing what is, perhaps, an obvious point: Chaplin did not hate capitalism, far from it. Indeed, as we will see, although he surrounded himself with several left-wing thinkers, he was able to distinguish between productive and predatory forms of free market activity. He was also someone people were as likely to ascribe to a victory of Adam Smith as they were Karl Marx.

Many linked the Little Tramp to capitalism at this stage. For example, in March 1921 an English Conservative Member of Parliament, W.H. Sugden, set out to define what capitalism was in a speech to local constituents. He told his audience that 'by capitalism he meant commodity production, profit-making and everything that furnished income'. And as to what personified this phenomenon: 'Charlie Chaplin and Sir Harry Lauder were both examples of Capitalism.'[2] At this stage he may well have said 'exemplars'. This chapter, therefore, sets out the twin tracks on which Chaplin's politics would be based: a belief that capitalism could be harnessed to positive ends, and how to nudge it in the right direction when it was not. We begin with the latter.

Max Eastman, Rob Wagner and Chaplin's early political development

Chaplin's generally capitalistic stance aside, it is undeniable that he was interested in the advance of the political left across the globe. Picking up any newspaper over the previous years would have furnished this fascination: the overthrow of the Russian Tsar in March 1917, the Communist takeover of power eight months later and a subsequent civil war between those seeking to preserve the old order and the revolutionaries desiring to protect their take-over would all be followed attentively by the screen comedian. This burgeoning interest was, however, helped by three left-wing intellectuals who had regular access to Chaplin in the period of his greatest fame: Max Eastman, Rob Wagner and Upton Sinclair. Sinclair we will deal with in the chapter on the 1930s, but it was the First World War that, one way or another, drew the other two into Chaplin's circle.

Chaplin's early political thoughts are worth teasing out partly because of the consistently pro-communist views that opponents would later attempt to pin on him. Much of this can be laid at the door of communist newspaper *The Daily Worker*. In 1944, that publication described him as 'a long friend of the Soviet Union since 1917'. During his visa problems in 1952 it noted that 'a year or so after 1917 Chaplin joined the ranks of artists and profes-sionals who upheld the world-shaking Russian revolution'.[3] Later right-wing opponents leapt onto these idle boasts, noting that 'the Daily Worker, official organ of the Communist Party, has reviewed the life and activities of Chaplin in the most glowing terms'.[4] This, they argued, was proof of Charlie's long-term disloyalty of Amer-ica. Yet as Rob Wagner and Max Eastman both found, it was harder to get Charlie to raise the red flag than his loose tongue occasionally made it appear.

In 1915 Rob Wagner began working with Chaplin, ostensibly aiding the comedian in dealing with the volume of correspondence his new-found fame had burdened him with. Wagner had worked for Keystone previously and was something of a polymath – spend-ing his days variously organising for the Socialist Party, writing bits of freelance journalism, working for major film executives in a variety of ways, including script writing, and teaching high-school wrestling. The two were no doubt connected by the fact that, in part, Wagner's conversion to the socialist cause had been expedited by a trip to London in 1901 – a location that had similarly done so much to influence Charlie's own life. The connection was crucial. For Joyce Milton, 'Wagner became [Chaplin's] political mentor.' However, while 'Wagner talked like a radical . . . he usually took care to keep his politics and his income producing activities separate. Charlie, however, lacked this self-protective instinct.'[5]

Wagner not only helped Chaplin articulate his preconceived opinions in a more concise manner, but also helped shape his thought in new directions. Recalling their early days, Chaplin wrote, 'I bought books on sociology and I began to realize that there were many unseen forces at work in our social system. It was not that I was for socialism. What I was against, as Rob Wagner pointed out, was the abuses of capitalism.' Chaplin continued: 'Socialism casts grey aura over everything, I would argue, and that if we did not work for profit there would be no incentive. Rob would counter my ignorance with the fact that "The Post Offices system throughout the world was not run for profit but for service."'[6] Advocating such a view then, as now, did not necessarily mean out-and-out communism. For one, nationalisation of the means of distribution was, by 1918, the official British Labour Party position – a party that was 'establishment' enough to see its first Prime Minister in office by January 1924. Yet by the early 1920s Chaplin was taking Wagner's line even further: 'It was one of the greatest mistakes the Government could make to restore the railroads to private ownership. The postal department is run by the government and I see no reason why the railroads should not be [too].'[7]

More difficult to explain – certainly to those out to label Wagner or Chaplin as communists – was the fact that, on 4 March 1919, Wagner and Chaplin would attend a lecture entitled 'Hands Off Russia' given by Max Eastman in Los Angeles. With both the British and Americans having intervened in the civil war on the side of the anti-Bolshevik 'White' army in Russia, such a stance was controversial if not without its supporters. In any case, after the lecture Chaplin would show Eastman around his studios on La Brea, and the two then went for a swim, and began horsing about for the studio cameras. According to one early Chaplin biographer

Theodore Huff, 'Max Eastman appears to have been the first political intellectual to influence [Chaplin].' Certainly, Eastman was, in his own words, 'the only Socialist agitator who opposed the world war and supported the Russian revolution and yet managed to stay out of jail'.[8] In what some would have taken as a tell-tale sign of his then political compass, Chaplin admired Eastman's 'restraint'. As editor of *The Masses* (forced to close after it was alleged to have broken the terms of the new wartime Espionage Act) and then its successor *The Liberator*, Eastman was Chaplin's link into the burgeoning intellectual climate of Greenwich Village, including thinkers such as Waldo Frank and the Jamaican-American poet Claude McKay.

As Huff noted, 'Having seen poverty in his own childhood, Chaplin was naturally interested in any plans for social betterment . . . he was drawn to any doctrine which seemed to promise or vaguely connote freedom.'[9] In the early 1920s, studio hand Jim Tully recalled that 'the radicals came for his attention and pity. He was worried constantly for the poor in Russia, when that unhappy country was mentioned. John Reed's name came in the conversation, and then Max Eastman's.'[10] Chaplin later described himself as 'intellectually a fellow-traveller' of such types. Since his vaudeville days he had begun to read political tracts, but 'being a slow reader, I browse. Once I am familiar with the thesis and the style of an author, I invariably lose interest.'[11] Plato, Locke and Kant were all read 'piecemeal' by Chaplin, but he much preferred the form of intellectual *conversation* with which Eastman was able to furnish him.

Very occasionally, Chaplin would attempt to pay his politics forward to others in the movie industry. One early witness to Chaplin's political conversion was his great rival Buster Keaton. As the two great silent comedians sat drinking a beer in Keaton's kitchen, neither could know that vague comments Chaplin would make between the two in 1920 would set the course for such a lengthy period of overtly leftist political engagement from the Englishman. By his own admission, Keaton had 'gone his whole life almost unaware of politics, and I only wish my old friend had done the same'.[12] Chaplin's financial partner at United Artists D.W. Griffith was another who sensed where the wind was blowing, telling Max Eastman after hearing the leftist firebrand speak that 'I take my hat off to you. You are a braver man than I am.'[13] Charlie did not demur from such utterances, however. As Keaton and Chaplin chatted away, Chaplin began 'going on at a great rate about something called communism which he had just heard about'. In light of the Russian revolution of 1917 and the Palmer Raids in the US of November 1919 and January 1920 (resulting in the deportation of more than 500 foreign citizens deemed 'radicals'), 'just heard about' must have been dramatic licence on Keaton's part. Nevertheless, on that occasion Charlie said that 'communism was going to change everything, abolish poverty. The well would help the sick, the rich would help the poor.' Becoming more agitated, Chaplin banged the table and exclaimed that 'what I want is that every child should have enough to eat, shoes on his feet, and a roof over his head!' Reasonably enough, Keaton replied, 'But Charlie, do you know anyone who doesn't want that?' Keaton may indeed have had a point. But with the ranks of the American unemployed swelling from an average of about 950,000 in 1919 to 1.7 million in 1920 to more than 5 million by 1921, the urgency that Chaplin was expressing was hardly unwarranted.[14]

By 1921 Charlie's various statements and friendships had cemented the idea of him as a political figure. When he returned to Europe to coincide with the release of *The Kid* that February he was bombarded with questions of this type in an impromptu press conference that took place in Cherbourg, France. A ping-pong game of political debate ensued: 'Will you visit Ireland?' 'I don't expect to do so.' 'What do you think of the Irish question?' 'It requires too much thought.' 'Are you a Bolshevik?' 'I am an artist, not a politician.' 'What do you think of Lenin?' 'I think him a very remarkable man . . . because he is expressing a new idea.' 'Do you believe in Bolshevism?' 'I am not a politician.'[15] Given his praise for Lenin, the Bolshevik question was perhaps understandable – but it spoke to a general misunderstanding of the complexity of Chaplin's world view.

As Chaplin had previously struggled to get across to Rob Wagner, much of his political advocacy, as such, was more about an enlightened capitalism than the dead hand of the controlling state. Throughout his career Chaplin's world view feared public-sector encroachment on individual liberty as much as the vicissitudes of the free market, and in the early 1920s it was no different. In 1921

Chaplin told Thomas Burke that while 'many people have called me a socialist my radical views have been much misunderstood. I am not a Socialist, nor am I looking for a new order of things.' The hero in this vision was a man he would later mock mercilessly in *Modern Times*: Henry Ford. In 1914 Ford had made the announcement that he would voluntarily shorten the working day for those in his factories from nine to eight hours, and, even more dramatically, would introduce a new wage scale that more than doubled the minimum daily wage for his workers from $2.34 to $5. In 1919 this became $6 and then by 1929 $7. This astonishing move was precisely the type of productive rather than predatory capitalism the early Chaplin so admired. 'For a long time,' Chaplin pronounced, 'capital has held sway and declared that the present order is the only one. But Henry Ford's methods rather disprove that, don't they?' Ford's new wage scale had 'made profitable sharing absolutely practicable' and he was justly 'getting all the business of the country because he is fair'.

The only question was how to increase minimum wages across the board: 'Henry Ford has proved the practical result of paying the workers well and keeping them happy.'[16] Eventually the motor industry indeed caught up with Ford's generosity in this regard. Although Chaplin would most seriously settle on theories of under-consumption a few years later, Ford also proved something of a vanguard here, too. Ford's justification for the new wage scale was after all to increase 'the buying power of our own people, and they increased the buying power of other people, and so on and on'. 'It is this thought of enlarging buying power by paying high wages and selling at low prices that is behind the prosperity of this country,' Ford concluded.[17]

And yet, given what we know about the car manufacturer's anti-Semitism, Chaplin's praise of Ford still rings oddly. In January 1919 Ford had taken over the running of the *Dearborn Independent* that he soon turned into a newspaper whipping up notions of a Jewish conspiracy on a weekly basis. In 1920 a compendium of these articles would be published under the title *The International Jew: The World's Foremost Problem*, and Ford would go on to be the only American to be mentioned (positively) in Hitler's *Mein Kampf*. But his views were not just aired to right-wing crackpots. Due to Ford imposing its sale on Ford car dealerships, by 1925 about 900,000 copies of the *Dearborn Independent* were in print. These did not include Ford's own writings from cover to cover, but the newspaper knew its job, often ran stories based on Ford's half-conceived anti-Semitic verbal rants and generally toed its proprietor's line until it was forced to close at the end of 1927 (under the weight of legal action against its controversial content).

Dearborn Independent rants included several against Chaplin. On 12 November 1921, for instance, the paper ran a story on 'The Gentle Art of Changing Jewish Names'. It asserted that 'the Jewish habit of changing names is responsible for the immense camouflage that has concealed the true character of [recent] Russian events'. 'The list of [Bolshevik] controllers of Russia,' Ford asserted, was replete with Jewish communists who had concealed their racial or religious identities. The *Dearborn Independent* went on to note that 'the same may be said with reference to Kaplan, a very common name. Charlie Chaplin's name was, in all probability, Caplan, or Kaplan. At any rate, this is what the Jews believe about their great "star" [whereas] Non-Jews have read of Charlie as a "poor English boy."' The name issue was part of a wider tapestry for those opposed to Chaplin's later political views to suggest he had something to hide. The fact that Charlie was neither a Jew nor a communist barely seemed to matter.

Charlie the anarchist

If – and it is an 'if' – Chaplin could be linked to any one radical ideology during the 1920s, some posit the case for anarchism over and above communism. On several occasions he told the loyal Harry Crocker that, if he was 'to become any form of political entity, he would be an anarchist'. By this he did not mean 'the form of anarchism now usually associated with the term – a war on human society as it is constituted at present, hatred of the bourgeois and propertied classes as such, and a systematic effort to establish, especially by means of explosive, a state of terrorism'. It was more a rejection of the state per se, rather than individual rulers or classes within it – a late Victorian populism taken into the Jazz Age. For Crocker, 'Charlie's dislike of rules led him to express himself in favour of that form of anarchy which means a negation of government . . . He objected to all authority.

If men must have government, any form of it was equally good and equally bad.' The 1920s was not the ideal time to set forward such views, however: 'It was his misfortune that the majority of those to whom he stated his views either thought he was joking or saw in him a bomb thrower.'[18]

Certainly from the early shorts the Tramp had often been an anarchic figure. His propensity to get one over on authority figures from policemen to employers, his regular lack of a fixed place of abode and even the violence and thieving he occasionally used to get what he wanted – these were evidence of a political philosophy projected onto the big screen. As Christian Delage notes, 'Charlie, the Little Tramp, often found himself on the wrong side of the Police, the Law, Big Business, the Church – all those who hold power in an organized society.'[19] Yet it was not all one way. The 'dream' of the Tramp is often shown to be a stable home life in the country – with Paulette in the kitchen while Charlie beckons a cow over to provide the milk in *Modern Times*, or in the saccharine ending with Edna and Scraps' puppies in *A Dog's Life*. The latter is indeed perhaps overly neat, but remains a rather moving contrast to the standard trope of the Tramp leaving down an open road, alone. The Tramp is anarchic because the state has failed him, not because he does not want what the rest of society does.

Certainly as the political establishment really went for Charlie from the mid-1930s onwards there was a more sharply defined anarchist streak to Chaplin's work and pronouncements. Keystone Chaplin was certainly an anarchist, and so too would be the world view of *Monsieur Verdoux*. But the lengthy stretch in the middle is rather more ambiguous.

Such ambiguity would be typified by a mini-speech he would give when staying with the Astors in 1931. He began by declaring that 'the world is suffering from too much government and the expense of it'. Certainly this view would accord more with anarchism than it would the communist regime in Moscow. That being said, it rather also suggested Charlie's belief in the Marxist principle of the state eventually withering away once its usefulness had expired. Yet in the next sentence Chaplin made a complete U-turn. While many anti-waste Conservatives at the dinner table probably nodded along the principle of the world 'suffering too much government', Chaplin suddenly remarked that he would 'have government ownership of the banks and revise many of the laws and those of the Stock Exchange. I would create a government bureau of economics, which would control prices, interests and profits.' In contemporary British terms this was almost exactly the position forwarded by the Labour Party at the 1931 General Election. As such, he was generally closer to that movement than the anarchist tendency.

Charlie the mogul

As some recognised, however, this encouragement of individual freedom was symptomatic of a barely submerged megalomania. For someone who hated the notion of empire, Charlie had become de facto Viceroy of his own cinematic fiefdom. Sick of being reliant on others' time, in 1917 Charlie decided to build his own studio. Buying Hollywood Orange Grove – which took up around a block on La Brea Avenue and nearly the same amount on Sunset Boulevard – he constructed a complex that still stands to this today (amusingly it is presently occupied by the Muppets). At the time, La Brea and Sunset were 'mere dirtroads' yet would come to form two of Hollywood's main arteries. Indeed, one of the few truly poor business decisions Chaplin would make was to not sell this land at the top of the market. Having bought it in 1917 for $34,000, in the late 1920s Charlie received an offer to buy the plot for $750,000 that he refused – thereby missing out on a large profit at a time his ongoing divorce case meant he sorely needed the money.

Yet these new buildings held a symbolic significance for Charlie. As Harry Crocker noted, 'The office buildings which lie along La Brea were in fulfilment of Charlie's plans, a bit of old England.'[20] As the romantic novelist Elinor Glyn wrote to a friend, 'He is an absolute autocrat in his own Studio, and that of course is why his Pictures are always such things of art and magnetize the public – they do not show the muddle which five or six separate wills produce.'[21] Having had so little control over his life as a young man Charlie was determined that no vision but his should permeate his pictures. As the ideas for feature-length business for the Tramp began to dry up by the 1930s this would subtly change, but at the height of his career in the roaring twenties the studios at La Brea served as his cinematic White House in which he alone was the boss.

Charlie was not the first South London boy to have achieved astonishing fame and wealth through the arts. As Alan Fischler has shown, Arthur Sullivan – of Gilbert and Sullivan fame – had experienced a similarly meteoric rise half a century or so earlier. Born in 1842 in Lambeth, music soon became to this composer 'a means not to money, but rather to social glory. Once he emerged as Britain's leading composer, he earned an ample income; but instead of buying himself houses with it, he made liberal donations to the coffers of the Monte Carlo casinos.' In doing so, rather like Chaplin, 'his companions on these Continental junkets mattered more to him than did the cost'.[22] Being seen with 'the right sort' of people was the real acme of power. For Charlie, if this could only be achieved through bossing about his underlings at the studio, then so be it.

As with Sullivan, there must have been an element of adopting the ostentatious trappings of wealth to try to communicate to it. In a sense, Charlie became such an interesting historical figure because he was always something of a nouveau riche fish out of water. An Englishman in Los Angeles. A movie maker among politicians. And a former pauper mixing with the global intellectual and economic elite. But this led to a series of faux pas that, although minor matters of form, likely embarrassed a man who was, to his core, always making up for the impoverishment of his childhood. During his 1921 trip to England he would meet only the 'most proper of intellectuals'. Through Lady Astor, this number included an introduction to George Bernard Shaw. Once she had introduced the two, Lady Astor noted, 'You two probably have a lot to say to each other, so I'll run along.' Crocker recalled what played out next: 'The Bard looked down; the comedian looked up. There was an electric silence which Chaplin feared to break, and Shaw failed to break. A butler announced that dinner was served and, relieved, both abandoned their posts on the grate. Without the exchange of two words.'[23] Charlie would get over such hesitancy in later years (Shaw would become a friend), but its early impact was crippling: he had ideas about how the world should change, and was still taking in new ones, but his nerves were holding him back. In the early 1920s he was always feeling his way from the silver screen into the intellectual sphere.

He could also be bizarrely petty about totally trivial matters. In 1920 *Punch* magazine printed an article about Charlie that suggested that he did not like the works of Shakespeare. Charlie fired off a terse letter to that publication's editor, Owen Seaman, stating that 'were that the case, I fully realize that the loss would be mine, but as it happens, the statement is lacking in accuracy, and just in this instance I should prefer not to be misquoted'. Informing the editor that 'what I told Mr Faulkner was that personally I prefer Shakespeare for private reading and never derive so much genuine pleasure from his works when I see them in a stage rendering', he demanded a retraction. 'I trust that you will give this statement of mine the publicity necessary to remove an entirely wrong and to me very unpleasant impression.' In the end, Seaman conceded the point, but it did not seem the be all and end all.[24] One wonders if Charlie had been more assiduous in correcting the *political* half-truths printed about him in the 1920s, he may well have benefited from it down the line.

To secure his ego some more, Charlie also erected a new house in Beverly Hills. This again had a touch of his homeland. Elinor Glyn reported, 'Charlie Chaplin's house is most beautiful but like England too – and they have the proper staffs of European servants – and everything is beautifully done, but this costs, in this country, simply a colossal sum of money.'[25] Allied to this slice of the old world were very much signs of the new – a cinema screen was concealed in the roof, to be let down as demanded, while Charlie's love for tennis was indulged with a new court.[26] His book shelves contained numerous prominent British and Irish authors, including Bernard Shaw, H.G. Wells, J.M. Barrie and Thomas Burke. These trappings helped foster an atmosphere where ambitious young types flattered and did not challenge Chaplin. As Jim Tully later wrote,

> Hollywood is the most crowded carnival in America. Too often the stale wine of an over-stimulated nation, there are far too many inside the tent who should never have joined in the first place. They come from everywhere, those with too much to give, and those with not enough – the big and the

small – the brave and the always defeated. In over twenty years I have heard the word 'genius' applied to more hams than Armour could supply the most patriotic of nations at wartime.[27]

This could have been applied to Chaplin more than any other. Like many a mogul, he had become powerful to the point where few would question his actions until it was too late. Unlike the democratic politicians with whom he would have dealings, there was no brake or check to Chaplin's power.

The most obvious and long-standing facet of Chaplin's mogul status was the foundation of United Artists, however. Initially this started as an artistic quarrel. After *A Dog's Life* and *Shoulder Arms* Charlie felt that First National were not backing the type of art he wanted to make to a significant enough degree. The extra funds he required were not 'much . . . an additional ten or fifteen thousand dollars a picture'. Given his 'Million Dollar a Year' contract he may have had a point. Still, meeting First National executives in Los Angeles he noted that 'exhibitors were rugged merchants in those days and to them films were merchandise costing so much a yard'. Charlie thought his requests reasonable, but later noted that he 'might as well have been a lone factory worker asking General Motors for a raise'. After a brief silence at the boardroom table, one First National executive merely muttered. 'Well, Charlie, you've signed a contract and we expect you to live up to it.' After angrily replying that 'you're not dealing with sausages, you know, but individual enthusiasm', Charlie 'could not understand their attitude, as I was considered the biggest drawing card in the country'.[28]

Perhaps he had a point, perhaps not. Either way, what happened next certainly illustrated Charlie's mettle for change. His brother Sydney had heard rumours that all the big motion-picture producing companies were looking to merge. The next day Sydney met with Doug Fairbanks and Mary Pickford whose Paramount contracts were expiring and the studio had as yet done nothing about it. All agreed that such prevarication probably had something to do with the impending merger and so 'we all agreed to hire a detective'. This detective, 'a very clever girl, smart and attractive looking', wormed her way into the attentions of 'an executive of an important producing company'. For three nights, staving off his affections, she gained a complete story of what the big companies were planning: 'a forty-million dollar merger of all the producing companies and . . . sewing up every exhibitor in the United States with a five-year contract.' This would mean a de facto monopoly over the entire industry, limiting what artists such as Charlie could both be paid and likely the types of films they could make.

To resist this, the plan was simply that Douglas, Mary, Charlie, D.W. Griffith and W.S. Hart should make an announcement that they would form their own company, sell their productions on the open market rather than through a block-booking system and remain independent. This was a bluff – 'our objective was only to stop exhibitors from signing a five-year contract with this proposed merger'.[29] Upon making this announcement, however, the next day the heads of several production companies offered to resign their posts and become President of United Artists. The front-page coverage the story received was further evidence that perhaps the idea could be a success. The bluff became a reality – on 5 February 1919 United Artists (UA) was incorporated with 20 per cent stakes for Pickford, Chaplin, Fairbanks and Griffith. The balance was held by William McAdoo, who had returned to legal private practice by this stage, but who had previously served as the US Secretary of the Treasury at the time of the Liberty Loans that Chaplin had helped sell.

Charlie's own contribution to the UA pot was actually relatively modest at first. Working out his First National contract until 1923, it was only *The Gold Rush* in 1925 that saw him deliver the first bone fide hit to the company. In the interim, Pickford (*Pollyanna, Little Lord Fauntleroy* and *Tess of the Storm Country*) and Fairbanks (*The Three Musketeers, Robin Hood* and *The Thief of Bagdad*) did much of the heavy lifting at the box office. Still, under the leadership of Joseph M. Schenck from 1925 the company was put on firm footing, negotiated the retention of its founding members and signed new stars such as Gloria Swanson. By the mid-1930s it was reporting profits of more than $1 million a year and had expanded well beyond its position as challenger company to the big studios. Charlie eventually cashed out his share in the 1950s for $1.1 million, in part to pay for back taxes owed to the Internal Revenue Service (IRS).

Within the very ethos of UA were signs of Chaplin's own world view, however. In short, he was sick of carrying what he considered to be 'lesser' filmmakers and having the studios shift mediocre products on the back of his own superior art. As such, Tino Balio notes, at United Artists 'each picture was to be sold and promoted individually. Block booking was out. In no way could one United Artists release be used to influence the sale of another UA product. Merit alone would determine a picture's success.'[30] Chaplin may have had some socialistic inclinations, but business was business. In many ways he embraced the 'dog eat dog' atmosphere of capitalism in deed as much as he protested against it in prose.

Chaplin and his money

Partially through UA, Chaplin had become an astonishingly wealthy man who clearly also had many ideas about the state of modern politics. However, there were two problems that Chaplin's early political interlopers soon found. The first was to get him to commit his ideas to paper. In the mid-1920s Jim Tully recalled that 'a London editor asked him for an article on social conditions in America'. Chaplin knew 'little of the subject' but was intrigued enough to agree. 'He labored valiantly for some time,' Tully remembers, 'but could not get his thoughts in order. A few lines of misspelled words were the result. He lost interest.' Tully would often wind his boss up: 'How's the article coming along, Charlie?' This did not go down well. 'His eyes narrowed at my barbed condescension. He did not reply.'[31] As we will see, particularly with reference to German war debt, this issue was to a large degree solved over the next ten years: Chaplin became more committed to setting his thoughts to the page, and, due to his increasingly slow rate of cinematic production, he had more time to do so.

But, second, if a fool and his money are easily parted, Chaplin was no fool. Max Eastman liked Charlie as a man and a comedian, but he also wanted his financial investment. When seeking to raise money for his journal *The Liberator* Eastman encountered an enthusiastic Chaplin. Charlie initially claimed he wanted to help: 'He said it with some warmth and then gave us $25.' Going by Charlie's then salary, this equated to about 12 minutes' pay.

This taught Eastman that although 'Charlie likes radical ideas; he likes talk about transforming the world, but [he] doesn't like to pay for the talk, much less the transformation'. As Harry Crocker recalled, 'Although Chaplin later gave Eastman $1,000 [to help with his publication], Eastman learned in 1919 what others were to learn years later.'[32] When interrogated by the FBI in 1948, Chaplin called any suggestions he had donated to the Communist Party an 'unmitigated lie' but did concede that he had donated to the Progressive Party campaign then being undertaken by former Vice-President Henry Wallace. Getting Chaplin to bankroll the hard left in any meaningful way, however, was a bridge too far.

This must have been particularly galling for his political friends and would-be allies because not only did Chaplin's films bring him astonishing wealth, he also managed to avoid the calamities of the Wall Street Crash. As we will address in more detail later, Chaplin was a huge fan of C.H. Douglas's system of Social Credit. To Chaplin, this work stated that 'basically all profit came out of wages. Therefore unemployment meant a loss of profit and a diminishing of capital.'[33] As a result, he later recalled that 'when American unemployment hit 1.4 million in 1928' Chaplin promptly sold all his stocks and bonds, preferring to keep his capital fluid. The day before Wall Street plummeted Chaplin dined with the composer Irving Berlin. Berlin's portfolio then compromised several million dollars' worth of investments that had made him a total of more than $1 million. Chaplin advised him to get out while the going was good, touting the Douglas argument at him. Berlin was furious: 'Why, you're selling America short!' A couple of days later, his investments in ruins, Berlin came round to Chaplin's studio 'stunned and apologetic, and wanted to know where I had got my information'.[34] Even when confronted with what must have seen like the utter vindication of his political world view, however, Chaplin was unwilling to part with any of his preserved gains to finance a party able to propagate them more widely.

These gains were also so large because, as Buster Keaton bemoaned, 'Charlie Chaplin and Harold Lloyd from the start were smarter businessmen than I. They became millionaires early in the game by producing their own pictures and retaining control of their film properties. They still own these properties. This means they are in a position to earn fresh fortunes for themselves any time they feel like leasing or selling the TV rights to their old silent movies.'[35] The UA example we have already outlined. But sometimes Chaplin wanted the industry to go even further. Indeed, when shooting the breeze with Harry Crocker, Charlie outlined a new scheme to bring movies to the masses – the big studios should be forced to sell their products to exhibitors at no more than 10 per cent above the cost their films took to make. Crocker kept his counsel, but 'Chaplin leaned forward and poked me between the shoulders to prod forth an answer.' Refusing to look his boss in the eye Crocker agreed with Charlie but added, 'and you are just the man to inaugurate the experiment. For years you have succeeded in upping the price on exhibitors for your films as a matter of prestige to them. You should therefore be the first to come to their aid in this matter.' Charlie recoiled: 'I should say not. This scheme is not for me. I'm not a business man: I am an artist!'[36]

Given his almost limitless wealth Charlie's retention of money verged on the pathological. When funds for his film projects were beginning to wane the English eccentric Ivor Montagu wrote to his friend asking for a helping hand. When he received no answer he angrily chased Charlie with a message of 'Wotthehell! When we wire you we need money you ought to take it that we do need it, and for some purpose you may be sure more important than you would be spending it on.'[37] In the case of the rather chaotic Montagu it may have seemed like throwing good money after bad, but it was indicative of a wider trend.

For a man so wedded to the idea of helping 'the people' through various social programmes, the greatest irony (or hypocrisy) was that Chaplin always remained incredibly reluctant to pay the taxes that would help fund them. As Sam Goldwyn noted of Charlie, 'His prejudge is against anything that interferes with his own personal freedom. The censor, the income tax, any supposed obstruction – these are hateful to him in the degree to which they infringe upon that coveted sense of power.'[38] As Charlie himself scribbled some years later, 'You can only tax and extract so much from people and no more. If it goes beyond a certain amount you are going into Socialism or Communism and the present system of society will collapse and change in spite of ourselves.'[39] To forestall later accusations about his political loyalty, Charlie claimed in 1942 that he had contributed more than $10 million in American income tax since his arrival in the country – 'every cent of it glad'.[40]

In fact, the connection between Charlie and tax went back many years. In the Britain he was beginning to prosper in, the then Liberal Government's famous 'People's Budget' of 1909 had mandated the principle of a graduated income tax where, the more one earned, the higher the marginal tax rate would be. On just over £500 a year by the time he emigrated to the States, Chaplin was nowhere near being pulled into the new higher rates of tax for incomes over £3,000 and £5,000, respectively, however. Indeed, it would be America where, because of his soon to be astronomical earnings, Chaplin would feel the effects of recent changes to fiscal policy.

The Sixteenth Amendment to the US Constitution in 1913 gave Congress the 'power to lay and collect taxes incomes, from whatever source derived, without apportionment among the several States'. Ironically, given later events, the poster boy for this shift in policy would be one Charlie Chaplin. In March 1916, Manhattan became host to a new branch of the IRS and to promote this undertaking Chaplin was persuaded to take part in a few publicity photographs as an official explained to him how to fill out the form. Given that he failed to provide a 1917 declaration to the authorities he probably should have paid some attention during these proceedings. In years to come things would only get much worse.

Chaplin's later claim to be 'glad' to pay 'every cent' of tax was clearly a lie. While he was in the midst of the second divorce woes that the next chapter outlines, in January 1927 the US government announced that it was placing a lien on his assets due to underpayment of income tax going back to 1918. The amount Chaplin had supposedly avoided was $1.35 million (equivalent to about $18 million in 2015), no small sum. Particularly egregious seemed to be his returns for 1924. Chaplin had various reasons to have filed a low return for that year – most obviously, the commercial failure of his first drama *A Woman of Paris*. But while other huge stars of 1920s Hollywood such as Douglas Fairbanks ($132,190), Gloria Swanson ($87,075) and Mary Pickford ($34,075) had been seen to make a 'fair' contribution to the IRS, Chaplin's payment for that year was the puny $345.81. That sum would not allow one to buy

a Chevrolet Roadster at the time, let alone form an adequate contribution from one of the richest individuals in America. Newspapers covered this payment as 'the biggest surprise in screenland'.[41]

The Chaplins were adept tax avoiders. Joyce Milton's analysis
of this murky topic covers it in expert detail, but, in essence, while
Charlie was using United Artists as a vehicle to minimise his own
income tax contributions his brother Sydney was concurrently
involved in a whole series of 'businesses' almost certainly designed
purely for tax avoidance. From 1918 to 1920, for example, Sydney
Chaplin purchased more than 400 former military planes from the
American government. At a time when air travel was in its infancy,
this was a laughable investment. As Milton notes, 'There was simply no way that any commercial air service at the time could have
used forty planes, much less four hundred. Either Syd was a very
great optimist or the purchase was part of a scheme to reduce his
tax liability [by claiming relief for buying from the government].'[42]

In early 1927 the combination of the tax affair and his crum-
bling personal life brought Chaplin to physical and emotional
exhaustion. The gates of Chaplin's studios were padlocked shut
and an audit was carried out to assess the value of on-site material should the government need to seize it. The IRS was willing to
forgo a criminal prosecution of Chaplin that could lead to prison,
but only should he sign a consent decree acknowledging his criminal activity and financial liability. Since this could mean deportation for the non-American Chaplin, he refused. By April 1927,
reluctantly, he, however, consented to the payment of just over $1
million in back taxes. Much of Charlie's then $16 million wealth
was not liquid and thus there was some difficulty in actually raising this sum, but eventually the payment was made. It would not
be the last time that Charlie would fall foul of the IRS – even, as
Chapter 9 will note, when he was in 1950s Swiss exile.

Taking him seriously

As this study notes at various points, many politicians, journalists
and authors took Chaplin entirely seriously. This book's message
that Charlie's comedy was only a means to an end was well understood at the time. But this was a view hammered home by the
increasingly serious nature of Chaplin's films. 1923's *A Woman*

of Paris was Chaplin's first and only attempt at a purely dramatic film. Posters for the film came with a message from Chaplin 'to the public' that 'in order to avoid any misunderstanding, I hereby announce that I do not appear [in the film]'. Other than the smallest of cameos as an unrecognisable railway porter, this was indeed the case. The self-proclaimed 'first serious drama written and directed by myself' proved a critical smash but box-office bomb. Getting on for a century after its release, *A Woman of Paris* holds up as a nuanced portrayal of romance in the 1920s where the main cad (played by Adolphe Menjou) is charming and charismatic and the sympathetic heroine Marie St-Clair (Edna Purviance, in a role that Charlie hoped would launch her dramatic career) is not above making terrible decisions. Roaring twenties Paris is a place of sex and debauchery; cigarettes and alcohol are everywhere, and the effect is mesmerising. For Elinor Glyn, invited to the Fairbanks' 'charming house in Beverly Hills' to watch it, the film 'brought real life to you across the footlights'. Chaplin's characters were 'presented as such people would be – no one gesticulates or goes through a pantomime'. Correctly, she assumed that 'the public in general will not like the picture' but felt it was one that 'all thinking minds must appreciate'.[43]

After the poor response to *A Woman of Paris*, Chaplin needed a hit and began work on *The Gold Rush*. The idea came to Charlie while spending a weekend with Mary Pickford and Douglas Fairbanks. Glancing through stereoscopic views of Alaska and the Klondike, Charlie's imagination was stimulated: 'Immediately ideas and comedy business began to develop, and, although I had no story, the image of one began to grow.'[44] Reading up on the Donner Party of 1846–7 – where prospectors who had taken a wrong turn into the Sierra Nevada mountains were forced into cannibalism to survive – Charlie began to conceive of one of his most famous scenes where the Tramp cooks his own shoe, the shoelaces functioning as make-do spaghetti. For six months, he toiled over the various pieces of comedy business, eventually enveloping them in a love story surrounding the Tramp's pursuit of Georgia Hale – who substituted for the heavily pregnant Lita.

The plot (which differs somewhat between the 1925 silent version and a later 1942 re-release with commentary from Chaplin) is simple enough, though takes in many twists and turns along the way. The basic elements are that a Lone Prospector (Chaplin's Tramp) and his reluctant new friend Big Jim have travelled north to take part in the Klondike Gold Rush that took place in the late 1890s – they know there is gold buried nearby, but the location has been masked by the snow. The search for gold was indeed arduous but alluring. During this period thousands of prospectors really had headed north hoping to find gold in this previously empty area of North-West Canada. For example, from a population of 500 in 1896 the settlement of Dawson City expanded to a total of nearly 30,000 just two years later. As depicted in *The Gold Rush*, the wealthier prospectors spent their money drinking in the saloons while the poor shivered in hastily constructed, isolated wooden huts.

The film narrows in on the issue of hunger on several occasions. At one point Jim becomes so delirious through lack of food that he imagines Charlie's Prospector as a giant chicken and attempts to shoot him. Snapping out of it, the two eventually kill a bear – no doubt tasting better than the Tramp's shoe that they had been forced to eat earlier. The search for sustenance apart, *The Gold Rush* also deals with loneliness. Certainly this had always been present in Chaplin's work, but the frozen Canadian backdrop provided an additional layer of poignancy. After being separated from Big Jim, the Prospector arrives at one of the hastily constructed Dawson City-type settlements, and enters a dance hall. In this building we then encounter Georgia who, irritated at the attentions of Jack, a big and aggressive ladies' man, decides to dance with the 'most deplorable looking tramp in the dance hall'. This, of course, is Charlie, who is instantly taken and does not understand the game she is playing. Later, he offers Georgia and her friends an invitation to his New Year's Eve dinner, which she breezily accepts with little intention of actually attending. The shots of the lonely tramp, sitting at his lovingly prepared table and dreaming of how the night should have panned out with laughter and merriment aplenty (including the famous 'roll dance'), are deeply poignant. When he then wanders the snowy streets, standing outside the dance hall as *Auld Lang Syne* plays, there had perhaps been no finer shot in Chaplin's work to this point.

Seeing the effort that the Prospector had put in, and increasingly aware of her own loneliness, Georgia has a change of heart and attempts to make contact with him. But just as the two see each other he is dragged off by Big Jim to go searching for their lost cabin, and the lost gold that lies nearby. He has enough time to shout that he will return as a millionaire, before they depart. Finding the cabin, they bunk down for the night but, unbeknownst to the pair, the cabin is then blown to the edge of a cliff – coincidentally right by the gold deposit. After much high-jinks as the cabin threatens to crash over the edge, the pair just about make it to safety. Finding the gold, the newly rich pair return to America on a boat where, again unknown to Jim and Charlie, Georgia is also on board. Time passes and the Prospector is asked to don his ragged old clothes for a 'rags to riches' photograph that will appear in a newspaper piece hailing their incredible story. After hearing that there is a stowaway on board and mistaking this for Charlie, Georgia attempts to hide him to save him from exposure. The misunderstanding cleared up, the pair then re-unite – hand in hand in the 1942 version, and with a kiss in the 1925 silent. Perhaps due to this happy ending the film was an astonishing success. On a budget of *c.* $923,000 it would gross more than six and a half million dollars worldwide. After Mary and Doug had been pushing for so long for Charlie to make a bankable hit for United Artists, he had well and truly obliged.

His last work of the 1920s, 1928's *The Circus,* seemed to mark something of a return to 'pure' comedy for Chaplin. Since its making coincided with the unhappy divorce from Lita Grey that we cover in the next chapter, it is not even mentioned in Chaplin's autobiography. To modern tastes, it remains Chaplin's most amusing film, however – the comedy that truly stands up to a twenty-first-century audience in both its inventiveness and execution. The film is more a meditation on Charlie's work than it is his politics. The Tramp unwittingly becomes funny when he is trying not to be so, but is unable to make his audience laugh when he is attempting to perform prepared 'bits'. Chased by the police when falsely accused of stealing a wallet, Charlie stumbles into a circus ring and becomes a smash hit completely by accident. Various high-wire and perilous comedic acts involving monkeys render the film perhaps Chaplin's best slapstick performance. More seriously, *The Circus* invoked several Chaplinesque themes, including the Tramp bowing out of a love triangle involving himself, Harry Crocker and Merna Kennedy in the belief he was the least suitable partner for the girl, and almost ends on a beautiful shot of the lonely Tramp, sitting on a box with the circus having left town, and exhaling deeply in sorrow. Unlike *City Lights*, however, Chaplin would follow this by slightly cheating the audience, having the Tramp stand up and walk away twirling his cane as if happy to be back on the open-road. It was something of a missed opportunity.

As film had 'grown up' so, in a sense, had Chaplin. Although his political views in the early 1920s were mostly relatively orthodox (albeit interspersed with the odd pro-communist remark), his art had clearly evolved. Making feature-length cinema without any elements of pathos would have meant plotting an hour of purely anarchic comedy, and this held little interest for Charlie who always wanted to be taken seriously. Had he confined this desire to be taken seriously to the silver screen his life would have been much easier. But this would not prove to be the case. Then again, as we will note in the next chapter, his problems were as much in the bedroom as they were in the salon, or the film studio.

Notes

1   *The Star*, 10 September 1921, MHL/HRC/1/9.
2   *Northern Daily Mail*, 15 March 1921.
3   'Fact Sheet Containing Pertinent Material Pertaining to the Communist Affiliations and Activities of Charlie Chaplin', Hoover Institute, Stanford University, California [HOOV], George Sokolsky Papers [SOK] Box 241 File 3.
4   Clipping of 1949 Senator Cain Speech, HOOV/Elizabeth Churchill Brown [ECB] Box 18 Folder 13.
5   Joyce Milton, *Tramp: The Life of Charlie Chaplin* (London, 1996), 127.
6   Scribbled note, undated 1950s, Cineteca di Bologna [CIN]/Charlie Chaplin Archive [CCA].
7   Undated newspaper clipping 'The Serious Opinions of Charlie Chaplin', 1921, MAM/CCP Book 12.
8   Theodore Huff, *Charlie Chaplin: A Biography* (London, 1952), 260.
9   Ibid.
10 'The King of Laughter' manuscript, Charles E. Young Research Library, UCLA, Los Angeles, California [UCLA]/Jim Tully Papers [JTL] Box 82 file 250, f.1.
11 Charlie Chaplin, *My Autobiography* (London, 2003), 244.
12 Buster Keaton, *My Wonderful World of Slapstick* (New York, 1960), 270.

13 Joyce Milton, *Tramp: The Life of Charlie Chaplin* (London, 1996), 154.

14 Stanley Lebergott, *The Measurement and Behaviour of Unemployment* (Washington, D.C., 1957), 215.

15 Charles Chaplin, *My Trip Abroad* (London, 1922), 37.

16 Undated newspaper clipping 'The Serious Opinions of Charlie Chaplin', 1921, MAM/CCP, Book 12.

17 Quoted in *Saturday Evening Post*, 3 January 2014.

18 Harry Crocker's unpublished memoir, 'Charlie Chaplin: Man and Mime', MHL/HRC, VII–17.

19 Christian Delage, *Chaplin: Facing History* (Paris, 2005), 14.

20 Crocker, 'Man and Mime', MHL/HRC, VII–2.

21 Glyn to 'X', No. 19, University of Reading [UOR], Elinor Glyn Papers [EGN] MS 4,059, Box 24.

22 All via Alan Fischler, 'Dialectics of Social Class in the Gilbert and Sullivan Collaboration', *Studies in English Literature*, 1500–1900, 48/4, The Nineteenth Century (Autumn, 2008), 829–37.

23 Crocker, 'Man and Mime', MHL/HRC, VIII–5.

24 Chaplin to Owen Seaman, 27 April 1920, Cambridge University Library [CUL]/Add. 8,990/118.

25 Glyn to 'X', No. 3. UOR/EGN MS 4,059, Box 25.

26 'King of Laughter', UCLA/JTL, 15a.

27 Tullygram, UCLA/JTL Box 84, f6.

28 Chaplin, *My Autobiography*, 220.

29 Ibid., 221.

30 Tino Balio, *United Artists, Volume 1, 1919–1950: The Company Built by the Stars* (Wisconsin, 1976), 28.

31 'King of Laughter', UCLA/JTL, 75.

32 Crocker, 'Man and Mime', MHL/HRC, VII–21.

33 Chaplin, *My Autobiography*, 324.

34 Ibid.

35 Keaton, *Wonderful World*, 127.

36 Crocker, 'Man and Mime', MHL/HRC, X–12.

37 Montagu to Chaplin, 4 October 1933, British Film Institute, London [BFI], Ivor Montagu Papers [IVM] Item 320.

38 Huff, *Charlie Chaplin*, 262.

39 Scribbled notes, dated 1932, within CIN/CCA.

40 *New York Sun*, 16 October 1942 via COP/CCP 64.

41 Milton, *Tramp*, 253.

42 Ibid., 269.

43 Glyn to X, No. 18, UOR/EGN MS 4,059 Box 24.

44 Chaplin, *My Autobiography*, 299.

4 Sex, morality and a tramp in 1920s America

In May 1924, *The New York News* asked Charlie for his chief interest in life. For all the political machinations of this book and the sublime films he crafted, the answer he provided was almost certainly the most accurate he could give. '[It is] Women. Because they are the most interesting, fascinating, and charming subject in the world.'[1] Indeed, the interplay between sex, celebrity and politics – for all the more modern escapades of a Kennedy or a Schwarzenegger – has rarely been as pronounced at any point in modern history as it was for Charlie Chaplin. If the studio was his workplace and the political salon his mental gymnasium, the bedroom was his pastime. And that pastime was highly controversial in a 1920s America still wrestling with its own conceptions of morality, and modernity itself. On the one hand, the age of the more sexually liberated flapper often found with a glass of alcohol in her hand suggested a society moving in the direction of the flamboyant Chaplin. As Adolphe Menjou recalled, 'When Hollywood discovered that sex was no longer a taboo topic, even in women's magazines, the producers took off the wraps and gave the subject an all-out whirl. Sex, libido, bath-tub gin, Freud speak-easies and joy riding were the new trends in the pictures as they were in America itself.'[2]

On the other hand, politically America was conservative with a small 'c'. The Republican Party won all three Presidential elections during the 1920s, held a majority in the Senate throughout the decade and were largely uncomfortable with the drift of urban America. Whatever the jazz or decadent nightclubs of some sections of its major cities, America remained a fundamentally conservative nation, typified by imposition of prohibition between 1919 and 1933. Chaplin's salons with their young women, freely drinking, smoking and adopting a looser than loose attitude to that most traditional of institutions – marriage – rubbed many up the wrong way. As the right-leaning journal *The Argonaut* noted in the late 1940s: 'Everything one learns about [Chaplin] proves to be a bad egg – a rotten egg in fact . . . Is it not time to deport Charlie Chaplin as an undesirable alien? We said so at the time when he was demonstrating that he had the morality of a billy-goat; and we say so again.'[3] For Charlie, sex and politics would be forever intertwined.

It is important to understand how this took hold. This chapter therefore considers his 1920s in three regards: his proclivity towards young women (or, in some cases, 'girls'), his disastrous marriage to Lita Grey and the wider moral climate in which these were conducted. As we will note, Chaplin's activities with the opposite sex would soon attract the attention of a powerful enemy, J. Edgar Hoover of the new Federal Bureau of Investigation (FBI). In short, Chaplin would not have been so politically exposed had he not been so sexually exposed, and this was a trend ingrained during the roaring twenties.

Chaplin's women

Chaplin's early encounters with women veered somewhere between the chaste love affairs of the Tramp and rather more seedy escapades. As we saw in Chapter 1, utmost in the first group was the young Hetty Kelly, whom he met when in his Mumming Birds days under Fred Karno. When they first locked eyes at the Streatham Theatre in 1908, Chaplin was nineteen years old and Hetty fifteen. There is no doubt this encounter scarred Charlie for life. Although Richard Attenborough's 1992 film *Chaplin* laid it on a bit thick in casting the same actress, Moira Kelly, as both Hetty Kelly and Chaplin's last wife Oona O'Neill, most women for Charlie would be measured against the youthful beauty he had loved and lost. In many ways, he remained trapped in that nineteen-year-old self, struggling to capture a romance that was largely the product of his own imagination.

This process seems to have started almost immediately. Contained in an unpublished account of his long-time aide Harry

Crocker (who also played the Tramp's love rival in *The Circus* of 1928), Chaplin gave the following description of an encounter that took place during his early music hall career and shortly after his 'split' from Hetty:

> While I was playing the Folies – I was nineteen at the time,' he recalled, 'I had a most violent crush on a girl only ten or twelve. I have always been in love with young girls, not in an amorous way – just as beautiful objects to look at. I like them young because they personify youth and beauty. There is something virginal in their slimness – in their slender arms and legs. And they are so feminine at that age, so wholly, girlishly young. They haven't developed the "come on" stuff or discovered the power of their looks over men. I suppose you might say that I had a crush on the little Parisienne. It was funny; not in a sex way – I just loved to caress and fondle her – not passionately – just to have her in my arms.[4]

Such language was not unusual for the man, and Chaplin's relationship with young women has been remarked upon by many – not least the female participants. One such example was the movie-star Louise Brooks who, one evening in 1925, could be found in Chaplin's suite at the Ambassador Hotel, New York. By this stage Charlie was married to Lita but, as we will see, this was hardly a massive encumbrance to him. In any event, Peggy Fears, A.C. Blumenthal, Jack Pickford and Winnie Sheehan joined Brooks in experiencing Chaplin monopolise an evening doing various imitations. After a while the crowd thinned and Chaplin suddenly 'became the hunted man, seeking [Blumenthal's] advice about what to do about the detectives he felt sure that [press baron William Randolph] Hearst had on his tail because of his love affairs with [Hearst's mistress] Marion Davies'. Blumenthal and Fears then left, leaving Brooks alone with Charlie. At this point, Brooks recalled, 'Charlie would go into his seduction scene with me. He had his sexes mixed up. Instead of playing the lazy, watchful tom cat (like [Buster] Keaton), he rolled and slithered and rubbed like the lady cat. This was a technique suitable only for innocent little girls.' Talking through his various conquests, Brooks noted that 'men's choice of women is always determined by the success of their particular love play'. In terms of Charlie's other dalliances of the time, '[Pola] Negri wanted publicity, [Marion] Davies wanted fun, Peggy Joyce . . . [was] whoring for stardom'. At this point, Brooks was at a just about legal eighteen years old, but Charlie's other affairs suggested this was scarcely a concern to an entertainer then in his mid-thirties.

For at least some balance it must be added that not every affair Chaplin had in the 1920s pushed statutory boundaries. Pola Negri and Marion Davies were twenty-something actresses where the only danger for Charlie was overlapping with other powerful men (Rudolf Valentino in the case of Negri, and Hearst for Davies). Edna Purviance, Georgia Hale and, later, Paulette Goddard combined being Chaplin's leading lady while being actual adults when sleeping with their director. With the partial exception of Goddard, even such legally sound liaisons were always emotionally one-sided, however. Georgia Hale, the Tramp's love interest in *The Gold Rush* (1925), later reflected on

> the callousness and coldness to those for whom he proclaimed deep affection. Mr Chaplin's so-called love was as whimsical, imaginary and unreal as was the Hollywood affection his flattering friends showered on him . . . There was no manliness in him . . . no unselfishness, no support, no carrying through . . . But he expected all from a woman. He criticized, but could not or would not see himself.[5]

Part of this distance, one suspects, must have come from the traumatic experiences of his childhood. Having his mother wrenched away from Charlie at such a young age must have had an emotionally scarring effect on the young man that led him to keep all future relationships at something of a safe distance. Hetty's rejection also obviously stayed with him. Yet whatever the cause, he was clearly a nightmare to be romantically involved with. His background may help explain such behaviour, but it does not excuse it. When the FBI later asked him all manner of questions regarding his prolific sexual exploits, Chaplin simply replied, 'What kind of reply is a healthy man who has lived in this country for over thirty-five years supposed to make?'

We will go on to discuss his marriage to Lita Grey shortly, but the general pattern of Chaplin's four marriages was that while the comedian would get older, the wives would remain more or less the same age. Before turning to Lita it is important to note that this trend was readily understood and acknowledged as odd at the time. According to census data, the average age of a first marriage for American women was 21.2 years in 1920 (24.6 for men).[6] Compared to this, three of Chaplin's four wives were eighteen years old or under at the time of marriage – and this received much press comment. Taking Lita as indicative, the *Montreal Gazette* pointedly noted that 'Chaplin's child bride' had completed the requisite education required of a California girl in 1924.[7] Likewise, in March 1926 *The Evening Independent* ran the headline declaring 'Screen Comedian's *School-Girl* Wife Mother of Seven Pound Boy'.[8] And when the marriage was about to end, the *Pittsburgh Press* wrote of the impending divorce from 'his girl wife'.[9] The very fact that these descriptive terms were used suggests that Chaplin's relationships were not as normalised as he liked to suggest. In and of itself, that remains as much a comment on contemporary mores – Chaplin was rarely challenged on such tastes beyond the inference previously noted – as it does his own predilections. In the wake of the famous Arbuckle case (outlined below), however, any suggestions of sexual impropriety did not sit too well with the American public.

Lita

When casting for a flirtatious angel to appear in a dream sequence in *The Kid* (1921), Chaplin came across the young Lillita Louise MacMurray – later known professionally, at Charlie's instance, as Lita Grey. Unbeknownst to Charlie he had actually met her before. On her eighth birthday in 1916 a kindly restaurant manager led Lita over to see him when the two happened to be lunching at the same tea room on Hollywood Boulevard. Charlie dutifully performed a magic trick for Lita, who ran back to her mother saying she found the Englishman 'spooky'.[10] Lita's early life was not without more serious trauma – her father had left when she was just two years old, and her mother's second husband had died in the bizarre circumstances of having accidentally burned down the hospital ward he was staying on (via an errant cigarette).[11]

Settling in a new home on De Longpre Avenue, the MacMurrays were neighbours of Chuck Riesner, Charlie's assistant director. Lita enjoyed playing with Chuck's new baby, and it was quite the cinematic neighbourhood all in all. Merna Kennedy, later the Tramp's love interest in *The Circus*, also often came round to see Lita. One day in the spring of 1920 Lita and Merna were sat doing their homework on the front porch. Chuck Riesner and Charlie walked by the house, and Chuck introduced Lita to the screen icon. After Chuck told Lita he thought she'd 'photograph well', Charlie then asked, 'Would you like to be in a movie?' Once her mother had extracted guarantees over her education, Lita was told to report to the studio at 10 the next morning.[12]

After a $50-a-week contract was signed to employ both Lita and her mother ('a small wage' according to Lita) Alf Reeves led Chaplin's newest actress over to Rollie Totheroh, his lead cameraman. There, Lita recalls:

> My hair was arranged and makeup applied in such a way that I appeared in my screen test to look several years older than I actually was, which is what Charlie had wanted. I was tall for my age, and the makeup and wardrobe enabled me to look old enough to play the role of the flirting angel who tempts the Tramp in the film's dream sequence. It was a role that Charlie had created just for me.[13]

At the time Lita was just twelve years old.

Given his previous marriage to Mildred Harris, neither Lita nor her mother can exactly have viewed Charlie as perfect husband material. Indeed, by the time that Lita began working for Charlie he was often away from the studio dealing with his divorce. On set, there was also a continual reminder of what becoming romantically involved with the man actually meant: Edna Purviance, who was playing the mother of the titular *Kid* in this endeavour. At the time, Lita recalled, Edna was 'getting bloated through excessive drinking'. Several times the shooting had to be called off on *The Kid* because 'Edna was so drunk – literally staggering – that he could not use her in the scene'.[14] This had no doubt been exacerbated through Edna's on–off relationship with Charlie.

After her success in *The Kid*, Charlie cast Lita in another minor role in his comedic romp *The Idle Class*. He then invited her to a birthday party he was throwing for the actress May Collins (another of his later conquests), and told the then thirteen-year-old that he had 'been watching you when you haven't been looking. You have very pretty eyes, my dear.'[15] When Lita's mother refused her permission to go without her as chaperone, Chaplin became furious. Unbeknownst to Lita's mother, she and Merna snuck back to Chaplin's studio where Charlie was 'astonished and full of enthusiasm' at seeing Lita once more. Lita 'noticed that his eyes were going up and down my body', but was pleased when he announced he was searching for his leading lady for his new picture – *The Gold Rush*.[16] Describing the screen test that followed, Jim Tully was not impressed: 'Though she had less acting ability than any other girl who applied, Chaplin exclaimed, "Marvellous! Marvellous! Seated next to him, and not wishing to endanger my insecure position by being too honest, I went [back] into my office." Still, Charlie caught up with him: "What do you think of her Jim?" "Evading, I asked in return, "What do you think of her Charlie?" "Marvellous! Marvellous!" was the answer. Eventually Lita was ushered in: "Would you like to be a leading lady?" Charlie teased "Very much," she exclaimed. Tully recalls that "there was more than admiration in his troubled gaze. He covered it with a warm smile . . . The comedian's eyes went up and down her lithe young body." "You're engaged," he said, laughing.[17]

Charlie told his new star that her then legal name Lillita-MacMurray Parker was too 'long [and] awkward . . . for such a pretty girl'. Lita Grey it would be from now on, and a salary of $75 a week was soon awarded to suit her new star status. To forestall any awkward questions, the studio publicity machine soon began giving her age as nineteen. It should be added that Charlie's policy of hiring inexperienced and young actresses was not merely the product of his sexual proclivities. On set the man was a tyrant. As Virginia Cherrill found when working on *City Lights* almost a decade later, 'He acted out every part . . . every glance, every movement, just as he wanted it played.'[18] Hiring inexperienced actresses meant that they had fewer lessons to 'un-learn', and thus Charlie's brand of obsessive micro-managing could be instilled at a quicker rate. Even so, it still took a record

342 takes to record the scene where the Tramp and the blind girl first meet in *City Lights* – covered in the next chapter.

Back in the early 1920s the relationship between Lita and Charlie soon crossed the lines of director and actress. Inviting Lita over to his house, he told her 'it might be fun' to try his steam bath. Closing the door of the bathroom behind him, Lita was left alone in a room where 'the steam was gushing out of a vent at a very fast rate. It was only a few minutes until I could not see my hand before my face.' Suddenly, the door opened and Lita 'could feel Charlie's hand gently going up and down my body'. Sensing Lita's hesitation, Charlie told her, 'Don't be ashamed – this is an ideal way to make love. We can't see each other.' After the deed was done, she told Charlie it had been 'a wonderful experience'. Still, she asked, 'Do the servants know what we've been doing in the steam room?' 'Perhaps,' replied Charlie, 'but it doesn't matter. They're close mouthed. That's the way the Japanese are.'[19] Kono, Charlie's Japanese chauffeur, then drove Lita home, one presumes keeping to that stereotype.

This arrangement continued for weeks, with Charlie never using any form of contraception: 'Charlie believed that there was no danger of my becoming pregnant.'[20] After the chaperone the two had been using to keep Lita's mother off the scent found out that she was being used for such an underhand purpose, Charlie and Lita had to find other ways to be together. Here Chaplin was utterly brazen – inviting Lita and her mother over to stay the night after one of his parties. Once Lita's mother had fallen asleep, her daughter tiptoed across the room, headed through Charlie's connecting bathroom and into the master bedroom where her lover was still awake. After a while the creaking springs of the bed awoke Lita's mother, who stormed into the room demanding to know, 'How long has this been going on?' Charlie was surprised but attempted to talk his way out of it. 'Please, Lillian. Don't cry. I love Lita. We've been together several times when you didn't know about it . . . If Lita gets pregnant, we'll get married.'[21] The timing was precipitous – two weeks later a doctor confirmed that Lita was with child.

With Lita's mother insisting that 'he has to marry you, that's all there is to it' Chaplin obliged (thereby making good on the precedent he had previously set with Mildred Harris). To get around

Californian statutory age limits, on 25 November 1924 Charlie married Lita in Empalme, Sonora State, Mexico: soon after Lita began to start 'to show'. Taking the Southern Pacific Railroad to this small coastal town two hundred and fifty miles inside Mexico, the trip must have seemed like what it was – fleeing the scene of a crime. Charles Spencer Chaplin Jnr would be born on 5 May 1925, putting the date of his likely conception in August 1924: or when Lita was aged sixteen years and four months. This was definitely illegal – the age of sexual consent in California then stood at eighteen years old (although twenty-five states and the District of Columbia maintained sixteen years as the limit). On this matter, according to Lita at least, Charlie showed some gallows humour on the train home from Empalme. Within earshot of his new bride, he told some of his hangers-on, 'Well, boys, this is better than the penitentiary: but it won't last long.'[22]

Interestingly, Lita later claimed that the two had become engaged in May 1924, and that 'thereafter' Charlie had 'seduced [her] under promise of marriage'.[23] If they had indeed become engaged in May then Chaplin did not, publicly at least, appear to be relishing the prospect. The very next month Charlie had told the *Atlantic Journal* that, when it came to marriage, 'I think it's terrible. It is about as fascinating and inspiring as a prune factory . . . I think marriage is the quickest and surest death to individuality known to humanity. Life becomes as humdrum and uninspiring as an old shoe.'[24] Again, as with his previous attitude to marrying Mildred Harris in 1918, this was hardly spoken like a man truly in love.

When news of the Mexican wedding got out the Hollywood rumour mill soon cranked into motion. In February 1925 Valeria Belletti, Sam Goldwyn's personal secretary at MGM, wrote that

> the gossip in Hollywood just now centers around Charlie You of course know about his marrying that 16 year old child. Well, he was compelled to. You see he wronged her and she threatened to advise the police, and since she was under age it was either marry or go to jail. So he married her in order to save his reputation and career. When he came back to Hollywood, he brought his wife to his home, and he has never got into it. He's been going around with Marion Davies

and I think Mr Hearst will soon cause some trouble. At least so it is rumoured.[25]

That trouble would include much of his later political woes – and losing the good graces of the Hearst press would prove to be a risky move as the media generally turned against him. But he had more immediate concerns: what to do about a child bride he had evidently lost any infatuation for. This was manifest fairly early, and Lita later recalled Charlie's extreme reluctance to buy her wedding ring, leaving her embarrassed to be 'bare-handed' at parties. By early 1925 the solution Chaplin probably would have preferred – an abortion – was beyond the realms of possibility. But, as we will see, his alleged desire to procure one was just one of many controversial aspects of the Grey–Chaplin wedding.

In May 1925, Lita gave birth to the newlyweds' first son, Charles Jnr. Charlie promptly disappeared from the scene to go to New York to promote the release of *The Gold Rush*. Yet this was not all he got up to. Louise Brooks would go on to be annoyed that Charlie did not discuss their aforementioned liaison – A.C. Blumenthal, Peggy Fears, the Ambassador Hotel and all – in *My Autobiography*.[26] It was hardly surprising. Charlie spent two months in New York barely going out, fearful that the Hearst press was out to expose his various sexual exploits by way of revenge. And to get around this he simply brought them into A.C. Blumenthal's apartment. While Blumenthal played the piano, Peggy sang and Louise danced. Charlie had other ideas. Retreating to the bathroom he produced a bottle of iodine. According to Brooks, 'He had studied the matter and was firmly convinced that iodine was a reliable VD [venereal diseases] preventative.' Normally, he would only apply a dab, but this evening he 'was inspired to paint the sum of his private parts with iodine and come running with a bright red erection'.[27] Louise and Peggy squealed; Blumenthal's reaction is not recorded.

Divorce trial

Unbelievably, his relationship with Lita did not last. Even after a second son, Sydney, was born in March 1926 it was clear that Charlie was looking for an early exit from his marriage. In

November 1926 he told Lita and Lillian to take a trip anywhere far away from him: 'Go away some place for a while; I can't think or work when you are here. You are ruining my career.'[28] Eventually, they settled on Honolulu. Upon their return from Hawaii, bowing to the inevitable, in January 1927 Lita served Charlie with divorce papers.

The complaint filed by Lita at the Los Angeles County Superior Court was explosive stuff. As Chaplin biographer Jeffrey Vance notes, it was 'designed not only to sway a judge but to so sully Charlie Chaplin's greatest asset, his reputation with his audience'.[29] The content was so outrageous that the popular press soon dumped stories about the Teapot Dome scandal and the threat of war with Mexico to put Charlie on the front page. Given the content of this incendiary document, such political machinations could understandably wait.

To begin with, the many accusations of adultery contained within the petition were at the vanilla end of proceedings. Indeed, the notion of the Hollywood leading man as philanderer and cad was relatively ingrained. Upon his first divorce in 1919, for example, Al Jolson had cheerfully remarked that 'outside of my liking for wine, women and racehorses, I'm a regular husband'. That said, once journalists got wind of the contents of Lita's petition, there was much speculation over who the 'prominent moving picture actress' who had allegedly exercised 'a very great portion of [Charlie's] time' in the first month of their marriage really was. This woman Lita later revealed to be Marion Davies. Indeed, it was the threat of revealing Marion's identity publicly that Lita suggested forced Charlie to concede a settlement of $825,000 ($100,000 was ringfenced in a trust fund for each of their sons). 'W.R. [Hearst] would go crazy!' Marion is alleged to have said when Lita suggested she may leak the news of their affair, and certainly Hearst would have been out for Charlie's career in a matter of minutes had their affair been more widely known.[30] But all that was not what buried Chaplin in the eyes of many.

Discussing the case in later life, Lita stated that 'most of the content [of the divorce petition] is correct. However the way it is presented, the words used, the descriptions of sex, was all drawn up by my attorneys.'[31] Given the earlier tale of the steam bath that she did not retract there was probably enough factually accurate material to have kept the press interested. Yet if unpicking the truths and untruths from the petition is not easy, we can certainly summarise its contents – not least because it was reported as 'the truth' at the time. In short, Chaplin was portrayed as a sexual deviant. 'At times too numerous' for Lita to mention, Charlie had 'urged and demanded' she 'perform and commit such acts and things for [the] gratification . . . of [his] abnormal, unnatural, perverted, and degenerate sexual desires'. Such acts were 'too revolting, indecent and immoral to set forth in detail'.[32] They, however, certainly included the demand that Lita 'commit the act of sex perversion defined by Section 288a of the Penal Code of California' – oral sex. At the time performing this act with someone under the age of eighteen was punishable by a year's imprisonment.

According to the petition, Charlie would brag to Lita about the previous actresses who had performed these (and other) acts. Although not named in the petition, Lita later suggested that these were Edna Purviance, Pola Negri, Claire Windsor, Peggy Hopkins Joyce and her own friend Merna Kennedy. Charlie's attempts to encourage Lita into a threesome with 'a girl of their acquaintance . . . [who] might be willing to commit acts of sexual perversion' may or may not have included one of these five. Certainly three of these – Purviance (the star), Joyce (whose pursuit of a wealthy husband had formed part of the inspiration for the plot) and Negri (his lover during filming) – had been around the director during the making of *A Woman of Paris* just before his courtship with Lita began. In any event, Lita later revised the number of actresses involved with Charlie as up to seven.[33]

Sex aside, the divorce petition also portrayed Chaplin as mentally deranged. Much of this was clearly trying to manipulate the court. While Lita was 'a virtuous and inexperienced girl' who nonetheless had a 'sense and duty of maternal protection and preservation', Charlie was a nightmarish prima donna.[34] On one occasion Chaplin allegedly suggested Lita take her own life, and on another 'he picked up a loaded revolver and menacingly threatened to kill her'.[35] When Lita tried to tell Charlie that they 'should make the best' of their marriage, he told her, 'I might suddenly go crazy anytime, and kill you.' After seeing Charlie wave a gun one too many times, Lita is said to have left the marital home, never to return. Later in life Charlie would make similar claims against

Joan Barry, as Chapter 8 will show. Before his fourth wife Oona his relationships were certainly rarely stable.

Threatening a woman, adultery and general sexual adventurism were not the only offences Lita tried to hang around his neck, however. As the legalistic language of Lita's petition put it,

> as a result of [Charlie's] seduction, plaintiff became pregnant with child at the time of said marriage; [and] upon the discovery of defendant of said delicate condition of plaintiff, defendant delayed the consummation of said promise of marriage for so long a time in an effort to induce plaintiff to prevent the birth of said child by submitting herself to a criminal operation.[36]

In short, Charlie wanted rid of their baby. Yet with Lita viewing abortion to be a 'great social, legal and moral wrong', this was not an option she would countenance. Charlie allegedly then tried the same prior to the birth of their second child, telling Lita that 'other women had done that much for him without any hesitation', and named 'one moving picture actress, whom, he stated, had such an operation performed twice for him' (this was likely Edna Purviance). This was a smart legal play from Lita's team. Not only could Charlie not disprove this allegation (it may well have been true in any case), it would alienate religiously minded, small 'c' conservative public opinion from Charlie while simultaneously angering those liberals seeing a man of influence and wealth trying to pressurise a poor young girl into a dangerous operation. In the late 1920s some 15,000 American women died each year from abortions. Much of these occurred at the type of hazardous, back-street clinic Charlie would likely have paid (if only to keep the story out of the papers) to have Lita avoid, but it was hardly a good look almost fifty years prior to *Roe vs Wade*. In his autobiography Charlie would deal with the Lita years in a sentence: 'For two years we were married and tried to make a go of it but it was hopeless and ended in a great deal of bitterness.'[37] At the least that latter claim was certainly true.

Censorship and the movies

This debauched lifestyle mattered so much because it went against the grain of much of Charlie's industry, or rather the direction that several influential groups were trying to take it. This was starkly illustrated on 5 June 1922 when *The New York Times* carried the dramatic headline: 'Ultimatum by Hays to Purify Movies'.[38] This referred to Will H. Hays who had served as President of the Motion Picture Producers and Distributors of America (MPPDA) since March that year, having left his previous position as Post-master General under President Warren Harding. Hays was a right-wing politician turned film censor – not exactly the ideal candidate for Charlie – and his ties to the White House ran deep. As Chairman of the Republican National Committee between 1918 and 1921 Hays had links to the Teapot Dome scandal then plaguing the administration. This had involved the selling of fed-eral naval oil reserves to private bidders at suspiciously low cost, and would engulf members of the Republican leadership through-out the 1920s. But even if Hays faced accusations that his own hands were far from clean, he was quite prepared to cast simi-lar aspersions on the motion-picture industry. The new MPPDA that Hays led sought to 'guarantee clean films to the public'. *The New York Times* reported that 'this ultimatum is the last word to a few Directors whose last few pictures have been questionable, and that the failure to comply would mean dismissal from the industry'.[39] Self-regulation of the movie industry was now in. A Republican broom would sweep clean.

The situation had reached this point due to three factors. First, undeniably, there was a political motivation. As discussed in Chap-ter 2, the potential if not always the realities of leftist sympathy within the movie industry meant that there was an incentive for some to de-politicise the business. And de-politicisation was often code for keeping things exactly as they were. In the wake of a global conflict where more than 100,000 Americans had been killed and a revolution in Russia that seemed to offer a nightmar-ish glimpse of alternatives to democracy, the world, it was thought, had been through enough. It was not for the movies to stoke the fires of radicalism any more than had already been the case. Race, labour–capital questions or gender: these were not issues that officialdom wanted filmmakers to visit without the most extreme caution.

Second, there was clear pressure from religious groups, par-ticularly Catholics, to censor the movies. In this regard, Hays was actually something of a brake on the advance of censorship. With statutory censorship boards already in place in Florida, Kansas, Maryland, New York, Ohio, Pennsylvania and Virginia by the time the MPPDA began its work, the religious lobby had had significant success across the country in narrowing the content that millions of Americans could see. Indeed, one of Hays's first key victories was to wage a $300,000 campaign to ensure that a referendum on delivering a new statutory censorship board in the significantly Catholic state of Massachusetts did *not* pass.[40] The industry-led MPPDA was strict, but state-run boards appealing to fervently religious populations could be even worse. Accommodation between the MPPDA and religious groups was therefore necessary if the body was to survive at all, and this led Hays's organisation in the direction of taking a morally tough stance. By 1929, as we will see, it would be two religious men – the Catholic layman Martin Quigley and the Jesuit Daniel Lord – who would draft much of what became the 'Hays Code' to censor cinema content. Religious lobbying had contributed to the implementation of America's experiment with prohibition from 1920 and significant restrictions on non-Western European immigration from 1924. In a sense the movies were just another platform for such small 'c' conservative battles.

Third, religious groups aside, the view that Hollywood may need some greater moral policing was not without some credence. Chaplin's own less than innocent sexual exploits apart, accusations of murder and rape against a similarly big name – Roscoe 'Fatty' Arbuckle – had rocked Hollywood throughout 1921. Lurid accusations regarding Arbuckle having used a piece of ice – later upgraded to a Coca-Cola or a champagne bottle – to rape an aspiring actress, Virginia Rappe, resulted in three trials for manslaughter over late 1921 and early 1922. Arbuckle was unanimously acquitted at the third trial after the jury had deliberated for just six minutes (five of those being used to pen a formal apology to Arbuckle for his ordeal). The press, particularly William Randolph Hearst's brand of populist 'yellow' journalism, had a field day throughout the arrest and trials, however. Arbuckle's weight was used to suggest a lecherous cad who would overpower innocent young maidens. The presence of alcohol and the suggestions of an impending orgy did not help matters. Buster Keaton stuck up for Fatty, as did Chaplin. When Keaton went to meet Arbuckle at the

old Santa Fe Railroad Station in Los Angeles to express his solidarity during the trials, a crowd – or 'hate-frenzied mob of 1500
men and women' as Keaton later described them – gathered to hurl
abuse such as 'Big, fat slob', 'Degenerate bastard' and 'Murderer'
at a man later found to be innocent of all charges.[41] His career
was, however, ruined. For some in 'respectable America', Arbuckle's unseemly antics – even if he was innocent of the actual murder
charge – demanded a response. The major innovation of Hays's
MPPDA was to make that response one of industry self-regulation
rather than federal censorship.

Even so, if FBI files are to be believed, Chaplin did not take setting up of the MPPDA particularly well. He was not the only one.
As Adolphe Menjou noted, 'On Hollywood Boulevard the opinion
was that people won't stand for any serious censorship.' In this
regard, they were, however, out of touch: 'In the rest of the country
civic groups and parent–teacher associations were holding more
and bigger indignation meetings, while editors were still fulminat-
ing against Hollywood.'[42] Here Chaplin was either deliberately
myopic, or simply thought it would all blow over. When the radical Marxist labour organiser William Z. Foster visited Los Angeles
in August 1922, Chaplin threw a welcoming party for him and
what the FBI dubbed fellow 'Parlor Bolsheviki'. At this gathering
Chaplin stated that neither he nor any of the stars associated with
him would have any use for Will Hays. Laughing, he claimed that
'we are against any kind of censorship, and particularly against
Presbyterian censorship'. Leading his guests through the Chaplin
studios, he showed them a pennant with the words 'Welcome Will
Hays', which he had affixed to the door of the men's bathroom.[43]
Initially, such animus was at least publicly restrained. When the
MPPDA had been set up, they had been eager to secure the membership of the big cinematic names, including Pathe and the Hearst
and Thomas Ince companies, to bolster their reach. But high on
that list had also been Charles Chaplin Productions and United
Artists.[44] By March 1927 United Artists had joined the MPPDA.[45]

Through his UA affiliation Charlie had to deal with the new list
of so-called 'Don'ts and Be Carefuls' produced by the MPPDA.
Signatories to this document were resolved that the contents of this
list 'shall not appear in pictures produced by members of this Association', and, to be fair, 1920s Chaplin rarely troubled the censors

here. With the main concerns of the 'Don't' list mostly alighting on blasphemy, racial mixing ('miscegenation', 'white slavery') and sexual conduct ('suggestive nudity-in fact or in silhouette; and any lecherous or licentious notice thereof'), Charlie was not a threat to the 'list' in this regard. *The Pilgrim* of 1923 – where Charlie has to improvise a sermon about David and Goliath – would possibly have bordered on the prohibited 'ridicule of the clergy'. Others would have seen *The Immigrant* as causing 'wilful offense to any nation' – that is, the self-aggrandising wing of America. But, for the most part, Chaplin's actual cinematic content would have passed the conditions laid out in 1927. In any event, the Studio Relations Committee that monitored such content performed a purely advisory function in the 1920s.

But there were harbingers for later troubles here. Where Charlie was already beginning to worry moral America was in the portion of the list that demanded 'special care be exercised in the manner in which the following subjects are treated' – the so-called 'be carefuls'. Here the need for 'good taste' was stressed in twenty-five areas from smuggling to surgical operations. While 1920s Chaplin had not yet begun to push the boundaries on some of these, the request to temper 'the use of the flag', 'international relations (avoiding picturizing in an unfavourable light another country's religion, history, institutions, prominent people and citizenry)' and 'techniques of murder' would all largely cover his content in the 1930s and 1940s. Scenes depicting 'sympathy for criminals' and 'theft [and] robbery' had arguably – albeit in a light-hearted setting – formed part of his output since the early days. The studios had defined, if not yet fully enshrined, what was 'normal' and 'acceptable' film-making, and Charlie was moving towards the edge of this window of acceptability.

In 1929 these 'don'ts and be carefuls' were re-drafted and extended through the combined efforts of the MPPDA, the Catholic layman Martin Quigley and the Jesuit Priest Daniel Lord Lord's view was that 'we can make pictures with our approval and break them with our disproval'. Why, he asked, were 'marvellous', wholesome pictures like Paramount's 1929 *Disraeli* box-office failures but *Hell's Angels* – which had 'no place in a civilized world' – or the 'filthy production' *Party Girl* such successes? It was because the Church had not thrown its moral weight behind the 'good' and thus the 'bad' was free to roam unchallenged. There was a need to imbue the movies with a more ecclesiastical, church-friendly tone – one that, in short, was not merely ambivalent to good and evil but firmly threw itself behind the former.

After an initial draft from Quigley, Lord set to work turning the 'Don'ts and be carefuls' into what became known as the Hays Code from 1930. This combined document began by noting that 'mankind has always recognized the importance of entertainment and its value in rebuilding the bodies and souls of human beings . . . But it has always recognized that entertainment can be of a character HARMFUL to the human race.' This had a particular dimension that was relatively benign in the days before the crash on Wall Street led to a worldwide Depression, but became ever more important as time passed. 'Correct entertainment', noted the Hays Code, 'raises the whole standard of a nation. Wrong entertainment lowers the whole living conditions and moral ideas of a race.' Motion pictures 'reproduce the morality of the men who use the pictures as a medium for the expression of their ideas and ideals'. Thus, Charlie's protestations that he was just a comedian was a defence that was beginning to wear ever thinner with official movie opinion formers. In the 1930s this would play out in a myriad of ways.

'Respectable' Hollywood

If Chaplin represented avant-garde, vaguely subversive Hollywood in the 1920s – foreign, leftist and debauched – this needs further contextualising. Part of this was again about notions of a global Jewish conspiracy – a concept that served its adherents so well because even when politicians or businessmen denied they were part of it, this was merely evidence of the so-called 'cover-up'. On 22 January 1921 Henry Ford's *Dearborn Independent* claimed that film and cinema was at the forefront of this plot. With 'gentile playwrights and actors . . . steadily diminishing in number for want of a market, at times the employment of Jewish actors has been so obtrusive as to endanger the success of the play'. It went on to note that 'some of the more prominent Jewish actors, many of them prime favorites, are Al Jolson, Charlie Chaplin . . . Ed Wynne, or to mention his real name, Israel Leopold'. Here, 'the cover-name conceals from the theater going public the fact that the actors and actresses who purvey entertainment are, in large and growing proportion, Jewish'.[46]

Against this secretive cabal of subversives, however, there was a body of cinematic opinion that was much more politically palatable. Foremost among this was Louis B. Mayer, born Lazar Burt Mayer to Jewish parents in the Ukraine (thereby ironically forming another Jewish name concealer for the Fords). According to the actor Ralph Bellamy, Mayer was a 'Jewish Hitler, a fascist' with 'no feeling for any minority, including his own'.[47] Although a movie mogul, as Ross persuasively shows, 'through his involvement in party politics and his careful mentoring of conservative stars, Mayer laid the groundwork that made it possible for actors such as George Murphy, Ronald Reagan, and Arnold Schwarzenegger to become successful politicians'.[48] That these were all of the political right was as much about the California Mayer made his mark in, as it was his own innate beliefs. With registered Republicans outnumbering Democrats by 3:1 in California, the so-called Grand Old Party (GOP) was the establishment party in a state that had a Republican Governor in Sacramento from 1917 to 1939. With an immigrant background and (unlike Chaplin actually) being Jewish, there was little more obvious sign for Mayer of having 'made it' in America than hobnobbing with and influencing the conservative, apple-pie eating and Protestant-worshipping political establishment.

After the official inauguration of Metro-Goldwyn-Mayer (MGM) in April 1924, Mayer joined the Republican Party and campaigned for the re-election of President Coolidge. Coolidge had famously declared that 'the chief business of the American people is business' and as capital flowed into the movie industry (more than $1 billion of capital by 1921) the alliance between Hollywood and the Republican establishment became ever more secure. Whereas Al Jolson had organised Broadway players to campaign for the Republicans in 1920 and 1924, it would be the election of Herbert Hoover as President in 1928 that would finally cement the pact between entertainment and the GOP, however. While Mayer had joined the Coolidge bandwagon rather late, he ensured that by 1927 he was firmly behind the presumptive next Republican nominee in Hoover. Appointed treasurer of the Republican National

Committee for California, Mayer went around the major studios soliciting donations from Cecil B. De Mille ($10,000) and United Artists president Joseph Schenck ($7,000) for Hoover's cause – the latter, albeit by degrees of separation, thereby seeing revenues from Chaplin films fund the Republican Party. At the 1928 Republican National Convention in Kansas City Mayer even promised to 'deliver the motion picture industry to the Republican Party'. Although the existence of Charlie Chaplin always rendered this an impossible task, Mayer was able to convince the even more important press magnate William Randolph Hearst to leave behind his last vestiges of Democratic sympathy and support Hoover's nomination for the Republican ticket. On 12 March 1929, the first guests Hoover would host after moving into the White House would be the Mayers.[49] With Republicans in the Governor's Mansion in Sacramento, occupying the White House and in control of both Houses of Congress in Washington, this was undeniably a smart political play.

By 1932 the extent to which Mayer had captured Hollywood for the Republicans would have been obvious to a child of ten. Indeed, one such ten-year-old was actor Jackie Cooper (later to achieve a second dose of fame as Perry White in Christopher Reeve's *Superman* films) who told a Republican sympathetic meeting of women's groups that he would vote for Hoover if he was old enough. During the 1932 campaign Lionel Barrymore, Buster Keaton, Jimmy Durrante, Conrad Nagel and Mae Murray all took part in a grand rally in support of Hoover at the Shrine Auditorium in Los Angeles six days before the election. That these activities were portrayed as patriotic and as decent Americans supporting their President would not be a luxury extended to Charlie Chaplin in later years. Now the American public had not liked what had gone on in Charlie's hotel rooms, they were about to get even more of a dose of what went on in his mind. In the 1920s he had begun to enter the political fray, but in the 1930s he would hurl himself headlong into it.

Notes

1 *The New York News*, 30 May 1924.
2 Adolphe Menjou, *It Took Nine Tailors* (New York, 1948), 129.

3   *The Argonaut* clipping, 2 January 1948 within National Archives, Washington, D.C. [NADC]/HUAC/RG 233.

4   Harry Crocker's unpublished memoir, 'Charlie Chaplin: Man and Mime', MHL/HRC, IV–16.

5   Georgia Hale, *Charlie Chaplin: Intimate Close-Ups* (New Jersey, 1995), 149–50.

6   Via US Bureau of the Census.

7   *Montreal Gazette*, 6 December 1924.

8   *The Evening Independent*, 30 March 1926. My italics.

9   *Pittsburgh Press*, 22 August 1927.

10 Lita Grey (Jeffrey Vance ed), *Wife of the Life of the Party*, (London, 1998), 5.

11 Ibid., 3, 8.

12 Ibid., 10–11.

13 Ibid., 13.

14 Ibid., 15.

15 Ibid., 27.

16 Ibid., 30.

17 Tully, 'King of Laughter', UCLA/JTL, 83.

18 Miranda Seymour, *Chaplin's Girl: The Life and Loves of Virginia Cherrill* (London, 2009), 76.

19 Grey, *Wife*, 42.

20 Ibid., 45.

21 Ibid., 50.

22 Divorce petition, Los Angeles County Superior Court (LACSC), Lita Grey–Charlie Chaplin Divorce Papers (LGLP) 2.

23 Divorce Petition, LACSC/LGLP, 3.

24 *Atlantic Journal*, 1 June 1924.

25 Valeria Belletti to Irma, 27 February 1925, MHL/Valeria Belletti Papers [VLB] 1–f.2.

26 Louise Brooks, 'Charlie Chaplin Remembered', *Film Culture*, 40 (Spring, 1966), 5–6.

27 Peter Ackroyd, *Charlie Chaplin* (London, 2014) 152–3.

28 Divorce Petition, LACSC/LGLP, 11.

29 Grey, *Wife*, 126.

30 Ibid., 104.

31 Ibid., 128.

32 Divorce Petition, LACSC/LGLP, 7.

33 *Reading Eagle*, 20 December 1992.

34 Divorce Petition, LACSC/LGLP, 3.

35 Divorce Petition, LACSC/LGLP, 20.

36 Divorce Petition, LACSC/LGLP, 3.

37 Charlie Chaplin, *My Autobiography* (London, 2003), 300.

38 *The New York Times*, 5 June 1922.

39 *The New York Times*, 5 June 1922.

40 Gregory D. Black, *Hollywood Censored: Morality Codes, Catholic. and the Movies* (Cambridge: Cambridge University Press, 1996), 32–3.

41 Buster Keaton, *My Wonderful World of Slapstick* (New York, 1960), 160.

42 Menjou, *Nine Tailors*, 130.

43 15 August 1922 report, Federal Bureau of Investigation [FBI], Charlie Chaplin file [CCF] part 7.

44 MPPDA Committee Minutes, 6 January 1922, Flinders Institute for Research in the Humanities, Flinders University, South Australia [FIRTH], Motion Picture Producers and Distributors of America [MPPDA] File no. 57.

45 Although Chaplin himself did not put his personal production company through their auspices.

46 *Dearborn Independent*, 22 January 1921.

47 Steven J. Ross, *Hollywood Left and Right: How Movie Stars Shaped American Politics* (Oxford, 2011), 53.

48 Ibid.

49 All via Ross, *Hollywood Left and Right*, ch.2.

5 Between Churchill and Gandhi: A comedian sees the world

If socially conservative America was beginning to baulk both at Chaplin's politics and his womanising, the man himself was about to re-assert some profoundly transnational connections. Centred on Chaplin's world tour to promote *City Lights* in the early 1930s, this chapter stresses the international thinking that informed his work. He was of course British rather than American – but it was more than that. Charlie's world view developed in the 1930s by drawing on thinkers from John Maynard Keynes to Mahatma Gandhi. He read widely, paid attention to the news and put much thought into how the world 'should be' as much as how it was. He was an autodidact whose sheer wealth meant that his political views were almost always about what was better 'for other people'. And, as a result, in later years some judged the political philosophy he portrayed on the screen as jejune in the extreme.

This was unfair. In artistic terms Chaplin's views were always more developed than, for example, his nineteenth-century predecessor Charles Dickens. When George Orwell wrote his 1940 essay on Dickens, he noted 'the utter lack of any constructive suggestion anywhere in [Dickens's] work. He attacks the law, parliamentary government, the educational system and so forth, without ever clearly suggesting what he would put in their places.'[1] In this regard Chaplin had a more developed *weltanschauung* than the nineteenth-century writer. More importantly, criticising the coherence of Chaplin's politics also somewhat overstates the specificity of the political world in which he interacted. Rather than the modern fascination with specific retail policy offers – cut this or that tax by a set amount, fund spending on this budget line by reducing it on another – interwar politicians in both America and Britain tended to set out their various principles in broad brush strokes. If Chaplin could be vague in his desire to help the poor, so too could elected officials. Thus, politicians talked of solving unemployment, poor housing, low welfare and so forth but did not often set out concrete programmes to reach these end goals, or how they would be paid for. By way of ballpark indication, in 1929 the British Labour Party manifesto would constitute 2,500 words of rather vague aims.[2] Chaplin spoke more politics than that during, say, his 1942 speech on a second front. Certainly in the intervening years politics has since changed dramatically. Indeed, in 2015 Labour would set forth a set of specific pledges totalling more than 16,000 words. But we should not judge Charlie by the modus operandi of the twenty-first century. The fact that Chaplin did not sit down and write *Das Kapital* in the 1930s should not preclude an acceptance of him as a coherent political actor.

This chapter therefore considers the international influences on Chaplin's thought in the crucial years after the Wall Street Crash, issues that we continue in the next chapter on *Modern Times*. Taking in Sergei Eisenstein, Ivor Montagu, Winston Churchill, Gandhi and the deputies of the pre-Nazi dominated German Reichstag, his travels when working on and then promoting *City Lights* would prove vital in shaping his politics. In a sense, it professionalised them, moving Chaplin from the type of man who could merely blether about communism over a cold beer with Buster Keaton to someone prepared to take on contemporary politicians more seriously. Whether this was a good thing for Chaplin's life is of course debateable, but it certainly changed it. To paraphrase the title of one of his later books, this was truly a time when a comedian saw a good deal of the world, and would bring much of it home to America.

Eisenstein in Hollywood

Before Chaplin saw the world, however, the world flocked to Chaplin. A theme of this work is that for a self-proclaimed non-communist (and certainly a very successful capitalist) Charlie Chaplin kept the company of a significant number of Bolshevik sympathisers. One of these was the Englishman Ivor Montagu, a public school and Cambridge-educated son of a Peer who had been in sporadic contact with Charlie throughout the late 1920s. Like Rob Wagner before him, Montagu was one of several poly-maths whose leftist politics was only part of their appeal to Charlie. A jovial man, after working for the Labour Party at the 1918 General Election Montagu later recalled that 'I put my top-hat away in the Underground cloakroom nearest to my public school when I went out canvassing'.[3] Like Charlie he never let leftist sympathy drift into a purely monastic existence. For example, as President of the International Table Tennis Federation, Montagu helped popularise the sport across the globe. He was adept with a much larger tennis racquet, too, always more Chaplin's game. As a film critic for the liberal-leaning *Observer* and *New Statesman* in London he had a natural affinity for the work of Chaplin, and attempted to ingratiate both himself and, more crucially, others of a leftist standpoint into Charlie's inner circle. Montagu had even directed three short comedic films himself – these were low budget, but had utilised a script written by Chaplin's acquaintance H.G. Wells.[4] After failing to make a breakthrough as a director in Britain, Montagu's eyes began to turn to Hollywood and the opportunities potentially out there.

Just as Chaplin would consider much of his economic phi-losophy on the beaches of the French Riviera in late 1931, Montagu's association with communism took a decisive turn in the equally salubrious location of the Swiss Alps. There, in La Sarraz, a late 1920s conference organised by the French philosopher and cultural theorist Raymond Aron saw various avant garde European filmmakers gather to, in Montagu's words, 'praise one another and admire one another'.[5] One such attendee was the 'slim, strong, handsome, fair-haired and golden-skinned' Serge Eisenstein, then still riding high on the success of the Russian revolution depicting *Battleship Potemkin* (1925) and *October* (1928).[6] Montagu declared Eisenstein and his collaborators (including Grigory Alexandrov) 'the supreme experimenters' who were convinced, 'not incorrectly, that the great cinema of those days, the cinema of industry and prosperity, was too complacent'. This artistic licence is what drew Montagu in: 'We were not "Reds" – the term was little used then – but we adored experiment.'[7]

Ingratiating himself with a smattering of Russian gained through two previous trips to the Soviet Union, Montagu invited Eisenstein to give a lecture at the Film Society in London. This was not the first connection Chaplin would have to Eisenstein – in 1926 Douglas Fairbanks and Mary Pickford had seen *Potemkin* in Moscow. So impressed was he with the film and keen to get its director to Hollywood Fairbanks had then asked the Russian, 'How long does it take you to pack your bags?'[8] Since the Soviet regime was grateful for the propagandistic potential of Eisenstein's recent output, he and Alexandrov were permitted to leave the Soviet Union to cross a Europe where 'notabilities in literature, the arts, academic circles, [and wider] society' were all eager to meet them. Like Montagu they were eager to get to Hollywood, however – particularly to learn from the new sound cinema that would so plague Chaplin. With a £500 loan from his uncle to sustain himself for a year, Montagu promptly proposed to join them.

Ivor Montagu's initial connection with Chaplin is difficult to ascertain. Certainly as far back as September 1925 he had been in touch with Soviet officials who had offered Charlie – presumably in the erroneous belief that Montagu was something of an insider – the opportunity to make a film there, or simply visit the country as a tourist.[9] But the initial tone of their correspondence seems to be Chaplin trying to fob off a Montagu looking for any angle into the famous filmmaker. Doubtless he received many such attempts. In November 1925 Montagu had written to Charlie, but Alf Reeves had simply issued a perfunctory reply on his behalf saying the 'letter has been placed on his desk to await his return'.[10] After H.G. Wells and George Bernard Shaw had agreed to pen letters of introduction to both the Fairbanks and Chaplin, Montagu appears to have led his Soviet friends to Hollywood in 1930 with the vague hope of parlaying them into something, but having no idea where it would lead. He was, in fact, something of a chancer. Chaplin eventually agreed 'to do something' for Montagu, but largely 'to show his deep respect for Mr. Shaw and Mr. Wells'.[11] Alf Reeves attempted to intercede to get a more proactive response from Charlie, partly due to Montagu's wife coming from the same South London hinterland as himself, but Montagu rebuffed the offer. Eventually, after what must have seemed like an interminable wait, Chaplin's chauffeur Kono rang Montagu asking him round for tea at his Beverly Hills house. A set of tennis later (Montagu won six games to three), a friendship was sealed.

This friendship did not necessarily mean business – formally at least Eisenstein had an initial agreement with Paramount for six months. This, however, merely provided expenses ($500 for Eisenstein a week, $100 for Montagu and others) while they searched for a film to make. This time seems to have been mostly spent attending the parties held by studio big-wigs, no doubt in the hope that one would produce a big cheque for them to finance some cinematic venture. At one such gathering the group encountered Upton Sinclair, whose wife told Montagu that 'whatever happens now to the Russian revolution, it has been a wonderful help to Upton and me in our propaganda'. Montagu saw Sinclair as something of a sell-out by this stage, however: 'The Red David who had challenged Goliath with *The Jungle* and *The Brass Check* had become pink by now.'[12] In any event, it was Chaplin's house that had now become their collective 'second home'. At another party Montagu encountered Jim Tully, the now ex-Chaplin employee, who inveighed against his former boss, 'sneering at him for intellectual pretension'. Tully spat that 'he has a library full of the books of the day, but he has never read any of them from start to finish'. Defending his would-be sponsor, Montagu noted that 'there is probably not another star of his eminence in the Hollywood of that day, or any magnate, who had a serious library at all or had even looked at any of those books'. Generally, Montagu believed, 'Chaplin had looked into them all and had ideas about them he could present with point.'[13]

If Montagu was not a communist (and his later CV listed communist membership from 1931) he was certainly facilitating their bidding.[14] The Soviet film agency Amkino kept pestering Montagu and Eisenstein to find out why Charlie would not sell any of his films to the USSR, 'and try to do something about it'. Ironically for a director accused of trying to export communism to the West, this was because he felt that the Soviet regime was short changing him: 'Charlie explained that it was not because he was in any way anti-Soviet, but business was business and the money they were offering was less than he would get for a film from one middling-size town in the United States.' Montagu tried to explain 'all about the five-year-plan, the need of the Soviet Union to import machinery, the shortage of valuta. He would not budge.' It was, Charlie noted 'the principle of the thing. Pictures are worth something. They give Henry Ford valuta for tractors and my pictures must be worth at least as much as several tractors.'[15] Montagu tried to broker a complicated deal whereby Charlie would receive furniture looted from the Tsar's palace in lieu of payment for distribution rights, but it came to nothing.

The more Eisenstein was seen around Hollywood, the more suspicious those on the American right became at his motives. Montagu eventually put the failure of Eisenstein to land a major Hollywood project as down to a mixture of 'mistrust of intellectuals (especially "foreigners"), tribal rival[ries], our own tactical mistakes, and political fears'.[16] As mentioned, Montagu himself personally denied being a communist. This was untrue. The British secret service was monitoring Montagu's mail constantly, he was described as 'the communist cashier' in the press in 1932 and, most crucially, by 1940 he had received the code name 'Intelligentsia' from Moscow.[17] Amusingly, the British became ever more suspicious of Montagu because of his advocacy of table tennis – which they considered a hobby so eccentric it had to be cover for something more nefarious. More worryingly, with Montagu's brother Ewen heavily involved in the planning for Operation Mincemeat (the diversion for what became the Allied invasion of Sicily in 1943), Ivor was considered something of a threat to national security by the 1940s. Despite (or perhaps because of) this, Charlie proved a loyal friend until death – a loyalty that was reciprocated. For his part Eisenstein eventually shuffled off to Mexico to link up with Upton Sinclair on a new film project, which we cover in the next chapter.

The talkies

Leaving Montagu and Eisenstein behind, Charlie took off to promote 1931's *City Lights*. In many ways Chaplin's 1931–2 world tour was initially intended to be as much about personal and artistic introspection as it was political development. The political writings would indeed emerge as this chapter will note, but there was a more immediate problem: Al Jolson's landmark performance in *The Jazz Singer*. Previously Chaplin had been the cinematic innovator. He had taken the one-note slapstick comedy he had encountered when first arriving in the States, and imbued it with a pathos that far exceeded those of his great contemporaries. He was, however pompously he expressed it, an 'artist'. Except now the rules of the cinematic game had changed. On 6 October 1927 Warner Brothers released *The Jazz Singer* to critical and commercial success. The major story here was not only the use of spoken dialogue in the film, but the fact that it had proven so successful. With a near four-million-dollar return on a $400,000 investment, the business case for moving to sound was clear.[18] The big question was where that left the Tramp, and was he now behind the times?

In the mid-1930s Winston Churchill speculated on this dilemma. On the one hand, he believed that 'had it not been for the coming of the Talkies, we would already have seen this great star in a serious role'. Chaplin remained, as Churchill knew, an anachronism in the post *Jazz Singer* age: 'He is the one figure of the old silent screen to whom the triumph of the spoken word has meant neither speech nor extinction.' And for all the huge US receipts *The Jazz Singer* had taken in there was a commercial argument for ploughing on as long as possible in the silent format: the international market. As the great imperialist Churchill knew, 'there are many countries which lack the resources to make their own talkies. There are millions of people whose mother tongue will never be heard in any cinema and who understand thoroughly no other speech.' Churchill's case then segued in slightly odd directions here:

> The English-speaking nations have a great opportunity – and a great responsibility. The primitive mind thinks more easily in pictures than in words . . . The films which are shown amid the stillness of the African tropic night or under the skies of Asia may determine, in the long run, the fate of Empires and of civilisations. They will promote, or destroy, the prestige by which the white man maintains his precarious supremacy.[19]

Churchill's words here may not chime with post-1945 norms, but at least they were consistent with his general world view. What is less clear is how he imagined that Chaplin would fit in to this agenda. Pointing to the need for studios to make the 'right type of silent films' to both hit 'an immensely profitable market' and provide 'a great service to civilisation', he hoped 'we shall not have to wait another four years for the next Chaplin picture'. If Winston was hoping for Charlie to make a silent version of, say, *The Lives of a Bengal Lancer*, he would be waiting a long time. But the point was that so too would any cinema-goers who wanted to hear the Tramp talk. From 1927 until 1940's *Great Dictator*, the Tramp – or a variant of him – appeared on screen without speaking a word of English (the gibberish song in *Modern Times* not withstanding). For thirteen years Chaplin rode out the talking storm, helped in large part by the fact that his immense wealth meant that he did not need to make many pictures, and his independence through United Artists meant that there were no executives to face down in any boardroom. By 1936 the *New York Evening Journal* found it 'curious to see the lips of the actors move and to hear no sound' in *Modern Times*, the last time that Charlie would chance such a tactic. But he had ploughed on regardless.

City Lights

As with much of his cinematic work, 1931's *City Lights* was the means and not the end. At least for our purposes it got him into the rooms to talk to various famous politicians and thinkers. But its sheer genius demands outlining even in a work on Chaplin's politics. In one sense, there was a major exception with this film – Charlie did not end up sleeping with his co-star. From Edna Purviance (1914–23) to Georgia Hale (1925) to Merna Kennedy (1928) to Paulette Goddard (1936–40) Charlie had always adopted co-stars as sources of potential affairs. This was not the case with Virginia Cherrill. Initially attracted by her 'shapely form in a blue bathing suit', Chaplin found that unlike other applicants he had tried, 'to my surprise she had the faculty of looking blind' – a key plot point for what would become his most moving film. Virginia's inexperience at acting was not necessarily a problem for Charlie – 'those with less experience are more apt to adapt themselves' – but her attitude to filming was. As she later noted, 'I don't think Charlie really liked me very much . . . we had almost no social contact of any kind.' For Virginia filming 'was boring in that there was so much waiting. One waited . . . sometimes for months, literally – three or four months – and Charlie would not come to the studio.' As a result, Virginia sat knitting or reading in her room while Charlie figured out how to resolve the film's plot.

Chaplin started pre-production on City Lights in early 1928, albeit soon halted after the death of his mother on 28 August that year. The film did not receive its premiere until February 1931. This was some delay, even for Charlie. As Ivor Montagu wrote to him just before its release: '[I am] beginning to get anxious about City Lights. Why isn't it ready? What is happening to it? I begin to have visions of you swallowing the negative inch by inch as you do your spaghetti [in one memorable skit in the film].'[20] This was not just a product of the poor relationship between Charlie and Virginia, however – many changes occurred in the overall structure of the story that delayed matters. When filming commenced in December 1928 it had originally been planned that the film should be set in London, but this was subsequently revised to a generic city, presumably in America. Similarly, although he had always planned the story to be about the theme of blindness and had an unusually strong sense of how it may end, he had originally conceived it as something of a follow-up to *The Circus* where he would play a clown that had gone blind and was attempting to conceal this fact from his young daughter. Even when he had settled on the importance of the blind girl, he toyed with various endings, including having the Tramp introduce her to the millionaire and for him to bow out of a love triangle once more. The plot and the cast were both a pain, Cherrill aside. The role of the millionaire had to be re-cast after four days when the Australian artist Henry Clive refused to jump into a river during the millionaire's aborted suicide attempt that sees the Tramp come to the rescue. There could be no revisiting of this plot element. It would be the association with the millionaire that enabled Charlie to assume the affectations of wealth so crucial to the arc of the picture.

In the end, *City Lights* began with a couple of scenes of comedic business before its central story is introduced: the mutual love between the Tramp and Cherrill's flower-selling girl. Although a comedy, the film derives its poignancy from the sheer lengths that Charlie will go to to earn the money not only to pay for the girl's rent, but ultimately to procure an operation to restore her sight. Against the backdrop of Chaplinesque slapstick, *City Lights* is ultimately an exceptional love story in which its heroine has no idea of the Tramp's poverty, and throughout begs the viewer to consider what will happen when her sight is restored, and she sees her pauper of a benefactor. This required careful craftsmanship. What Chaplin could not figure out for a long time was how, in the scene depicting their first meeting, the girl should be shown to be unaware of the Tramp's lowly social status and, equally crucially, to show that the Tramp knew this and would thus decide to affect the habits of a rich man to win her over. As Charlie later wrote, 'Logically it was always difficult to get a beautiful girl interested in a tramp. This has always been a problem in my films.'[21] In the end, the simplest indicator of 1930s wealth, a car door slamming (and the two characters' reactions to it), was used to communicate these crucial plot signals that drive the whole film. It is an incredibly efficient gem of a scene. But it took time – contributing to Virginia's general frustration and partly accounting for her being temporarily fired before Charlie realised he had shot too much film and was forced to bring her back.

The second story arc concerns the Tramp's friendship with the millionaire, now played by Harry Myers. Having saved him from committing suicide (presumably because his wife has left him), the millionaire is grateful and gregarious towards the tramp when drunk. The two go out on the town, host an opulent party at the millionaire's house and drive around the city together without a care in the world. When under the influence of liquor the millionaire hands over his money willingly whenever his new friend asks, but crucially he does not recall doing this, or indeed the Tramp at all, when sober. Because of the millionaire's erratic ways, the Tramp is forced to take on a series of jobs (from street sweeper to amateur boxer) that not only pave the way for much hilarity, but illustrate the lengths he will go to to help his beloved. In this sense although *City Lights* aims no direct pot shots at particular leaders or policies, the fact that the only two people to treat the Tramp in a humane manner are a drunkard and someone who cannot see him lend the film an overarching class emphasis.

Whatever the politics, the film remains a classic from beginning to end. Indeed, even the economy of the scene depicting the protagonists' first meeting and the pacing of the story thereafter do not compare to the film's justly famous climax. After taking on various demeaning jobs to try to help his sweetheart, the Tramp eventually manages to get the funds from his millionaire friend to give to the blind girl that will pay for her rent and help restore her sight. After being wrongly imprisoned for stealing this money, the Tramp wanders the streets aimlessly: alone once more. Passing by a prosperous flower shop now run by Virginia, her sight restored and middle-class manners affected, he is initially met with derision and then pity. Recognising his sweetheart, the Tramp is clearly moved at her beauty and how well she is now doing, but tries to scuttle off before she works out who he is and presumably has her dreams shattered. Cherrill, however, manages to grab him by the hand with the intention of giving some change to this poor wretch. But, as she does so, she recognises his touch. Slowly it dawns on her that this Tramp – not the handsome Prince Charming she had previously been shown to be imagining – had been her hero all along. She takes in her benefactor with a mixture of despair and gratitude. Through tears the Tramp asks, 'You can see now?' 'Yes,' she replies, 'I can see now.' She draws his hand to her heart and sighs. On Charlie's face, a mixture of delight at seeing her again, but utter fear at what comes next, we fade out.

For every ounce of criticism that may be lodged at Chaplin the man, it is difficult to deny the genius of his work after scenes like this. As Charlie later noted, 'The reason it hasn't the usual fade-out is because it would have been laying it on too thick for me to walk away in this picture.'[22] Many praised the efficacy and restraint of the work. After inviting him to the film's London premiere, Charlie recorded that Albert Einstein was blubbing like a baby as the film reached its moving crescendo. More broadly, in *The Listener* the writer Francis Birrell was effusive in his praise for this mesmerising picture. Given the financial crash over a year and a half before the film's release, *City Lights* is surprisingly a-political on the surface. Its class message is implied but not hammered home. Partly this was because the Depression had not yet reached its peak. And yet, despite this, Birrell read much into it:

> Take another tiny moment, when Chaplin is being led off to gaol – by a misunderstanding of course. Just as he is going through the squalid doorway he kicks away his cigarette stump with the heel of his boot. The whole of human expression, the whole of the sense of powerlessness of man in the grip of the machine is in this perfectly timed gesture. It defies analysis, but it is utterly significant and beyond criticism.[23]

Even when kicking away a cigarette people could imbue Chaplin's work with deep meaning. Again, after a flower pot is knocked by a cat on to Chaplin's head, Birrell noted that

> Chaplin fades, and the scene is empty save for the sinister wagging of the cat's tail on the sill up in one corner. There is, I suppose, about two inches of tail exposed in the right hand top corner of the screen, yet there is something terrible about its slow, self satisfied wagging, its complete indifference to its own selfishness, to the ruin it has caused, the havoc it has worked on human dignity, to the happy dream it has destroyed. This tail seems to signify the whole farce of selfishness and unconscious cruelty in the world.

Again, perhaps so, perhaps not. Soon enough critics were going to have more overtly political films from Charlie to chew over. As the lights dimmed on Europe's cities, to be illuminated again by fascists carrying torches, Charlie could not contend himself with cats and flowerpots. Politics, he sensed, was moving in a far more immediately sinister direction.

Back to Britain

As the painstaking ordeal of *City Lights* finally moved close to fruition, and with the stinging publicity of both his divorce from Lita Grey and the tax-evasion case still hanging around, a world tour seemed an utterly agreeable idea. If in trouble: run – an option not open to Charlie in his youth. And so on 13 February 1931 he set sail from New York to arrive in Plymouth, England six days later. The itinerary of his world tour is painstakingly reproduced in Lisa Stein Haven's excellently produced and annotated version of Chaplin's *A Comedian Sees the World*, and his travelogue published in *Women's Home Companion* across late 1933 to early 1934. To give something of the political flavour of this trip the following engagements are listed within it for 1931:

February 1931

23/   . . . Lunch at Quaglino's with Randolph Churchill and Lord Birkenhead

24/   Lunch at House of Commons with Philip Sassoon and Lloyd George
25/   Luncheon at Lady Astor's Cliveden; meets Bernard Shaw
26/   Dinner overnight at Churchill's Chartwell

March 1931

1/   Visits Thomas Burke
3/   Luncheon at House of Commons with Lady Astor, Lloyd George, and Kirkwood; first economic speech;
13/   Meets ministers of the Reichstag, Dr Joseph Wirth among them [in Berlin]
15/   Tea with Einstein
16/   Visits Vienna; visits workmen's apartments
21/   Attends tea with British consul [in Venice]
23/   Arrives back in Paris . . . lunch with Countess Noailles and Aristide Briand
27/   Receives Legion d'Honneur back in Paris from Aristide Briand

June 1931

Stays with H.G. Wells in Grasse

August 1931

14/   Dines with Winston Churchill in Biarritz

September 1931

7/   Meets Prince of Wales for the first time at a benefit for the war wounded
19–21/ Weekend with Churchill at Chartwell
22/   Meets Gandhi at home of C.L. Catial in Beckton-road, Canning Town

October 1931

9/   Meeting with Ramsay MacDonald outside the House of Commons
23/   Attends Conservative election meeting at Plumstead in disguise
27/   Attends election night party at Selfridge's

November 1931

14–16/ Spends weekend with Viscount and Viscountess Astor at the Eliot Terrace, Plymouth
14/   Attends whist drive and dance of the East End Conservative Association
20/   Visits the House of Commons with Lady Astor

We deal with the international elements of this schedule later in the chapter, but the British dimension is worth reflecting on. While Britain remained a beacon of democracy in a Europe that saw most countries fall to totalitarian regimes of left and right in the years up to 1940, its politics were not without dramatic incident – particularly during Chaplin's visit back to his homeland in 1931.

Throughout the 1920s unemployment in Britain had remained stubbornly more than 10 per cent of the labour force. Through that decade policy makers of both left and right had wrestled with how to tackle the 'intractable million' of the unemployed, with post-war fiscal retrenchment being largely the policy prescription enacted by Conservative-dominated administrations to try to restore the nation to financial rectitude. This had been mirrored by the return of several industries – including the mines and the railways – to private ownership after being taken under state control during the war. As such, in the late 1920s Charlie made a rather accurate prediction:

> The next election, mark my words, will see the Labo[u]r Party more strongly in power than heretofore. Why? Because the government has made a tremendous mistake in its treatment of the unions, in refusing to negotiate, in letting affairs drift into an impasse, in letting the strike be called.[24]

Here Charlie referred to the General Strike of May 1926, which had seen in the region of 1.7 million British workers from transport workers and railwaymen to steelworkers and dockers down tools for nine days in solidarity with the demands of their mining colleagues to avoid wage reductions. Together with a general impression that the Conservative government led by Stanley Baldwin had been inert to the poverty faced outside the greater south-east of England, this indeed led to a Labour victory in the General Election of 1929.

But when Chaplin arrived back in his homeland in February 1931 he most certainly did not walk into a socialist paradise. A few months after Ramsay MacDonald had become Labour Prime Minister his government, like so many, had to deal with the effects of the Wall Street Crash and the subsequent desire of American banks to repatriate capital they had previously lent to Europe. Allied to this was the problem of parliamentary maths – Labour was certainly 'more strongly in power than heretofore', but this still meant a minority government reliant on the votes of other parties to pass any legislation. Britain had therefore to deal with a fast-moving crisis with a government that had to negotiate hard for every inch of policy space. It is in this light that Chaplin's various meetings during his British trip are potentially so fascinating.

Certainly, Charlie always enjoyed dinners with aristocratic Tories. Their conversation, manner and even accent impressed him. But it was the politicians of the left who bear most attention. By the time of his meeting with Ramsay MacDonald in October 1931, the Labour government had already fallen from power after several of its ministers refused to countenance further spending cuts to help balance the budget and a National Government (led by MacDonald but heavily populated by Conservatives) had taken its place. Yet Charlie's meetings earlier in the year with Oswald Mosley, David Kirkwood and David Lloyd George were more telling than his more 'official' dealings with the Prime Minister. We will deal with the Mosley conversation in our chapter on fascism (which Mosley would later adopt), but suffice it to say that speaking to a figure advocating dramatic government intervention to curb unemployment was both formative, and hardly unique. Lloyd George, the former Prime Minister turned vocal proponent of Keynesian deficit spending, was very much of a similar mind set to Mosley and in his 1929 Liberal Party manifesto had set forward dramatic schemes to bring forward future infrastructure investment under the slogan *We Can Conquer Unemployment*. David Kirkwood, a member of the Independent Labour Party (which sat well to the left of the more mainstream parliamentary force) would have had much in common with Charlie's American political allies like Henry Wallace and Upton Sinclair, too.

There was no little irony that these conversations about the plight of the masses took place during tea at parliament or on the French Riviera. Such a dichotomy brings to mind Charlie's conversation with Harry Crocker regarding his leftist friend Max Eastman. Asking where Max was, Crocker replied, 'in Southern France writing on the the technique of revolution'. 'He certainly sets himself some lovely subjects,' laughed Charlie in reply.[25] As we will see, when others started to mock Charlie for similar divergence between his political content and the locations from which it was delivered, this fired his radicalism. But, for now, it should simply be stressed that this British sojourn mattered. The 'respectable' soft-left, pro-orthodox economics of MacDonald were failing before Charlie's eyes. Meanwhile, charismatic and seemingly eminently plausible politicians like Lloyd George and Mosley were offering solutions regarding greater intervention that Charlie was beginning to believe would ultimately be necessary to avert economic meltdown. When Charlie arrived in February 1931 British unemployment stood at 21.3 per cent of adult workers; by the time he headed off in December it had barely budged (20.7 per cent).[26] The politics of MacDonald and Baldwin – best articulated by Baldwin's 1929 election slogan of 'safety first' – did not seem to be working. New solutions were needed. Yet if Britain was ailing, Charlie would encounter even worse examples of democratic mismanagement on this world tour.

The German question

For all the economic difficulties faced by Britain, it was Germany, Chaplin correctly diagnosed, that was the major problem facing the Western world. In 1921 he had visited the country during his tour to promote *The Kid*. Passing into the country on his train to Berlin, Chaplin noted, 'Germany is beautiful. Germany belies the war. Men, women, and children are all at work. They are facing their problem and rebuilding.'[27] Although, with the notable exception of one-time conquest Pola Negri, there were 'a few pretty girls, but not many' in the German capital, he generally enjoyed his time in the land of Britain and America's recent enemy. Asking to be taken 'through the German slums' he was even rebuked by being told that 'they have long such disappeared'.[28] Certainly the night-time was more rough around the edges – 'the streets are dark and gloomy, and it is then that one gets the effect of war and defeat' – but Charlie's general impression was of 'a great people, perverted for and by a few'.[29]

When promoting *City Lights* a decade later he encountered a different country. On the plus side, he caught up again with Albert Einstein, and his films (and therefore Charlie himself) were far more known in Germany than they had been in 1921. Hearing shouts of 'Gold Rush Charlie' and 'Circus Charlie' it was clear that his silent films had penetrated far beyond the English-speaking world. Yet storm clouds loomed on the horizon. Visiting the German Reichstag to take tea with several parliamentary deputies, he was given a rather gloomier vision of the new Berlin. He recalled that 'every member seemed pessimistic of the future' and heard it repeated that 'it was impossible to go on for another year'. When Charlie enquired what this meant, he was told simply 'bankruptcy'. The future did not look bright: 'We shall have trouble,' the deputies told him. 'We have young men graduating in qualified professions and passing their examinations, only to leave college and stand in the bread line with the rest of the unemployed.' Charlie summarised that this would lead to 'anarchy and Bolshevism. Their plight seemed pretty awful and their future dark.'[30] Less than two years before Hitler became Chancellor of Germany this seemed a reasonable assessment.

All this required a solution. As we will see, part of this involved a sustained interest in the politics of Social Credit and the theories of C.H. Douglas. But an equally large part saw Chaplin sit down and actually sketch out a plan to solve the 'German question' for himself. Writing to contacts at the *Daily Mail* in London, he had them send him financial data from the newly formed Bank of International Settlements (which then, as now, monitored transnational flows of capital) and John Maynard Keynes's 1919 volume on *The Economic Consequences of the Peace*.[31] Keynes's work had argued as to the folly of punishing the Germans too harshly at the Treaty of Versailles, and would prove particularly formative for Charlie. Thus whereas Jim Tully had mocked Charlie in the 1920s for not putting pen to paper on his vague political musings, with the exotic back drops of Bali, Japan and Singapore in 1932, he finally set to work.

By 17 June 1932 the *Los Angeles Times* had him noting that 'on my travels I talked my idea over with renowned economists and none was able to find a flaw'. He continued, 'I think it can be made practical. I am now preparing a paper on the subject which I will release in a few days.'[32] In the early drafts of this paper that survive in Bologna, Chaplin wrote that 'the most stupid and blind theory existing today is the belief that we must protect the high value of our currency, even at the sacrifice of our commodities, for what we know is that it is the inexorable law of cause and affect that if money is dear, commodities are cheap and vice versa. So where is your standard of values?'[33] The previous September Charlie's homeland of Britain had – after avoiding the measure for some time – devalued its currency against the US dollar by almost a quarter in coming off the gold standard. But Charlie proposed to go further.

By 27 June 1932 it became clear that his willingness to sacrifice the value of 'our' (presumably America's) currency meant printing new money. This transnational form of quantitative easing was the inventive twist to an 'economics manifesto' that Chaplin published that day to widespread media coverage across the United States. Chaplin proposed a new global issue of $35 billion worth of currency, with the new currency to have the same value as gold. This money would be paid to the Allied powers, in lieu of the sum then comprising Germany's total war debt, which would be cancelled. Germany would cover the administrative cost of launching the scheme, and it would simultaneously provide 'added capital to the world'.[34] Chaplin's scheme would not only redress Germany's problems, but America should consider that 'Europe's recovery is our recovery – Europe's prosperity is our prosperity'.[35] With the world being 'without money', it was time, in Charlie's mind, to create some. The timing here was not precipitous: at the Lausanne Conference underway as Chaplin published his manifesto, German reparations under the Treaty of Versailles were subsequently cancelled altogether. Technically, when Congress rejected the Lausanne Plan in December 1932 Germany was, however, still liable for its debt to America, but Hitler would be in no mood to pay this when he came to power barely a month later. If Charlie's famous speech at the end of *The Great Dictator* was sometimes derided as being a little flowery, it is worth considering that he had issued a very practical (or at least specific) scheme to try to arrest the rise of Nazism in the first place. As to resolving the German question he was, at least initially, a Keynesian – certainly in terms of *The Economic Consequences of the Peace*.

Chaplin and Empire

If Charlie took his economics 'manifesto' from elements of C.H. Douglas and J.M. Keynes, he also looked outside the West to inform his world view, too. Back in September 1931 two global icons had met in a humble little house in London's East End. Sitting on a sofa in a modest room, no more than twelve-feet square, sat Charlie Chaplin. A taxi pulled up outside the house, met with 'hooraying and cheering' as the figure he was about to meet entered 'that crowded little slum street'.[36] The man was Mohandas Gandhi, known by his honorific title of Mahatma (the venerable) who was greeted by a throng of East Enders desperate to see him. Although Charlie agreed with his new acquaintance on several points, two issues place this meeting as a little odd.

First, Charlie had just come from his stay at Chartwell with the Churchills (see Figure 5.1), not the biggest fans of Gandhi to say

Figure 5.1 Chaplin's stay at Chartwell in September 1931 saw much political discussion, not least about India. Here Charlie is pictured with, among others, Winston Churchill, his wife Clementine and his son Randolph.

Courtesy of the Churchill Archives Centre, Cambridge, UK

the very least. The previous October Winston Churchill had joined a lobbying organisation called the Indian Empire Society that argued that 'too rapid advance towards self-government [for India] would be fraught with the utmost danger'. Later he would join a parliamentary off-shoot of this body, the India Defence League, which would strenuously oppose the devolution of power to the Government of India in 1935. To go from Churchill to Gandhi in 1931 was to travel from one end of the political spectrum to the other, and this irony had been discussed at the Churchills' dining table. Brendan Bracken, a Conservative follower of Churchill's, told Charlie that 'we've catered to this man long enough. Hunger strikes or no[t], they should put him in jail.' Charlie replied that 'if you imprison one Gandhi, another will arise. He is a symbol of what the Indian people want, and until they get what they want they will produce another Gandhi after another.' Churchill smiled, and noted diplomatically that 'you would make a good Labour Member [of Parliament]'.[37]

Second, Chaplin actually thought Gandhi's visit to London 'a mistake'. This was less for reasons of policy than presentation. While Chaplin had 'always respected Gandhi for his political astuteness and his iron will', he felt the trip had tarnished the Mahatma. 'In the cold dank climate of England, wearing his traditional loin-cloth . . . [Gandhi] seemed incongruous.' For Chaplin, 'his legendary significance evaporated in the London scene . . . One's impressiveness is greater at a distance.'[38] In a sense this was rather like Chaplin's desire to keep the Tramp from talking – as soon as he talked the mystique of what he may sound like was lost. 'Gandhi' the concept, Charlie felt, was more impressive than Gandhi the man. Better, in other words, to stay on that pedestal.

In any event, after the obligatory photographs the two got to talking. For Charlie 'now came that uneasy, terrifying moment when I should say something astutely intelligent about a subject I knew little about'. Knowing he could not wait for 'the Mahatma to tell me how much he enjoyed my last film . . . I doubted if he had ever seen a film', Charlie began to interject. 'Naturally I am in sympathy with India's aspirations and struggle for freedom,' he ventured, 'nonetheless, I am somewhat confused by your abhorrence of machinery.'[39] For a man set to release *Modern Times* six years later this anti-Luddite view was perhaps surprising. 'After all,' continued

Charlie, 'if machinery is used in the altruistic sense, it should help to release man from the bondage of slavery, and give him shorter hours of labour and time to improve his mind and enjoy life.'[40] Gandhi considered the notion, and then gave Charlie a 'lucid object lesson in tactical manoeuvring in India's fight for freedom, inspired, paradoxically, by a realistic, virile-minded visionary'. Machinery, Gandhi argued, had made India dependent on England, 'and the only way we can rid ourselves of that dependence is to boycott all goods made by machinery. That is why we have made the patriotic duty of every Indian to spin his own cotton.'[41] This was doubt-less something of a political education for Charlie – only mildly undermined by then watching the Mahatma at prayer: 'His astute legal mind, and his profound sense of political reality . . . seemed to vanish in a sing-song chant.'[42] Yet even in September 1931 Charlie evidently was not fully reconciled to his *Modern Times* view of the world, telling reporters, 'I was not able to follow [Gandhi] in all that he told me, but I was none the less anxious to impress upon him my view that machinery was a heritage of mankind, and we could not wholly depart from its usefulness.'[43]

Homeward bound

Gandhi provided one insight into contemporary Asia, but within a year Charlie would have a far more sustained one. As his world tour wound its way through Ceylon, Singapore, Java and Bali, Charlie encountered 'the realization of all of my exotic dreams' in the sights and rickshaws of Kandy, and the 'fantastically beautiful scenery' the further he ventured into south-east Asia.[44] Most significantly, in May 1932 Charlie visited Japan and received a rapturous reception. In Kobe harbour Charlie's boat was greeted by aeroplanes circling overhead, dropping leaflets of welcome, with thousands of Japanese cheering on the docks: 'It was as excited and emotional as any crowd I have ever seen anywhere.' With the government putting on a special train to transport Charlie to Tokyo, at every new station the train pulled up in the crowds became ever larger. By the time the Chaplin party arrived in the Japanese capital, an estimated 40,000 people had gathered to greet the English star.[45] Although Charlie found the Japanese 'generous and hospitable', he was almost witness to a rather darker side. On 15 May Charlie attended a sumo wrestling match with Takeru Inukai, known as Ken. His father, Prime Minister Tsuyoshi Inukai, had been experiencing a long running battle with the Japanese military for control over foreign and defence policy. Many within the Japanese Army wanted a full-scale invasion of mainland China (after the previous conquest of Manchuria), and Inukai was seen as an impediment to this. As Charlie and Ken watched the sumo, six naval cadets broke into the Prime Minister's palace and shot Inukai Snr dead. Had Ken not been with Charlie he would have been assassinated, too, but the military coup held even more significance for the creator of the Tramp. The ring-leader of the plot, Seishi Koga, later confessed that the plan had been to kill Charlie because, ironically, 'Chaplin is a popular figure in the United States and the darling of the capitalist class.' He believed that 'killing him would cause a war with America, and thus we could kill two birds with one stone'. Eventually they reasoned that the death of Chaplin was unlikely to draw a declaration of war from President Hoover – a reasonable call. Chaplin later wryly commented, 'I can imagine the assassins having carried out their plan, then discovering that I was not an American, but an Englishman – "Oh, so sorry!"'[46]

Eventually, Charlie made it back to American soil safe enough. Landing in Seattle and making his way down the coast on land, he passed 'through the rich farmlands of Washington, the dense pine forests of Oregon, and on into the vineyards and orchards of California'. In doing so 'he found it impossible to believe ten million people wanting when so much real wealth is evident'. He felt glad to be 'home in Hollywood' and contended that 'in America lies the hope of the whole world'. Given the upheaval he had witnessed from the triumph of small 'c' conservatism in Britain to the violence of militarist Japan, the radical in Chaplin likely meant such words utterly sincerely. At this time at least, he felt that 'whatever takes place in the transition of this epoch-making time, America will be equal to it'.[47] In some turbulent times that remained to be seen.

Notes

1 Orwell's work is readily available for free online, including via the Project Gutenberg site: http://gutenberg.net.au/ebooks03/0300011h.html#part10 (accessed 7 November 2016).

2 It is fair to add that the Liberal Party and its leader David Lloyd George – who Chaplin would meet on this tour – had set out rather more costed schemes.

3 Richard Weekes biographical essay of Montagu, within Communist Party of Great Britain Paper Archives [CP], People's History Museum, Manchester [PHM], IND/MONT/1/1.

4 Ivor Montagu, *With Eisenstein in Hollywood* (Berlin, 1967), 18–20.

5 Ibid., 14.

6 Ibid.

7 Ibid., 15.

8 Ibid., 28.

9 See correspondence in BFI/IVM item 324.

10 Reeves to Montagu, 19 November 1925, BFI/IVM item 324.

11 Montagu, *Eisenstein*, 66.

12 Ibid., 87.

13 Ibid., 92–3.

14 See Montagu's CV within PHM/CP/IND/MONT/1/1.

15 Montagu, *Eisenstein*, 96–7.

16 Ibid., 141.

17 See, e.g., TNA/KV/2/598 and TNA/HW/15/43.

18 See Richard Carr and Bradley W. Hart, *The Global 1920s: Politics, Economics and Society* (London, 2016), ch.4.

19 'The Future of Charlie Chaplin's Contribution', *Collier's Weekly* [undated 1934/5], Churchill Archives Centre [CAC], Cambridge, UK, Winston Churchill Papers [CHAR] 8/521.

20 Montagu to Chaplin, 26 January 1931, BFI/IVM Item 320.

21 Charlie Chaplin, *My Autobiography* (London, 2003), 208.

22 Paul Duncan (ed.), *The Charlie Chaplin Archives* (London, 2015), 338.

23 *The Listener*, 11 March 1931.

24 Harry Crocker's unpublished memoir, 'Charlie Chaplin: Man and Mime', MHL/HRC, XIII–12.

25 Crocker, 'Man and Mime', MHL/HRC, VII–22.

26 James Denman and Paul MacDonald, 'Unemployment Statistics from 1881 to the Present Day', *Labour Market Trends* (January 1996), 5–18.

27 Charles Chaplin, *My Trip Abroad* (London, 1922), 114.

28 Ibid., 118.

29 Ibid., 116, 114.

30 Ibid., 57.

31 Chaplin to *Daily Mail*, 26 February 1932, via CIN/CCA.

32 *Los Angeles Times*, 17 June 1932 via COP/CCP/39.

33 'An Idea for War Reparations', June 1932, CIN/CCA.

34 *Washington Herald*, 27 June 1932 via COP/CCP/39.

35 *Los Angeles Examiner*, 27 June 1932 via COP/CCP/39.

36 Chaplin, *My Autobiography*, 335.

37 Ibid., 334.

38 Ibid., 335.

39 Ibid., 336.
40 Ibid.
41 Ibid.
42 Ibid., 337.
43 *Nottingham Evening Post*, 23 September 1931.
44 Charlie Chaplin (Lisa Stein Haven ed.), *A Comedian Sees the World* (Missouri, 2014), 126–7.
45 Chaplin, *My Autobiography*, 366.
46 Ibid., 369–70.
47 Chaplin, *A Comedian Sees the World*, 144.

6 *Modern Times* and the Great Depression

Let us jump forward a moment. As our ninth chapter will note, Charlie's final years would be spent closer to Lausanne, Switzerland than Los Angeles, California. From this Swiss exile of the 1950s, with the scenic Alps in view, Chaplin had ample time to reflect on the maelstrom that had gripped the world two decades earlier. In one of the many jottings he wiled his days away producing, he argued that the Great Depression had been a classic example of the cyclical nature of capitalism. Chaplin was certain that

> the majority of us want to do right. But the law of supply and demand which derives profits from scarcity, must eventually end in disaster of some kind. I have never quite been able to divest myself of this thought. I have never read Karl Marx, nor have I studied socialism. But it is clearly recognized that the abuses of capitalism accelerated the depression of the 1930s.[1]

The impact of the Wall Street Crash would be writ large over two of his later films, the semi-silent *Modern Times* of 1936, and his first film explicitly not to feature the Little Tramp, *Monsieur Verdoux* released some eleven years later. These films were of a profoundly left-wing persuasion, no question. The communist *Daily Worker* even (wishfully) reported in 1936 that Chaplin had submitted the script of *Modern Times* for prior approval from the Moscow Cinema Board.[2] But Chaplin's response to the Depression went beyond these high-profile examples. This chapter considers Chaplin's economic thought between 1929 and the outbreak of the Second World War. If sex helped blacken his name in the public eye and his flirtations with communism rendered him beyond the pale as the political general climate changed, it was his 1930s critiques of capitalism that provided something of a gateway to this nightmarish pincer movement. As we will note, this was a period of artistic triumph, but also concrete engagement with ideas to arrest the decline then gripping many areas of America, and beyond. He had seen the problems of the world, and now it was time to solve them.

The Depression and Charlie

When the stock market collapsed in New York in late October 1929 Chaplin was still attempting to get *City Lights* over the finishing line. He had liquidated his investments in 1928 so was financially protected, but artistically he was still struggling with the impact of the crash and what, as a creative individual of a leftist leaning, he should do about it. With filming wrapped up in October 1930, little of the Depression's impact could be included in a film whose class rifts are clear, but that take place in a world whose titular 'city' was utterly generic. Initially, he was therefore accused of ducking the major political questions, both on- and off-screen. Indeed, in August 1931 the *New York Telegraph* even referred to the fact that 'Charlie Chaplin can well afford to sun himself on the sands of Juan-les-Pins [in the South of France] with $7,000,000 to guard him from a poverty stricken old age'. It continued: 'All this talk of depression is being greeted with a vague and wondering stare by film players as they trot down to their favourite bank to indulge in a little coupon clipping of their favourite and most productive bonds.' With Harold Lloyd having amassed a $12 million fortune during the 1920s, this was not just aimed at Chaplin.[3] A few months later the *Boston Globe* reported that 'pockets bulging with goodily returns financial from his Europe expedition, Charlie Chaplin is headed homeward'.[4] It was not only his diagnosis of the Depression, but the initial fear that he had been seen to do nothing about it that would drive much of his 1930s radicalism.

Action of some kind was clearly needed. Through seeing Europe Charlie had in a sense seen America's possible future – and it did not look too rosy. As Eric L. Flom notes, as Charlie returned to California he had come to believe that America, 'contrary to his early feelings during the vaudeville days, [had become] a place of uncertainty. No longer did the country seem to hold the promise it once did.'[5] This was an impression reinforced in everything from newspaper headlines to the dole queues. Indeed, the annual estimates of unemployment in the United States record an astonishing rise in the early 1930s. From 1930 to 1933 unemployment as a percentage of the civilian workforce was recorded as 8.9 per cent, 15.9 per cent, 23.6 per cent and finally 24.9 per cent, respectively. By 1933, almost thirteen million Americans were officially recorded as out of work – an astonishing increase of about eleven and a half million on the number seen in 1929. Yet to imply that Chaplin was totally oblivious to this was rather unfair on the part of papers such as the *New York Telegraph*, for the spectre of unemployment haunted Chaplin's work almost from its beginnings. The Tramp, after all, had been employed in every capacity from impromptu circus performer to boxer to gold prospector to glazer, all to stave off the impoverishment that American capitalism could bring.

This would continue in the 1930s as evidenced by a document prepared by Donald Gledhill, the executive secretary of the Academy of Motion Picture Arts and Sciences (AMPAS) in Los Angeles. Gledhill would type up a list of the 221 most popular films released that decade. This 1939 list, which was circulated to members of the House Un-American Activities Committee (albeit with the jovial note, 'don't take it too seriously'), included reference to three of Chaplin's works. Both *City Lights* and *Modern Times* were deemed 'socially significant' by the author, touching as they did on issues such as poverty and the Depression (and 'The Dictator' was listed as a 'Propaganda Film talked about but not yet made').[6] Chaplin may have liked lounging on French beaches, but his 1930s were about more than that. If Chaplin indeed wanted to change things in America he had three options: make politically challenging cinema, endorse President Roosevelt's New Deal, and explore politically even more interventionist alternatives to those pursued by the White House. As this chapter sets out, starting with the last, he stepped up to the plate on all three.

Social Credit

As for radical ideas, Charlie Chaplin was an enthusiastic convert to the movement known as Social Credit – propagated by the English engineer Major Clifford Hugh (C.H.) Douglas. The origins of this philosophy were primarily located in the Great War, although Douglas acknowledged his own debt to previous theories of under-consumption propagated by thinkers such as J.A. Hobson. When Major Douglas was put in charge of organising the work of the Royal Aircraft Establishment in Britain during the First World War he began to conceive that there was a fundamental flaw with the capitalist system. Since the work of the nineteenth-century theorist David Ricardo, perceived economic wisdom had it that all costs associated with producing a particular good would be distributed simultaneously as purchasing power. But in his war-time work Douglas began to conclude that this was not true – that the cost of producing goods was greater than the various salaries, wages and dividends paid out to the workers and management who produced them. Coming from a practical engineering back-ground, Douglas set out to do something about this imbalance, and his theories promptly gained widespread international atten-tion. For his part, Chaplin was certainly reading Douglas as early as his European tour of 1921.[7]

The precise rationale for Social Credit was expressed through Douglas's so-called 'A + B theorem'. By way of brief explanation, Douglas believed that the cost of producing any given good is made up of two groups of costs. 'A' costs denote all those pay-ments made to individuals – wages and salaries to employees, potential dividends to investors and/or managers. Added to this, the 'B' costs equate to everything else – raw materials, machin-ery, bank charges and other external costs associated with making a product. With the growth of industrialised economies and the increased use of machinery in the mode of production, 'B' was growing as a proportion of production costs. And since 'A' would always be less than 'A+B' this meant that capitalism had a funda-mental (and growing) flaw: costs were not being distributed suf-ficiently to ensure that purchasing power was maintained among the masses. The solution was simple: replace the lost money with a direct transference payment from government to worker. In other words, the state should top up wages, salaries and dividends with a sum necessary to allow people to purchase the relevant good they had helped produce. This 'National Dividend' proposal formed the most high-profile aspect of the Social Credit movement. Tax credits form something of a modern political equivalent.

Chaplin bought into this policy offering wholesale. When on his world tour in 1931, he stopped by Albert Einstein's house in Berlin. Describing the economic crisis then engulfing the Western world, Chaplin told the great professor that 'the business world has acquiesced and welcomed the fundamental industrial change from man power to machine power, which has cheapened the cost of all our commodities. But it stands resolute against any fundamental change in the capitalistic system that might cheapen money and facilitate the means of buying those cheap goods.'[8] Einstein scoffed: 'You're not a comedian. You're an economist. However, how could you cure all this?' Chaplin response was to 'reduce the hours of labor, print more money, and control prices'. At this point he was 'fascinated with the possibilities of the Douglas Credit Scheme'.[9]

Even as Roosevelt's New Deal began to arrest American unemployment, Chaplin maintained a 'keen interest in the Social Credit theory'. In a conversation with the American war veteran and playwright Laurence Stallings, Chaplin expressed such enthusiasm that an associate of Stallings, Gorham Munson, reached out to the film director on the back of such praise. Writing to Chaplin in June 1934, Munson pointed to the 'acquisition of very influential supporters' for the Social Credit movement. 'Among them Senator Bronson Cutting of New Mexico, Dr Paul de Kruif, and the Reverend Charles E. Coughlin who spent four hours in conference with Major Douglas last April.'[10] This was an odd set of supporters to say the least. A relatively bipartisan Republican in Cutting and microbiologist in de Kruif certainly lent the movement a degree of credibility, but Reverend Coughlin was more of a wild card – if, given one in four Americans listened to his broadcasts a popular one.[11] Initially a fervently pro-New Dealer, Coughlin turned against Roosevelt from 1934 and gradually began to deride the 'cash famine' in the United States being exacerbated by usurious elements (a similar path taken to Rep. Martin Dies, whom we will encounter later). As the decade progressed Coughlin increasingly linked responsibility for many contemporary ills – including communism – to American and global Jewry. In some ways Coughlin's anti-capitalism had similarities to Chaplin's own, but his views on Bolshevism and sympathy towards the anti-Semitic regime in Germany certainly did not. By May 1939 C.H. Douglas himself was writing of the horrors of the 'Jewish Financial System' and urged Hitler to 'destroy the power of the international financier – a power which only increases and which, if not destroyed, will destroy civilisation in Europe'.[12] Here again Chaplin could not follow – but he remained interested in the theory of Social Credit well into the 1940s. Chaplin was not a people person, but rather an ideas man. Whoever could solve unemployment and raise the conditions of the working class – he was at least willing to give them a hearing.

Upton Sinclair and taking a political stand

So Chaplin wanted to change capitalism, but to do so (short of standing for office himself, which he occasionally joked about) he would have to find a concrete vehicle to support. Despite being a communist in the eyes of many, Charlie never joined the Communist Party – or at least, as the House Un-American Activities Committee later acknowledged, there was 'no evidence' for his having done so.[13] Indeed, his most direct political endorsement came not for a Communist but for a Democrat: the 1934 Democratic Candidate for Governor of California, Upton Sinclair (see Figure 6.1). This point is an important one – Chaplin was in essence a liberal Democrat, someone certainly on the far left of the mainstream political spectrum, but still fundamentally within it. In more contemporary times he would have been a Jeremy Corbyn or Bernie Sanders fan, not a communist.

Upton Sinclair and Chaplin had been in contact for several years, and shared friends such as Max Eastman. In August 1918 Sinclair wrote to Chaplin to thank him for their first meeting: 'When I came to meet you, it was with no intention of butting in on your affairs, except as a Socialist always butts in everywhere – to make the other fellow into a Socialist!'[14] In 1920 and 1922 Sinclair ran unsuccessfully for the House of Representatives and then for the Senate on the Socialist Party ticket. Throughout the 1920s Sinclair ramped up his political engagement and, by 1923, was openly courting Charlie for money to help do so. On the back of fighting 'big business interests' through supporting a Maritime Strike in San Pedro (and the rights of protestors to organise without the fear of imprisonment), Sinclair wrote to Charlie to ask for

Figure 6.1 Chaplin was both a friend and a fan of Upton Sinclair's. Here he is at his studio lot with Sinclair and, among others, the white supremacist former Governor of Mississippi, James Vardaman. Even beyond Chaplin, the political connections of this era could be unexpected.

Courtesy of Lilly Library, Bloomington, Indiana, USA

$500 to help fund a new branch of the American Civil Liberties Union (ACLU) in Monrovia, California where he had moved.[15] Getting actual cash out of Charlie was never easy. As Chaplin threw himself into his divorce case and *The Circus*, the latter half of the 1920s did not, as Harry Crocker recalled, see much politics discussed at the studio. But one such conversationalist who could get a rise out of Charlie was a 'professional looking man . . . dressed in rough tweeds' who appeared 'far too mild looking for a socialist'.[16] Upton Sinclair's appearance aside, he regaled Charlie with his views on 'France . . . drifting into bankruptcy and a state of anarchy worse than Russia. If things break, all of Europe will be in a mix-up which will be worse than the last war.'[17]

Through the Ivor Montagu and Sergei Eisenstein machinations outlined in the previous chapter, Upton and Charlie almost became business partners. With his options to make a picture in Hollywood running out, Montagu 'knew Eisenstein had a hankering for Mexico'.[18] Upton Sinclair had obviously heard enough in his cocktail-party conversations with the Soviet filmmakers to back them financially, and formed a legal corporation entitled The Mexican Film Trust that signed Eisenstein, Grigori Alexandrov and Eduard Tisse to a contract in November 1930. The proposed Eisenstein film was to be an episodic montage of Mexican culture and politics from pre-European Conquest Mexico to the Mexican Revolution that had begun in 1910. Filming was supposed to be wrapped up in April 1931, but by the time that more than 170,000 feet of film was in the can the Mexican Film Trust – and Sinclair personally – were growing weary at the costs involved. Informal enquiries to Chaplin about stumping up some of the additional cost came to nothing. Eventually, footage Eisenstein had shot was released by Sinclair as three shorts, *Thunder Over Mexico*, *Eisenstein in Mexico* and *Death Day*. As he did so, Charlie simply wired to Upton: 'Sorry I could not join you in Mexico – success to the picture.'[19]

By 1933, Charlie's politics had been radicalised through the reading, writing and table talk that had taken place on his *City Lights* world tour, and Upton Sinclair was about to launch his own campaign for public office. Sinclair's campaign was something of a glorious failure: an exercise in shifting the Overton window of the Democratic Party to the left and, arguably, paving the way for Roosevelt to accelerate the interventionism of the New Deal. It is easy to see how Charlie was drawn to Upton – for Chaplin was certainly a fervent New Dealer in these early years. In October 1933, he even took to the nationally syndicated airwaves to deliver a nine-minute speech endorsing Roosevelt's new National Recovery Administration (NRA). The NRA was a landmark part of the National Industrial Recovery Act passed that summer, and was an exemplar of 1930s corporatist planning. Get industry, workers and the government around the negotiating table and jobs could be protected while paying decent wages. On the latter point, so-called 'blanket codes' attempted to ensure a maximum working week (at most forty-five hours), a minimum hourly wage (at least 20 cents, depending on the industry) and the complete abolition of child labour. By increasing productivity in the factories and purchasing power among ordinary workers, unemployment could be averted, or so the ambition remained. And so Chaplin took to the radio to endorse the new policy. Referring to the virtual army of 'eleven million unemployed' (it was likely even higher), Chaplin claimed it was incumbent on the 'ninety million people in America, myself included, who have the means – who have the purchasing power to buy now and can help put those unemployed back to work'.[20] Directly naming the nation's saviour, he noted that 'the people cried for action. Now President Roosevelt has given us that action. The Government has given us a program, and now it is our turn for action.' There was clearly a strong degree of respect there. Indeed, by 1940 *Liberty Magazine* noted that 'Charlie Chaplin owns no orthodox political allegiances. He is still a British citizen, although his personal political hero is Franklin Delano Roosevelt.'[21]

This was not a view held by all of Charlie's associates. For Waldo Frank, whom Chaplin encountered in Greenwich Village via Max Eastman, the NRA was 'the beginning of American Fascism'. This would not take the form of jackboots and uniforms, but rather 'may be so gradual in the United States that most voters will not be aware of its existence'. Instead, America would be conquered by 'judicious, black-frocked gentlemen; graduates of the best universities; disciples of [Columbia University President] Nicholas Murray Butler and of [journalist and public opinion theorist] Walter Lippmann'.[22] It is interesting, given his general antipathy to the overreaching intrusive state, to see Chaplin endorse a programme that others had criticised along these lines, but it identifies unemployment as the central concern in his world view once more. The early 1930s was not a time for kind words, but for action. In this regard Charlie rather agreed with another fascist sympathiser, the future British King Edward VIII: 'something must be done' about those out of work.

Upton Sinclair was one man putting noble intent into concrete action. Switching his affiliation from Socialist to Democrat in September 1933, Sinclair published a best-selling pamphlet entitled *I, Governor of California, And How I Ended Poverty* two weeks later. This *True Story of the Future* laid out the framework for Sinclair's campaign to 'End Poverty in California' – whose acronym EPIC and its actual message became known nationwide. In later life, Sinclair claimed he had no intention of winning the election, but was merely running for the governorship to educate the people in the socialist cause. By this stage Chaplin needed little such education. In December 1933 Sinclair wrote to Rob Wagner asking him to 'help me to persuade [Charlie Chaplin] to take a public stand' in formally backing him.[23] Wagner wrote back that he felt Chaplin was 'essentially an entertainer. If politics get hot and he is publicly lined up, he'll lose half his audience. As it is now, his Red stuff leaks out, helps the cause and doesn't [cramp] his profession.'[24] Eventually, Chaplin himself got in touch: 'After thinking over your request to use my name endorsing your political program, I realize it would be a mistake for me to identify myself in politics. As in the past, my principle is to maintain a non-partisan attitude.'[25]

This must have been a blow. Certainly, Sinclair's under-consumptionist analysis of the Depression ('one of abundance, not of scarcity') and the need to give 'workers access to the means of production' were two of several points within the twelve-point EPIC programme with which Chaplin wholeheartedly agreed.[26] Sinclair's more detailed prescriptions regarding a new state income tax, increased inheritance levies and other taxes on wealth to make up the state's deficit doubtless could have found favour with Charlie, too (particularly since he may well have found some scheme to avoid paying them). As it was, without Charlie's support, the right-leaning movie moguls soon hit Sinclair hard: producing movie reels depicting transients flocking to California on freight trains with the intention of remaining (and presumably living off welfare payments) in the event that the EPIC plan was ever implemented. After winning a stunning victory in the Democratic Primary (gaining almost 150,000 votes more than his nearest challenger, George Creel), Sinclair would go on to comfortably lose the gubernatorial contest itself to the Republican incumbent Charles Merriam.

Small victory though it may have been, Sinclair's campaign did succeed in bringing Chaplin out of his political foxhole. Despite his earlier protestations, in early 1934 Chaplin agreed to have his name appear on several leaflets supportive of Sinclair and, that June, he gave a speech endorsing Sinclair's candidature. Could he have done more? Certainly – but by then Charlie's sights were set on getting *Modern Times*, his own political oeuvre, out to the masses. When he got around to seeing it, Sinclair himself argued that 'the part about the factory was very interesting and charming, but the rest just repeats Charlie's old material'.[27] Few would take such a balanced view on this controversial product.

The making of *Modern Times*

When it came to *Modern Times* Charlie had initially intended to make a fully fledged talkie. After producing a rather so-so script, however, he eventually plumped for a mixture whereby the Tramp himself would not speak (save a song delivered in gibberish near the end), but other characters would be heard through the use of machinery such as the radio and a proto-television screen. This in itself was one of the more minor metaphorical points that Chaplin would make about machinery. *Modern Times*' themes of mechanisation and the de-humanisation of labour were most famously highlighted when the Little Tramp fell into the factory's great machine (we never learn what it is making; for Chaplin it barely mattered) and, in profile shot, we see him flow effortlessly through its cogs. Humankind, in short, had become part of the machine. As Gandhi had told him in 1931, machines that were supposed to be serving humankind had turned out to enslave them.

Such views had long been known to Chaplin's confidants. One day Charlie was chatting to Harry Crocker over tea at Santa Barbara. During this discussion, he decried the virtues of 'Efficiency! It is a terrible thing. In Detroit I went through a huge automobile factory [where] each man is told that he is a partner in the company.' Here Charlie was describing his visit to the Ford Motor Company in 1923. Doubting the validity of this arrangement, Chaplin presaged the nut-tightening wreck of the Tramp of *Modern Times* when he talked of the American worker being 'assigned individual tasks . . . For eight hours the man does one job, the same movement, the same effect.' Crocker indulged Charlie as

> he visualized each member of the sales force living under his individual Damoclean sword. [Charlie] was outspoken in his criticism of such a system. At this period of his life, he was not inherently serious on the problem, but even his semi-light hearted comments were construed as socialistic. Competition was the shibboleth of big business. Big Business was America's sacred cow, and he who ventured criticism of the ordered, machine conduct of Big Business was, to the industrial tycoons, a radical.[28]

Well before its release, the press had wind that *Modern Times* was going to be more overtly political than *City Lights*. Its initial title, which the British left-wing politician John Strachey (more of whom later) thought 'of often', was the almost political tract worthy *Mass Production*. 'I'm quite sure it will be the biggest thing you've done,' noted Strachey.[29] But it was more than the title. When asked about the Depression in 1934, Alf Reeves told *Screen Book Magazine* that although 'Charlie's basic purpose is to entertain[,] of course he is intensely interested in such problems. And it's impossible, isn't it, to completely pass over them even in a picture that is intended as entertainment only.'[30] Reeves was not merely stalling or being deliberately evasive here. Charlie's erratic working method meant that the construction of what became *Modern Times*' plot took time, and thus it was difficult to predict how the film would actually turn out. As Charlie later told Max Eastman, the film 'started from an abstract idea . . . an impulse to say something about the way life is being standardized and channelized, and men turned into machines and the way I feel about it'. He confirmed that he 'knew that was what I wanted to do before I thought of any of the details'.[31] As ever, those could be worked out on set.

In February 1935, Charlie's leftist credentials were given a shot in the arm when Boris Shumyatsky, de facto head of the Soviet film industry in the 1930s (until he was executed by the regime as a traitor in 1938), spoke out on the class content inherent in Chaplin's work. The *San Francisco Daily* professed itself sceptical at such a notion:

> 'Well, now, who'd a thunk it,' as the old Yankee farmer said. Here for years we've gone on believing that Charlie Chaplin was a great comedian and a great clown, but if you are to believe a gentleman by the name of Shumyatsky, all those years Chaplin has been working to show how 'honestly and truthfully the American [working] class is carrying on a struggle against capitalism.'[32]

Eighty years later, by way of curiosity, then Venezuelan President Hugo Chavez professed himself in agreement with the Russian's assessment, however. Showing the film to thousands of its workers in 2006, the Venezuelan Labor Ministry believed *Modern Times* laid the groundwork for 'socialism for the twenty-first century'. As Jhonny Picone, the Labor Ministry official sent out to answer a curious Western press, put it: 'With Charlie Chaplin it is easier to catch the attention of workers who are often too tired or don't trust government in the first place.'[33]

This was demonstrably true in the 1930s – and *Modern Times*' role as a gateway drug to more radical political views was worrying many. Certainly, many a political figure took Chaplin seriously. Before seeing *Modern Times*, Winston Churchill was of this mind: 'All [Charlie's] greatest pictures are tragedies, in spite of the richness of their comedy.' He believed they showed 'man in the grip of Fate – a longely [*sic*], pathetic figure who is perpetually at odds with circumstance, a rebel for whom there is no place in the modern world'.[34] Churchill did not make the connection that this was partly, even predominantly, engendered by free-market capitalism – but Charlie was rarely shy in doing so. This had been no more overtly the case than it would be in *Modern Times*, at least to this point.

The film itself begins with the dramatic description that it is a 'Story of Industry, of individual enterprise – humanity crusading in the pursuit of happiness'. Chaplin then juxtaposes shots of sheep being herded (including one black sheep, presumably Charlie) with workers trudging out of a factory. For Chaplin scholar Chuck Maland, this opening metaphor remained confusing: is it that capitalism treats its workers as livestock, or that the worker meekly accepts their fate without questioning it?[35] Either way, working in such a factory we find the Tramp who is subject to all manner of indignities including constant supervision from an overly attentive boss (who looks suspiciously like Henry Ford), and being subjected to a force-feeding machine. The latter piece of apparatus was called a 'Billowes feeding machine' in the film, a nod to inventors such as Charles Bedaux who were seeking to introduce increased efficiency into the workplace and quantify the performance of each worker.[36] By the 1930s – for Chaplin at least – even a worker's lunchtime was no longer sacrosanct.

In any event, running amok in this Bedaux-esque factory Charlie is eventually committed to a hospital before unwittingly becoming the leader of a workers' demonstration and being thrown in jail by some heavy-handed policemen. The story then pivots into a love story between the Tramp and Paulette Goddard's gamin (Chaplin would marry the real-life Paulette in 1936, only to divorce her in 1942) where the two try to resist the forces of capitalism as best they can: looting goods from a department store (and distributing some to hungry, unemployed workers), living in a deserted Hooverville old shack, and finally singing in a café to earn a living. Such distinctions are important, notes Eric Flom, because they situate *Modern Times* as a film that shows that 'everyone is impacted by the hardships of the Depression, even the employed' and that 'some crime is driven not by want, but by need'.[37] The film eventually ends with a trademark shot: the Tramp and the gamin, hand in hand, walking down a deserted road towards an uncertain tomorrow.

On that famous ending, the aforementioned Soviet official Shumyatsky had met with Chaplin during the filming, and even claimed to have influenced a creative change of heart regarding its content. According to the Russian, he had 'prompted Charlie Chaplin to make drastic changes in his latest film'. Previously, 'the fatalistic endings of all Chaplin's films, the individual's withdrawal to a position of resigned hopelessness, was in this film even more sharply pronounced than in all the others'. Yet after Shumyatsky's apparent intervention,

> when, after the privations and sufferings of the world, the heroes finally meet, they promise each other never again to part from one another. They decide to work and fight together against the "machine of time," a euphemism for capitalist society – and walk off, hand in hand, into the "blue distance."[38]

As a result, the Soviet regime resolved to buy the picture for showing in the motherland (the first to be shown since 1923's *A Woman of Paris*): 'the [Soviet] trust's officials boast that they have persuaded Chaplin to alter the end of his film. It will finish on a note of communistic optimism instead of being pessimistically American, as intended.'[39]

Here Alf Reeves was sent out to immediately dampen down such talk. 'The Russian story reads deep, terrible social meanings to sequences that Mr Chaplin considers funny.' In a nod to Chaplin's capitalism, he assured viewers that 'this picture is intended as entertainment, and perhaps it might be said too, that Mr Chaplin's purpose in this picture is to make money'. Reeves acknowledged that they were 'concluding the picture on a somewhat more optimistic note than was first designed', but this was down to Charlie having 'his own way and . . . his own ideas – always'.[40] The film's ending is often compared to Charlie's early work – and the much-repeated template of the Tramp walking away from shot down a road, once again alone. In *Modern Times*, it is true, he walks away with a beautiful woman. Yet perhaps the better comparison is with *The Gold Rush*. In 1925 the Tramp becomes rich through his prospecting, and eventually gets the girl (who herself wants to better her lot as a 'dance hall girl'). By hook or by crook he gets by, and the ending is unambiguously happy. Yet in the 1936 film Charlie and Paulette attempt various means to circumvent the capitalist system, but all end in failure. They may leave together, and Charlie may tell her to 'smile', but they have lost. As Paulette says, 'What's the use in trying?'

Upon its release in February 1936, *Modern Times* struggled domestically – taking about $1.4 million at the box office against a $1.5 million budget. Three years after lounging on Chaplin's boat in the Pacific, Alistair Cooke was called upon to review the film for the British publication *The Listener*. In a mixed review Cooke enjoyed bits of business including when Charlie sprinkles 'his food with dope which he thinks is salt', but noted 'with firmness and regret that *Modern Times* is never once on the plane of social satire'. Deriding those who found the Tramp an anachronism in a now sound age, he said that 'for the first time in Chaplin's history, we have a film that looks and sounds as if it came from only one place – from Hollywood . . . since he has yielded these two integrities – the looks and the sound – he has yielded much of his strangeness'.[41] As to what it all meant politically, the *Chicago Illinois Times* provided a balanced reaction. First, it noted the irony that the American public 'get excited when a broadcasting company permits an admitted communist to sound off over a nation-wide hookup, but we take our children to see the uproarious Charlie give capitalism a $2m razz'. And this, they scoffed, was 'a razz that makes [American Communist Leader] Comrade Browder's mournful numbers sound like a piece on a penny whistle'. Still, 'we don't think Charlie is a communist. Not with his bank account.' Instead, the paper praised Chaplin's consideration of the problems inherent in 1930s America: 'Apparently he has been reading the news and has concluded that no country is stable where too much misery abides.' He may even have been at home in the Roosevelt administration: 'Instead of denouncing agitators. Charlie gives a look at the thing that makes agitators. In other words, Charlie is a [Roosevelt backing] brain-truster teaching sociology with a slapstick. So far it hasn't got him into much trouble.'[42] That, of course, would change.

All in all, *Modern Times* would again prove something of a staging post on his artistic development. As we saw in the 1910s and 1920s, Chaplin was a willing and very able practitioner, not an opponent, of capitalism. *Modern Times* would see him take pot shots at aspects of the industrial production process – and certainly provide more opposition than he had previously mustered to Henry Ford. But the film ultimately remains 'Chaplinesque', and not merely because it includes the Tramp and a pretty girl. To borrow Steven J. Ross's descriptions, while it contains flashes of a 'radical' filmmaker advancing the cause of socialism, and certainly was 'liberal' in its implicit call for a more humane capitalism, ultimately it rests on Chaplin's perhaps widest trope of 'anti-authoritarianism'. In *Modern Times* the main fall-guys and targets of mockery are factory foremen and policemen, not the owners of the means of production. Only in *Monsieur Verdoux*, made in the wake of the HUAC attacks on Chaplin and the Second World War, would Chaplin really go for the artistic jugular.

The Napoleonic diversion

For all the controversy over the films he *did* make during the 1930s, another project remains of key interest despite not coming to fruition. More broadly, Charlie's willingness to help the Montagu–Eisenstein party in 1930–1 should not be taken as the limit of his outreach to various collaborators. Charlie was an autocrat in the studio, but he long struggled for the ideas to actually get him back in said studio in the first place. To rectify this, he knew that his own creative juices were often more likely to flow through conversations with politicians as they were with fellow actors or directors.

As Alistair Cooke knew, 'those who have seen him re-create scenes in the life of Napoleon have no fears for his popular reception as a dramatic actor'.[43] Charlie was obsessed with the Corsican dictator, telling Harry Crocker rather eccentrically, 'Do you know Napoleon and I have a lot of characteristics in common? He was nervous. He could not bear to unbutton things, he ripped them off, he left his clothes where they fell. He loved hot baths.'[44] Chaplin read Emil Ludwig's famous 1915 study of Napoleon and began to envisage various scenarios in which he could play him.

A great historical curiosity is that his collaborator in this instance could well have been Winston Churchill. During Churchill's visit to Los Angeles in September 1929 Charlie not only showed him around the set of *City Lights*, but the two sat up one night drinking and smoking. Winston's son Randolph recorded in his diary that 'Papa and Charlie sat up till about 3. Papa wants him to act the young Napoleon and has promised to write the Scenario.'[45] This would likely have been some form of comedic farce, as Charlie later noted:

> Take the case of Napoleon: I would not portray him as the mighty general, but as an undersized gloomy, silent, almost morose individual, who is always in trouble with members of his family. Heavens! There is humor throughout all his life! His efforts to marry off his brothers and sisters and step-children, and keep on good terms with his mother and his wife, and fight a few wars in the meantime, provide a wealth of material for a play. I would not burlesque him, you understand, but I'd re-enact all the messes he got into and all his efforts to extricate himself and keep peace in the family.[46]

In mid-1933 he tried to purchase a Napoleon scenario from an unnamed source through Ivor Montagu.[47] This may well have been Jean Weber's *La Vie Secrète de Napoleon 1er*, which he eventually did purchase in 1935. In any event, with Churchill evidently not stepping up to the plate (ironically, he was then seeking to preserve Britain's own empire, particularly in India), Charlie needed a collaborator to help him bring the idea to fruition.

In February 1935 one guest at Charlie's house in Beverly Hills would be John Strachey. If there was a politician who most mirrored Charlie's interwar politics, then Strachey would not be far off. A British Labour Party MP first elected in 1929, he resigned the party whip a year later to join Oswald Mosley's New Party. After losing his seat at the 1931 General Election, Strachey would not follow Mosley into fascism from 1932 and instead furthered his own intellectual credentials, publishing a series of works including *The Coming Struggle for Power* (which forwarded the standard Marxist critique that fascism was merely a vehicle to stave off a successful communist revolution) and drifted towards the Communist Party through the early 1930s. By the time he stayed with Charlie, Strachey viewed Roosevelt's New Deal as 'politically clever' and constituting 'relief' that had bought off 'revolution'. Letters in Strachey's privately held papers to global communists, including the American Earl Browder, Swedish-Indian Rajani Palme Dutt and Charlie's own friend the Englishman Ivor Montagu indicate that his Popular Front-esque sympathies were not unlike Charlie's own.[48]

During his stay with Charlie and Paulette, Strachey discussed the Napoleon project and agreed to return to England to write it. Strachey noted that his 'only object in writing it – aside from my own amusement – was to have something in front of us to knock about, if and when you come over here in the autumn'.[49] With the delays in production for *Modern Times* this visit did not pan out, but the script was still useful: Strachey 'always found it much easier to have some sort of manuscript in front of one, even if one scraps every word of it in the end, rather than start with a blank sheet of paper'. While the 'whole idea' Strachey felt to be Chaplin's 'from start to finish', it had 'so fired me . . . that it simply wouldn't stay still in my head'. Producing a script in short order (no doubt, in part, because Strachey was always scrabbling around for money in the mid-1930s), he sent over his thoughts to Los Angeles. Leaving the comedic 'business' to Charlie, Strachey concentrated on trying to flesh out his ideas for Napoleon the man: 'What do you think of Lodi still hearing Bounapart's [*sic*] voice in the garden? Has that idea of dividing the time and place of the visual and aural impression been done on the talkies yet?' Having read the script, Charlie judged 'it is wonderful – will write in detail later'.[50]

By early 1936 the script had been finalised and was registered for copyright on 9 April. In the surviving Chaplin–Strachey draft can be seen something of both men's philosophy. At one point the script has Napoleon, in a long-winded peroration, declare:

> There is something wrong with the whole political situation
> of Europe. Governments and Constitutions are old fashioned,

> obsolete . . . mechanical science is running away with us . . . steamboats, railroads and barges . . . all these things spell revolution and we must prepare for the future . . . The man of the future will be a scientist . . . Future governments will realise that the religious and moral principles are problems for the individual, but the economic problems of the individual are the affairs of the State . . . Countries will combine forces for the protection of the trades.[51]

In this prose we see much of the type of political rant that would mark Charlie's output from *The Great Dictator* of 1940 to 1957's *A King in New York*. Through Napoleon, the Chaplinesque manifesto of breaking down national borders and adapting to the pace of technological change come through clearly in a film that is, ostensibly, set in the nineteenth century.

Strachey and Chaplin were undeniably politically sympathetic to each other – albeit with Charlie the more fervently pro-New Deal. Personally they were both gregarious, and doubtless got along. And yet Chaplin's association with the man indicated much of the troubles to come. During his American tour Strachey not only met Charlie and Paulette but gave a series of speeches where 'he advocated the overthrow of the capitalistic system'. After finishing one such address to a 600-strong audience in Glencoe, Illinois, Strachey left the stage to be greeted by Col. Daniel W. MacCormack, the US Commissioner of Immigration and Naturalization, who arrested Strachey on the grounds that he had entered the country 'by means of false statements'. Upon his arrival in New York in December 1934, Strachey is reported to have answered in the negative 'questions intended to bring out whether visitors or immigrants advocate or believe in overthrowing the United States government by force or violence or whether they are members of organizations which have such aims or beliefs'.[52] Strachey had stopped short of advocating such violent revolution and he was not a member of the British Communist Party (both sides felt it more useful for him to appear 'neutral' from outside). However, he did declare Soviet Russia to be 'the hope of civilisation, and I believe the sternest measures were justified to safeguard it'. A move towards communism would be, he noted, a step 'forward'.

The anti-communist press soon denounced Strachey's views as those 'pleading for . . . FREEDOM FOR HIMSELF AND HIS FELLOW FOREIGN RATS TO UPSET OUR FORM OF GOVERNMENT'. They noted that 'HIS MASK IS LITERATURE. HIS FACE IS THE FACE OF STALIN'.[53] Released on bail, Strachey subsequently continued to tour the US denouncing 'W.R. Hearst, Father Coughlin' and others as 'decidedly and dangerously Fascistic'. Reversing the anti-communist charge against him, he argued that 'fascism has the mask of radicalism but the face of William Randolph Hearst'.[54] On 30 March 1935, US Immigration indicated they were willing to drop all charges against him, provided that he left the country. In later years, Martin Dies's HUAC Committee would continue to list him as one of the 'leading radicals admitted to the United States'.[55] Yet before boarding the *Berengaria*, Strachey turned to address reporters. He was 'profoundly grateful for the wide sympathy and support I have been given by the people of America'. It remained his fervent 'hope . . . that the whole case has done something to clarify the issue of free speech in America as applied to alien visitors'.[56] Sitting in the Californian sun, Charlie Chaplin may well have been nodding vigorously.

Notes

1 Undated note, 1950s, CIN/CCA.
2 A fact included within the 'Fact Sheet Containing Pertinent Material Pertaining to the Communist Affiliations and Activities of Charlie Chaplin', HOOV/SOK/240/3.
3 All via *New York Telegraph*, 30 August 1931 via MHL/CCS/24.f.231.
4 *Boston Globe*, 25 March 1932 via MHL/CCS/24.f.231.
5 Eric L. Flom, *Chaplin in the Sound Era: An Analysis of the Seven Talkies* (London, 1997) 83.
6 Gledhill note: 'Sing Me a Song of Social Significance, All Other Tunes Are Taboo', circulated 17 August 1939, NADC/HUAC/RG 233/Box 1,105.
7 Charles Chaplin, *My Trip Abroad* (London, 1922), 147.
8 Charlie Chaplin (Lisa Stein Haven ed.), *A Comedian Sees the World* (Missouri, 2014), 61.
9 Clipping within COP/CCP/39.
10 Munson to Chaplin, 15 June 1934, Wesleyan University, Middletown [WES], Gorham Munson Papers [GMN] Box 1 Folder 37.

11 For Coughlin listening figures see Gallup Poll, 18–23 December 1938, USAIPO1938-0141.

12 *The Social Crediter*, 6 May 1939.

13 See 24 January 1965 information sheet on Charles Chaplin within NADC/HUAC/RG 233/Box 42.

14 Sinclair to Chaplin, 18 August 1918, LLBI/UPS Box 2.

15 Sinclair to Chaplin, 29 May 1923 LLBI/UPS Box 5.

16 Harry Crocker's unpublished memoir, 'Charlie Chaplin: Man and Mime', MHL/HRC, VII–22.

17 Ibid.

18 Ivor Montagu, *With Eisenstein in Hollywood* (Berlin, 1967), 128.

19 Chaplin to Sinclair, 24 May 1933, LLBI/UPS Box 22.

20 *Boston Globe*, 24 October 1933.

21 'The New Mystery of Charlie Chaplin', *Liberty*, 2 June 1940, MHL/HRC/CCS/1/9.

22 Waldo Frank, 'Will Fascism Come to America?' *Modern Monthly*, 8 (1934), 465–6.

23 Sinclair to Wagner, 5 December 1933, UCLA/Rob Wagner Papers [RBW] Box 17.

24 Wagner to Sinclair, 8 December 1933, UCLA/RBW, Box 17.

25 Undated telegram – Chaplin to Sinclair – within UCLA/RBW, Box 17.

26 Upton Sinclair, *I, Governor, And How I Ended Poverty* (Los Angeles 1934), 10.

27 Sinclair to Wagner, 17 March 1936, UCLA/RBW, Box 17.

28 Crocker, 'Man and Mime', MHL/HRC, X–12.

29 Strachey to Chaplin, 14 July [1935], PRIV/STCH.

30 *Screen Book Magazine*, undated 1934, via MHL/CCS.

31 Max Eastman, *Great Companions: Critical Memoirs of Some Famous Friends* (Toronto, 1959), 224.

32 *San Francisco Daily*, 10 February 1935.

33 *Eugene Register-Guard*, 9 July 2006.

34 'The Future of Charlie Chaplin's Contribution', *Collier's Weekly* [undated 1934/5], Churchill Archives Centre [CAC], Cambridge UK, Winston Churchill Papers [CHAR] 8/521.

35 Charles J. Maland, *Chaplin and American Culture: The Evolution of a Star Image* (London, 1989), 151.

36 Michael R. Weatherburn, *Scientific Management at Work: The Bedaux System, Management Consulting, and Worker Efficiency in British Industry, 1914–48* (PhD thesis, Imperial College London, 2014), 78.

37 Flom, *Talkies*, 100.

38 *Motion Picture Herald*, 7 December 1935 via COP/CCP/44.

39 *Daily Telegraph*, 3 December 1935.

40 *Motion Picture Herald*, 7 December 1935 via COP/CCP/44.

41 *The Listener*, 19 February 1936.

42 *Chicago Illinois Times*, 15 March 1936 via COP/CCP/55.

43 *The Atlantic Monthly*, August 1939.

44 Crocker, 'Man and Mime', MHL/HRC, XI-23.

45 Diary entry, 21 September 1929, CAC/Randolph Churchill Papers [RDCH] 11/24.

46 Clipping within COP/CCP/52.

47 Montagu to Chaplin, 4 October 1933, BFI/IVM Item 320.

48 See, e.g., Strachey to Browder, 18 May 1936, Strachey to Palme Dutt, 10 October 1931, and the August 1940 correspondence with Montagu, all via PRIV/STCH.

49 Strachey to Chaplin, 14 July [presumably 1935], via PRIV/STCH.

50 Chaplin to Strachey, 19 July 1935, PRIV/STCH.

51 David Robinson, *Chaplin: His Life and Art* (London, 1992), 477–8.

52 *New York Herald Tribune*, 13 March 1935.

53 *The Chicago Herald*, 13 March 1935.

54 *Philadelphia Public Ledger*, 28 March 1935.

55 HUAC Hearings, 75th Congress on H. Res 242, 1,938/vol. 1, 700.

56 *The New York Times*, 30 March 1935.

7   The Tramp and the dictators

By the end of the 1930s Chaplin's homeland of Great Britain stood on the brink of war with Nazi Germany. By then the Wehrmacht had already been on the march across Central and Eastern Europe, radically overturning the Versailles order as it did so. Appeasement of the dictators by the Western European democracies was only seeming to delay the inevitable. With Prime Minister Neville Chamberlain having acquiesced to Hitler's demands to annex the German-speaking Sudetenland through the Munich Agreement the previous October, the German Army had moved to occupy and partition the remainder of the Czechoslovakian state in March 1939. In response, Chamberlain promptly guaranteed the independence of Hitler's next military target – Poland – meaning a conflict between Britain and the Nazi state was now likely just a matter of time.

Sitting in Los Angeles, the fifty-year-old Charlie Chaplin was too old to be asked to fight for his country in any impending war, but that did not mean that he was divorced from the march of European diplomacy – far from it. In April 1939, an extraordinary message was cabled from the British Foreign Office in London to their consulate in Los Angeles. It read, 'We wonder whether it might be possible for you to approach the Company making the film, and prevail upon them to treat the subject in such a way that it could be exhibited in this country without giving offence to Germany.'[1] The 'Company', of course, was Chaplin's United Artists, and the film was soon to take the name of *The Great Dictator*.

We will outline how this request panned out shortly (making *The Great Dictator* 'without giving offence to Germany' was certainly a tough ask). But first it is worth recapitulating the relationship between the world's biggest film star and perhaps the twentieth-century's most infamous figure, Adolf Hitler – the subject, through the thinly veiled moniker of 'Adenoid Hynkel', of Chaplin's 1940 satire. Like anyone even vaguely aware of the political climate of the thirties, Charlie had his own views on the German regime. A scribbled note now held in Chaplin's archive in Bologna, written late in the Second World War, saw Charlie give his take on the rise of Nazism:

> From the beginning of Hitler's regime, national dementia set in. Its pathological signs were classic. It started with exhibitionism, mass herding of military, goose steppers, packing into city squares by the hundreds of thousands, just to impress themselves and their Fuehrer. Jew-baiting and book burning followed which led to mass torturing and murdering of innocent people. And now that madness is being subdued, strait-jacketed and enhanced forever.[2]

This negative account was hardly unexpected and conforms to the broad themes of *The Great Dictator*. Yet, as this chapter makes clear, before the advent of Hitler's Nazi state Chaplin was not without a kind word to say for those on the road to fascism. Even more surprisingly, if a man named Konrad Bercovici is to be believed, this even extended to Hitler himself. Charlie's bravery in making his anti-Hitler film cannot be questioned. But we should first consider the slightly crooked path he took to get to this point. For many in the Anglophone world it was easier to see fascism's evils in 1940 than it was ten years earlier, and this even applied to Charlie himself.

Charlie and two fascists

An interesting example of Charlie's early views on fascism concerns Sir Oswald Mosley, later to lead the British Union of Fascists from October 1932, and drifting in that direction when he encountered Chaplin at a 1931 lunch on the French Riviera. The two had several mutual acquaintances – from the very political David Lloyd George to more artistic types such as the photographer Cecil Beaton.[3] Furthermore, the poet Blanche Oelrichs knew

Mosley's wife Cimmie and had encouraged Charlie to drop her a line whenever they were in the same location.[4] But Chaplin's descriptions of Mosley during this period went beyond the perfunctory acknowledgement reserved for a friend of a friend. In unpublished drafts of what became *A Comedian Sees the World*, Chaplin called Mosley 'one of the most promising young men in English politics in spite of his momentary defeat. He is one of the few dynamic forces to be considered in the future of English politics.'[5]

In 1931, this would have been a reasonable call – Mosley had resigned from MacDonald's Labour government over its refusal to bring forward capital spending to curb unemployment, and was viewed by many as a future Prime Minister. But by the time of publication it was no longer 1931, and Mosley's political alignment had decisively changed. The 1933 published version of *A Comedian Sees the World* eventually removed the second sentence in the above recollection of their meeting, but still remained an upbeat description given Mosley had by this time openly adopted the fascist ideal. A few months earlier, for example, in his book *The Coming Struggle for Power*, Charlie's potential co-scriptwriter John Strachey had denounced Mosley as 'stand[ing] for fascism naked and unashamed'.[6] For all this, Chaplin no doubt admired Mosley's political adventurism and on aspects of government intervention to create jobs the two had much common ground at the time.

Indeed, Chaplin's later re-writing of the meeting says much about their points of political overlap, and some possible retrospective sleight of hand. From the perspective of the 1960s, Charlie recalled the lunchtime encounter with Mosley rather differently to the positive noises he had made in the early 1930s:

> One guest stands out, a tall, lean man, dark-haired with cropped moustache, pleasant and engaging, to whom I found myself addressing my conversation at lunch. I was discussing Major Douglas's book, *Economic Democracy*, and said how aptly his credit theory might solve the present world crisis – to quote Consuelo Balsan about that afternoon: 'I found Chaplin interesting to talk to and noted his strong socialist tendencies.' I must have said something that particularly appealed to the tall gentleman, for his face lit up and his eyes opened

so wide that I could see the whites of them. He seemed to be endorsing everything I said until I reached the climax of my thesis, which must have veered in a direction contrary to his own, for he looked disappointed. I had been talking to Sir Oswald Mosley, little realizing that this man was to be the future head of the blackshirts of England – but those eyes with the whites showing over the pupils and the broad grinning mouth stand out in my memory vividly as an expression most peculiar – if not a little frightening.[7]

The notion of Chaplin the committed anti-fascist clearly has much behind it. He would risk his career to make a film critiquing the Nazi dictatorship, and loathed the treatment of the Jews in the Third Reich to the point where he would refuse to answer questions about his own ancestry to show some semblance of solidarity with these unfortunate souls. But there was something in Hitler the individual that drove Charlie's antipathy, too. With the more socially gregarious Mosley or Mussolini, Chaplin perhaps detected a spark of humanity that at least made the men – if not every aspect of their movements – explicable to him. And in the early 1930s the horrors of the Second World War remained years away. To someone curious about alternatives to Anglo-American capitalism, making pleasant conversation with such figures made logical sense.

This cross-political praise cut both ways. As noted, in American political terms Chaplin was essentially a slightly eccentric left-wing Democrat along the Upton Sinclair or Henry A. Wallace model (both of whom he supported in their runs for high political office). There were elements in which this could be said about early fascism, too. In his review of Wallace's 1934 book *New Frontiers* Benito Mussolini found it 'a declaration of faith and an indictment of economic liberalism'. Asking where America was headed, Mussolini concluded that 'this leaves no doubt that it is on the road to corporatism, the economic system of the current century'.[8] The corporate state in Italy appeared to many to have successfully walked a middle road between laissez-faire capitalism and out-and-out Marxism. It had harnessed the private sector in the national interest, and enacted the type of big public works schemes the Roosevelt administration would later ape. Given that democracy was always something of an abstract to Charlie – he could not vote in America, and was rich to the point where whoever was in the White House would have little impact on him economically – it is entirely feasible that he would have been sympathetic to aspects of Italian fascism.

In fact, Chaplin almost met Benito Mussolini, and the pair probably would have had much to talk about. This was true cinematically and politically. For one, as Thomas Doherty notes, Mussolini 'inspected foreign films as censor-in-chief [of Italy] and meddled with the scripts and casting-decisions of Italian-made feature films'.[9] This ran in the family – in the 1930s Mussolini's young son Vittorio served as the screen columnist for his father's newspaper *Il Popolo d'Italia*, and later travelled to Hollywood to seek to co-produce an Italo-American film. But even Vittorio may have failed to match his father's enthusiasm for the movies. In April 1929 *Il Duce* had told the American press of his love for

> [c]omedies – American comedies. I care for no other films. The attempt to create serious movies in America leaves me unmoved. They are nearly all sickly in their sentimentality, puritanical and filled with such unbelievable bunkum as to make any European burst with amazement to find such [trash] still existing. But your comedies! Need I mention Carlino Charles Chaplin? That is where the American film approaches a great art and has a value. The American comedies are among the best thing from America and I never miss them.[10]

This was several years before Chaplin would lampoon Mussolini as Benzino Napoloni in *The Great Dictator* (albeit through the softer form afforded by Jack Oakie than he himself gave to Hitler). But for all the speculation as to whether Hitler ever actually saw that film (it seems unlikely), smart money for having done so would have gone on the Italian dictator. A meeting between Chaplin and *Il Duce* was even scheduled for early March 1932 in Mussolini's office, but was cancelled at the last minute by the Italians. Although it could not take place a press release was issued for the event that made the American papers, including Hearst's *Los Angeles Examiner*: 'Premier Mussolini received Charlie Chaplin this afternoon in his study in the Palazzo Chigi, and the two conversed informally for 15 minutes.'[11]

Again, this may well have been a meeting of mutually appreciative minds. Chaplin's published account in *A Comedian Sees the World* was certainly very favourable to the home of fascism: 'on crossing the border into Italy I was impressed with its atmosphere. Discipline and order were omnipresent. Hope and desire seemed in the air. In the midst of these medieval surroundings, a new life has crept in.'[12] In 1928 Chaplin had even named Mussolini as one of the great personalities of the year, not merely for his general importance but 'because he took a nation and put it to work'.[13] In this sense Charlie was arguably similar to the historian Wolfgang Schivelbusch's verdict regarding FDR: 'In contrast to Hitler, with whom he always felt a world of social, ideological, and political difference, Roosevelt had nothing but "sympathy and confidence" in Mussolini up until the mid-1930s.'[14] In any case, always the businessman, before the fascists banned his work (from *Modern Times*) Italy formed a significant market for Charlie. Democracy was not all that important when there was lira to be made.

Before *The Great Dictator*

As mentioned, Hitler was a rather different case. Born in the same week, adopting the same toothbrush moustache for their 'character', and subsequently achieving global fame, Chaplin and Hitler's world views would be radically different. We will deal with *The Great Dictator* and Adenoid Hynkel in a moment, but it is important to note that much of Chaplin's early understanding of Hitler seems to have come from his friend, the newspaper publisher Cornelius Vanderbilt. During a journalistic visit to see the 'New Germany' Vanderbilt had managed to get into a concentration camp 'on some pretext', and returned home to publish 'stories of brutality [that] were so fantastic that few people believed them'. Sending Charlie postcards depicting Hitler making a speech, it is likely that Vanderbilt provided something of the inspiration for *The Great Dictator*.[15] Upon seeing these, Charlie 'could not take Hitler seriously . . . The salute with the hand thrown back over the shoulder, the palm upwards, made me want to put a tray of dirty dishes on it.' He thought, 'This is a nut,' although when

Thomas Mann and Albert Einstein were forced to leave Germany Charlie began to view that 'nut' in a more 'sinister' light.[16]

Not everyone felt this way. When in 1934 Vanderbilt released the anti-Nazi documentary film *Hitler's Reign of Terror*, *The New York Times* was scathing: 'Hitler's methods are scourged by Messrs. Vanderbilt and Hill, but their words would be infinitely more effective if they were endowed with a slight degree of subtlety and a sense of humor.'[17] As Thomas Doherty recently notes, when it came to showing the totalitarian regimes on film, in the early to mid-1930s reviewers still 'felt duty bound to pan a work whose good intentions were no compensation for its dreadful artistry'.[18] Equally, film reviewers were not above praising documentaries that were apologies for fascist regimes. Barely a year prior to panning *Hitler's Reign of Terror*, *The New York Times'* Mordaunt Hall described the 1933 pro-fascist documentary *Mussolini Speaks* as one where 'even those in the audience who are not Italians cannot resist a surge of patriotic feeling'. Hall further noted that 'as each point of the Fascist program is taken up in the dictator's flaming oratory, the camera moves out over the country to illustrate what has been done in that particular direction and how Mussolini has kept his promises to his people'.[19]

Part of this feeling came from the general perception that perhaps Germany and even the victorious Italy had been rather hard done by through the Treaty of Versailles. Such a view marked British and American elites, who in later years began to feel that perhaps they had listened too much to the French desire for vengeance in the post-war treaties. Richard Law, briefly a British Cabinet Minister under Churchill, recalled that

> in 1933, when Hitler came to power, we did not know that he was Hitler. We thought he was Charlie Chaplin; we thought he was a pathetic little man with a toothbrush moustache who went about in a rather curious chauffer's uniform. We rather pitied him, and felt that in some way he was speaking for the underdog.[20]

As we will shortly note with reference to Konrad Bercovici, it is by no means impossible that Chaplin himself shared something of these sympathies. The fact that his previous visits to Germany in 1921 and 1931 coincided with periods of economic downturn for that nation (sandwiching the more prosperous, 'golden years' of Weimar) was likely significant. On his 1921 world tour, as noted in Chapter 5, although Charlie enjoyed himself he also encountered 'many cripples with embittered, sullen looks on their faces' – the physical and emotional scars of the war.[21] Likewise, ten years later he had met with various Reichstag deputies bemoaning a Germany on the verge of total bankruptcy. Expectations of Germany were not high for Charlie.

His views on Hitler the 'performer' also shifted when it came to researching the film. After watching reels of Hitler's speeches, Chaplin conceded that he

> was impressed when I saw some of his gestures – I didn't understand what he was talking about – I'd say what he talked about was bloody rot – but he made certain gestures which were very effective. I didn't see any sort of orator do that. Churchill was sort of in the grand manner – in the grand tradition – English style, you see – [whereas Hitler said] "I will take Europe!" and it came over.[22]

His Hynkel character would go on to deliver speeches in a ludicrously over-the-top manner in the film, and certainly his words would be stage managed in their English translation, but the cheers of his audience – and Hynkel's ability to stop them with a wave of his hand – could be read as genuine enough. At one stage, he is even able to seduce his secretary merely by cartoonishly snorting. That at least was always more Chaplin's domain than Hitler's.

Yet, for Charlie, the anti-Semitism that was at the foundation of Hitler's regime was all too personal. Both Charlie's half-brother Sydney and then partner Paulette Goddard had Jewish fathers, and he simply never understood the irrationality of baiting Jews simply because they were Jews. As he later told American investigators looking into his communist sympathies: 'All this racial business – I am not a Jew – nevertheless the mere picking on a minority people incenses me more than the ideology, more than the work movement, or anything else – just because they were crazy – they were mad men.'[23] In part thanks to Nazi prejudice, Charlie was also himself again accused of being a Jew. During a trip to Berlin in January 1934 the genuinely Jewish Ivor Montagu happened across a book whose 'contents are almost unbelievable and not the least fantastic thing about it is that numbers of people in it are, like yourself, not Jews at all'. This book was Johann von Leers' notorious *Juden sehen dich an* (The Jews are Looking at You), in which Charlie was described as a 'nerve killing fidgeting Jew'. Although Montagu was 'sad to say there are some real crooks in it, it's surely not unhonorable to be included amongst so many noble and maligned'.[24] Albert Einstein and Emil Ludwig were at least two Jews within the book Charlie would have considered in the latter, more honourable light.

But if the Nazi regime's anti-Semitism clearly both angered and mystified him, Charlie took a reasonable amount of time to convert such antipathy into meaningful action – particularly given, unlike Italy, there was no economic concern since the new regime in Germany had banned his films from the outset. Even after the Nuremburg Laws of September 1935 formally excluded Jews from being citizens of the Reich, Charlie rebuffed those trying to convince him into helping Germany's Jews. One such body was the Society for the Protection of Science and Learning (SPSL), which throughout the 1930s sought to place German-Jewish academics at British universities and other institutions to get them out of the clutches of the Nazis. In October 1935 SPSL General Secretary Walter Adams wrote to Chaplin's acquaintance H.G. Wells letting him know that they wished to help 'displaced scholars, whether German or other national' but would require initial contributions of £100,000 to do so. They went on to say that

> if you were able to interest Mr Charles Chaplin in the work of the council, we shall be extremely grateful. If Mr Chaplin were interested, members of my Council would be pleased to explain their plans in greater detail to him on the occasion of his coming visit to this country.[25]

Wells 'was not at all hopeful Mr Chaplin would give a sum like £100,000 but said he would do his best', and the SPSL pinned their hopes on getting some face-to-face time with him after a proposed London premiere of *Modern Times* in December 1935.[26]

The biologist Julian Huxley was soon brought into this lobbying effort. Chaplin knew both Julian and his author brother Aldous (who Charlie liked very much as

> the cynical young man of the twenties'). Huxley wrote to tell Adams that '[the] last time he was here I tried to get in touch with him to ask him to a meal, but my letter was simply not

acknowledged! Apparently he has gangs of secretaries, who sit on almost everything. If you can find means of getting over this, I should be glad to do what I can.[27]

This seems certainly plausible – in his 1948 interrogation by the American Immigration and Naturalization Service Chaplin noted that 'we get tons of mail . . . we get a million things here for all sorts of donations . . . a lot of these things are all carried down to the studio and they more or less apportion some of these things out you know'.[28] It is certainly true that with a powerful man the underlings often hold much sway. Still, when H.G. Wells was able to reach the man personally, he noted that he 'regrets Mr Charles Chaplin is not disposed to assist in the project discussed'.[29] Adams replied that 'the news is of course disappointing but we are by now completely used to this sort of thing'.[30]

Indeed, the journalist Hedda Hopper – admittedly no sympathetic source, as we will see – suggested that Chaplin's reluctance to help the Jews lasted even longer. She recorded that a meeting took place at Twentieth Century Fox where 'a little man from Palestine [was] trying to win sympathy and raise funds . . . to arm one hundred thousand Jews in Palestine before we got into World War II'. Hopper provided her own donation, but when Chaplin was called upon 'he got up in a white heat of hate and said, "I am not a Jew; I am not a citizen of America; I am a citizen of the world, I will give nothing to this cause. I deplore the whole thing."'[31] In light of the film he would later make, this perhaps appears somewhat surprising. Yet against this we must, however, balance one crucial piece of evidence. In July 1939 Charlie would be hailed as a 'Twentieth Century Moses' after he signed over the foreign revenues from his pictures to aid Jews in Milan who had fled Germany and Austria and were awaiting the chance to emigrate to safer territories. Many American newspapers reported that 'according to Jewish quarters in Vienna, a part of this fund[, which ran into several millions of dollars,] recently was placed at the disposal of the Jewish community in Milan'. And 'for each of 1,000 Jews who left Germany under this arrangement last week, the Milan Jews posted a $50 bond with the Italian government so that the Jews would not become public charges in Italy'.[32] The material effect of this is difficult to ascertain – *The Great Dictator* would not be released (and therefore make any money) until after the Italian entry into the war had brought a clampdown on such emigration – but the gesture mattered. In July 1940, it was further reported that Chaplin was among those luminaries who collectively deposited $6 million in a Milan bank to aid Jews fleeing Austria after the Anschluss. Unpicking the financial flows of the time remains difficult, but we can at least hypothesise that the presence of such funds played a role in slowing the pace of Fascist Italy's conversion towards the Nazi dogma on the Jews. If any money from Charlie provided the time and space for one Jew – Austrian, German or otherwise – to escape the spectre of the gas chamber, then he was clearly on the right side of history in some catastrophic times. His conversion to this position, however, took time.

The Bercovici case

The Great Dictator would form Chaplin's quintessential statement of anti-fascism. While, however, we know when he announced the film (October 1938), there remains a question mark against when Charlie actually came up with the idea for it. Years after the event a Romanian-born author named Konrad Bercovici claimed to have distributed to Charlie (via Zeppo Marx) a script outlining, in essence, the plot of *The Great Dictator* in March 1938. There was nothing necessarily unusual with that scenario – we have seen that Chaplin had frequently toyed with different co-writers from Alistair Cooke to John Strachey as he made the difficult transition to sound. Orson Welles would even help Charlie with the scenario for the later *Monsieur Verdoux*. Yet in this instance *The Great Dictator* became the subject of an infamous legal case. In the early 1940s, having received no credit on the film (or, crucially, royalties) Bercovici would sue Chaplin for $6,400,000 in lost earnings. This case would eventually be settled by Chaplin in 1947 (albeit for the more modest sum of $90,000), partly no doubt due to Charlie having so many other legal and political troubles at the time.

The actual case was pretty flimsy as Chaplin's legal team laid bare – all Bercovici had was 'a [verbal] contract made in secret with no one present, no witnesses, no writing'.[33] Yet during the civil suit that was set to judge on the matter there were extraordinary accusations about Chaplin's politics, and ones that seem to fly in the face of everything we understand about the man. After Bercovici had finished his proposed script for Charlie, he claimed that he and Chaplin encountered each other at the house of a mutual acquaintance in April 1938. Charlie wandered in as Bercovici was discussing the Nazis and, surprisingly, 'his words right off the bat [on Hitler] . . . were: "Well, there must be something to the man. Look at what he has done for Germany."' Bercovici objected to this strenuously: 'I had been in Germany and I knew what was going on there.' But Charlie continued: 'You can't make fun of Hitler, make fun of a man who has done so much as he has, [or] such as Mussolini who has made something out of Italy.' 'In Italy,' Charlie is alleged to have said, 'The trains run on time, and look at what the Versailles Treaty had done for Germany. Hitler is bringing order out of chaos.'[34] This startled Bercovici: 'I knew [Charlie] to be somewhat of a liberal and took it for granted that he detested the Nazis. Before he had seemed to agree with me, but this time he disappointed me.' Having planned to thrust a copy of his script directly into Charlie's hands, Bercovici thought better of it.

Bercovici left the party having harangued Charlie: 'You sympathize with dictators because you have become soft and bloated.' Given that Charlie's economic manifesto of 1932 had been inspired in part by such accusations of lethargy in the face of global crisis, this was a smart play. Others at the gathering allegedly backed up Charlie's anti-fascist credentials, but Bercovici was not to be browbeaten and retained 'very little' respect for the comedian's opinions. Later that evening Bercovici went around to Charlie's house where his host 'suddenly seemed very anxious to talk about the dictator situation in Europe; there were things that he did not know about; what was really happening in Germany.' As time passed and the atmosphere mellowed, Bercovici outlined the general scenario behind his proposed script and how 'Hitler and all the other dictators could be killed with ridicule'. At the time Charlie was 'mildly opposed' to such a concept, but 'could see there was something in it'. As Bercovici went on Charlie asked more questions about Germany and Italy, 'who Hitler was, his background'. Bercovici duly obliged with such information and claimed, in so doing, that he was the first individual 'to acquaint Chaplin with the relationship between Hitler, Goering and Goebbels' – later lampooned to great effect in the film. He also suggested that the idea for Charlie escaping a concentration camp in the film was his alone.[35]

Bercovici's case was certainly full of half-truths and contestable statements. For instance, he claimed that 'Charlie impersonating Hitler is original with me.' That can hardly have been true. During the later trial Charlie's lawyer handed over to the jury a scrapbook of clippings from 1936 related to Chaplin – 'He keeps a scrapbook of press notices, as all important people do.' This book was full of

> scores of editorials and reporters' notes of stories in every newspaper in the United States and every paper in Australia, Canada, and England comparing Hitler and Chaplin . . . why the thing was as open as day. Did[, therefore,] Chaplin need Bercovici to implant the idea . . .? Nonsense.[36]

There was much in that view. Alexander Korda, for one, had proposed the idea at least a year before Bercovici.

But Charlie's alleged praise for Hitler and particularly Mussolini has arguably been glided over too quickly. Certainly it is odd to hear Charlie say, 'You have got to admire Hitler's efficiency, if nothing else, and Mussolini has done some good things for Italy, and I am not at this time trying to discredit him.'[37] In Joyce Milton's highly critical (although equally readable) biography of Charlie, she describes this as the action of someone 'ever the contrarian'.[38] Given that other sources, his son Michael not least, frequently point out that Charlie simply liked to argue for the sake of it there may be something in the notion that Chaplin was simply winding Bercovici up. But it is as likely that these simply represented Chaplin's views at the time. Bercovici later softened his description of the April 1938 conversation:

> I don't think Chaplin [defended] Hitler and Mussolini. I think Chaplin said, more or less, the picture is not as black as I had painted it; that they were not just gangsters . . . I would not say he defended Nazism or Fascism, but I would say he was not opposed to it in the sense I was opposed to it.[39]

As extraordinary as that may appear in light of the film he released two and a half years later, that description broadly seems to hold up. While it is easy to dismiss Bercovici's evidence, or indeed ignore it as many accounts of Chaplin's life do, it does at least deserve due consideration. Simply because it does not fit the narrative of brave Charlie standing up against the dictators, that does not mean it is fiction. Indeed, given his early statements on fascism, it seems entirely plausible. Contemporary difficulties or not, Chaplin did after all settle the case with Bercovici, indicating that there may have been something there.

It is undeniable that Chaplin would come to hate the dictators – and aspects of them were always inexplicable to him. For instance, when the Nazi bureaucrat Adolf Eichmann was put on trial in Jerusalem in 1962, displaying what Hannah Arendt famously called 'the banality of evil', Charlie was livid. As his son Michael recalled in typical 1960s idioms, this was 'a regular topic while his trial was going on and my father was choked with rage and would be just lost for words about what he'd like to do to that cat'.[40] But this was after the Holocaust had taken place. In the late 1930s fascism had seemingly conquered domestic unemployment, restored downtrodden nations' place on the diplomatic scene and projected an albeit pompous sense of hope for the future. The fact that Charlie may have imbibed some of that does not in any meaningful sense detract from his later work.

Putting America first

The odd pro-fascist utterance may even have done Charlie some good before the Second World War. Aside from machinations involving the communist baiting House Un-American Activities Committee (covered in the next chapter), Chaplin's output was so controversial in late 1930s America because he would come, in essence, to advocate a position explicitly contrary to existing statute: war with Nazi Germany. In 1935, Congress had passed the first of four Neutrality Acts, the first of which forbade America trading with any belligerent involved in a war. In 1936, this was extended to all forms of loan and credit. Finally, in 1939, with Britain and France now at war with Nazi Germany, 'cash and carry' sales were finally allowed – in effect meaning that the United States would only permit the sale of arms to belligerents if the other party to the transaction paid up-front, in cash, and managed the transportation of the goods themselves. Yet even this change of emphasis came with caveats. Until the passage of the Lend-Lease Act in March 1941 (passed partly because the British were running out of gold with which to pay under 'cash and carry'), America kept its dealings at the very least to a degree of plausible deniability when it came to the war erupting in Europe.

Gallup Polls suggest that the American people strongly supported such an isolationist stance. In September 1938 a survey of more than 3,000 Americans revealed that two-thirds did not think President Roosevelt should criticise Hitler's 'war-like' actions during the Sudetenland crisis.[41] By September 1939, with Britain and France now at war with Germany, only 6 per cent of Americans thought that Roosevelt should lead America in joining them.[42] By October 1939 this figure had even fallen to 5 per cent.[43] When Charlie Chaplin began work on *The Great Dictator* he was crafting a film that would likely fly in the face of received opinion – an undeniably brave move. *Modern Times* had been controversial, but this new film seemed to be pushing boundaries much further.

As a result of this isolationism Hollywood was generally careful about its output. There were several reasons for this. First, as Ben Urwand has recently shown, Nazi officials such as Georg Gyssling buzzed around Los Angeles in the 1930s discussing with the major studios what would and would not be acceptable for release in the Third Reich: 'He told the studios to make changes to their pictures about Germany, and he threatened to expel them from the German market . . . if they did not co-operate'.[44] By the end of the decade, as diplomatic pressures exerted a further such influence, Gyssling barely had to express his displeasure: studios knew what would not pass German censors, and acted accordingly. But it was more than that, for the American MPPDA itself urged strict neutrality during the conflict, and not out of fervently pro-Nazi feeling. In an open letter to Hollywood film producers on 15 September 1939, two weeks after the German invasion of Poland, Will Hays expressed his belief that 'no propaganda on the screen shall be the contributing cause of making this industry assume the dreadful responsibility of sending the youth of America to war'.[45] This was sent a year prior to President Roosevelt's famous pledge to the American people that 'your boys are not going to be sent into any foreign wars'. It also predated the formation of the anti-interventionist America First Committee – whose approximately 800,000 members included Hollywood figures such as Walt Disney and Lilian Gish – by roughly the same timescale. The movies broadly fell into this generally pacifistic spirit. Hays worried that 'there is no law' covering the issue of 'federal neutrality', and noted, 'We do very well, indeed, to keep our responsibilities constantly in mind now.' The films were about 'entertainment' and '"hate" pictures have no place on America's amusement screen'.[46] Such self-regulation by the MPPDA was convincing enough to forestall an amendment to the Neutrality Act that would have established a formal censorship board to police 'all Hollywood films with a war theme or setting'.[47]

While this was not Chaplin's view about film's role in the coming struggle, it is important to set out the ambiguities of the time. For one, the varying opinions as to what actually constituted cinematic propaganda were given interesting light by a survey sent to ten staff members of the self-regulating censorship body the Production Code Administration (PCA) in June 1938. This was undeniably a small sample, but this collective's views on what actually was 'propaganda' and whether particular texts were 'self-serving' are worth repeating. A small sample is given below in Table 7.1.

Table 7.1 Instances of 'propaganda' as defined by the Production Code Administration, June 1938

	Total replies	Propaganda?		Self-serving?		Uncertain
		Yes	No	Yes	No	
Texts						
United States Declaration of Independence	9	3	6	1	5	3
Communist Manifesto	7	5	2	3	3	1
Das Kapital	6	4	2	1	3	2
Mein Kampf	7	6	1	4	2	1
Franklin D. Roosevelt's *On Our Way*	6	6	0	2	3	1
Upton Sinclair's *The Jungle*	8	8	—	2	5	1
Films						
Birth of a Nation	9	3	6	1	4	4
Potemkin	7	2	5	0	3	4

Survey appendix of 'A Study of the Effect of the Production Code and its Administration and Content of American Motion Pictures, and Certain Other Basic Industry Policies and Their Current Application', 22 June 1938, FIRTH/ MPPDA No. 1,192

There are some interesting conclusions here. First, the notion that *Mein Kampf* was a less obvious form of propaganda than that propagated by Upton Sinclair or the sitting President is certainly odd. Yet, conversely, communistic texts by Marx were viewed as less overt forms of propaganda than those by Hitler.

Such confusing findings may arise from the fact that many of the respondents had difficulty precisely defining what propaganda actually was. While one respondent to the PCA survey noted that 'propaganda in common usage is a very confusing term which should probably be abolished altogether', others took more dogmatic lines. Another commented that 'anything today for or against Communism or Fascism or religion or even Prohibition, any of which subjects would tend to arouse the hatred and feelings of one group of American citizens against another, constitutes the type of propaganda that should be kept off the motion picture screens'. Even within the cinematic world, therefore, there were extremely divergent views as to what good cinema 'should' do during this difficult time.[48] Chaplin, to his credit, ploughed on regardless.

Censoring *The Great Dictator*

Making *The Great Dictator* amidst such debates was an unquestionably brave step. As his old friend and sailing partner Alistair Cooke knew,

> *The Great Dictator* will be more than an artistic risk. It is a daring business venture, for his change of theme almost certainly blights him of any prospect of showing the film in Poland and Portugal, in most of South America, in the Soviet, and in Japan – to say nothing of Italy and Germany.[49]

Certainly the commercial implications were stark. For example when Harry Warner, then President of Warner Brothers, wrote to Roosevelt's advisor Harry Hopkins in March 1939 to note that 'in South America, the American motion picture reigns supreme' he was telling the blunt truth.[50] With Argentina (90 per cent of films shown being American made) and Brazil (85 per cent equivalent) combining militaristic dictatorships with a public who liked a good glut of Hollywood, there were key markets at risk in making a film where an ally of such regimes, Hitler, was being ridiculed mercilessly

Although the diplomacy was rather different, this was also potentially true of the United States. When Bercovici had allegedly brought up the prospect of making *The Great Dictator* in early 1938 Charlie told him that 'he could not do it, that there would be trouble with the State Department, that we were at peace now with Germany and Italy, that these two men – Hitler and Mussolini – were heads of governments – we dare not satirize them'.[51] If this is true, Chaplin's stance had certainly changed by September 1938 when he engaged the writer Dan James, fresh out of Yale, to bounce ideas off with regard to the film's plot. After the October announcement that the film was going ahead, full production (the ordering of sets, costumes and so forth) would commence in July 1939.

The intervening period between these two dates would come to matter enormously. By December 1938 the German Propaganda Ministry was receiving reports that an 'impudent satire' of the dictators was being prepared by Chaplin. According to German internal memoranda, 'the joke of this film is that Chaplin, the "little big Jew," is mistaken (!) for the Fuhrer (!) by the guards and thereby ends up in the position of Adolf Hitler(!)'.[52] In a rare break from his détente with most of Hollywood, Hitler himself issued something of a direct response to Chaplin and other perceived anti-Nazi films such as the Three Stooges' *You Nazty Spy*! Subsequently, this 30 January 1939 speech by Hitler to the Reichstag would become known for promising 'the annihilation of the Jewish race in Europe' in the event of a world war, but it also contained a much less high-profile attack on the American film industry. He thundered that 'the announcement of American film companies of their intention to produce anti-Nazi – i.e. anti-German – films, will lead to our German producers creating anti-Semitic films in the future'.[53] In late 1938 and early 1939 Charlie was supposedly wavering about whether to make the picture, and more pressure was about to follow.

By this stage news of the planned film had reached Charlie's homeland of Britain. On 27 February 1939, a Conservative MP Edward Keeling wrote a letter to Rab Butler, Under Secretary of State at the Foreign Office and then a rising pro-appeasement star within the British government. Keeling had been contacted previously by one of his constituents, and told of 'a film now in preparation in Hollywood which is to be called "The Dictator" and in which Charles Chaplin is to portray Herr Hitler satirically'. According to this unnamed source,

> It is obviously most undesirable that such a film should be exhibited in this country and I venture to think that the Government should make it known immediately to the persons financially interested in its production and distribution that its exhibition in Great Britain will be forbidden, the necessary instructions being issued at the same time to Lord Tyrrell's Board.

In essence, this was a request to kill off what became *The Great Dictator* lest it prove offensive to the Nazis.[54] Butler promised Keeling he would look into the matter and get back to him.

What followed was a paper trail studied in ambiguity. On the one hand, the official line was very much as Rab Butler later told Keeling: 'Film censorship in this country is under the control of the Film Industry and, as we have repeatedly pointed out in the House of Commons, is in no way subject to government control.'[55] This general rule of thumb applied even into the Second World War. When Soviet Ambassador to London Maisky complained to the British about the content of King Vidor's comedy espionage film *Comrade X*, Harold Nicolson at the Ministry of Information deemed it to be 'vulgar and it is most vulgar to the Soviet system'. Yet he still 'warned' Maisky that we really did not have powers to do anything about it' and that the head of his department (Alfred Duff Cooper) 'does not feel that we should be justified in taking steps which are beyond our powers to prevent the showing of a film produced in America and for which we are in no possible way responsible'.[56] Had the government stood back from all involvement in what films could or could not be released, this would at least have been a consistent position.

In reality, however, it is clear that Chaplin was leant on by British sources to tone down his portrayal of Hitler. In early March 1939, the Foreign Office began to make enquiries about the nature of the film through its Washington Embassy, a request subsequently relayed to the British Consulate in Los Angeles.[57] This was a tumultuous time. Two weeks after this letter Hitler marched his troops into what remained of Czechoslovakia and by the end of the month Prime Minister Neville Chamberlain had issued his guarantee of Polish independence. The film's importance and sensitivity had therefore only grown. Indeed, when Jack L. Warner (of Warner Brothers fame) met with President Roosevelt around this time, he found a President hoping that Chaplin's picture would still come to fruition.[58] Warner assured the Commander in Chief that this was indeed so. On 21 March Chaplin issued a statement stating that 'owing to erroneous reports in the press that I have abandoned my production concerning dictatorship, I wish to state that I have never wavered from my original determination to make this picture'. He was not worried about 'intimidation, censorship or anything else'.[59]

That was fortunate because the British were not about to give up. On 28 April 1939 the Foreign Office in London wrote to their Los Angeles Consulate to note that

> while we have no wish to suggest that you should wish being charged with interference, we wonder whether it might be possible for you to approach [the Chaplin Company] . . . and prevail upon them to treat the subject in a way that it could be exhibited in this country without offending Germany.[60]

After having some presumably tense conversations with Chaplin on the matter, Los Angeles reported back two weeks later. The Consulate contended that he was 'entering into the production of "The Dictator" with fanatical enthusiasm'. His 'racial and social sympathies' were with the 'classes and groups who have suffered most in the dictatorship countries', and he was prepared to put a million dollars into the film to make sure this was hammered home on-screen. In something of a massive understatement, they reported that Chaplin's 'political outlook is not of a quality which is likely to influence him in favour of propitiating the personalities whom he burlesquing. Indeed, the directness of his attack would seem to be, to him, the picture's only motive and reason.'[61]

By June 1939 the Foreign Office had recognised the difficulty of their convincing Chaplin to change his film but still, again in the mannered language of diplomats, began to work on British censors to try to get them to refuse to pass the film. A 16 June letter sent from Rowland Kenney at the Foreign Office to Joseph Brooke-Wilkinson at the British Board of Film Censors certainly suggests as much. Relaying the news from Los Angeles that Chaplin was determined to make the film come what may, Kenney told Brooke-Wilkinson that 'Mr Chaplin recognises that the Hays

Office may refuse to pass the film for exhibition in the United States of America, and that it may be banned almost everywhere else'. Presumably just to be helpful, he 'thought it as well to draw your attention to these reports in order that you may be prepared – if you have not already heard of them – to give the film the most careful scrutiny should it be presented to you for a license in this country'.[62] This was a classic British fudge. By the letter of the law, Kenney had not overstepped statutory bounds here. But by urging 'the most careful scrutiny' for a product likely to be 'banned almost everywhere' he was giving the censors a firm nudge as to which side of the fence to come down on. Unbeknownst to Kenney, however, Brooke-Wilkinson was already sympathetic to this position – and he had independently already sent a telegram on Chaplin to his counterpart Joseph Breen, the anti-Semitic head of the Production Code Administration in America. Back in March 1939 Brooke-Wilkinson had contacted Breen to point out 'the delicate situation that might arise in [Britain] if personal attacks were made on any living statesman', and asking what contact could be made with Chaplin.[63] As Chaplin continued to work up his anti-Hitler scenario, therefore, British officialdom already was on the same page as to its likely response.

Events overtook matters, however. With the British declaring war on Hitler on 3 September 1939 such concerns were soon swept aside, and a product lampooning Nazi Germany was now useful rather than undesirable. But the early concerns among the British establishment should not be forgotten. Charlie had forged ahead with the expense of making a film with the very real prospect that it would be banned from his key markets. *The Great Dictator* would form a powerful legacy for many different reasons.

Content and release

Charlie later told a friend that he had 'put everything into this picture. It may be my monument.'[64] As ever, he shot and shot until he felt the scenes were right. It is said that he shot a million feet of film for a film that ended up using less than 7,000.[65] Even by Charlie's standards this was picky – but this film clearly mattered more to him than any other up to that point. While even the very political *Modern Times* had embedded itself within a world recognisible to the early Tramp, *The Great Dictator* was all too 'real'.

On 31 August 1939 screen tests for the film were started with Charlie seeking Jewish actors who could speak Yiddish for extras and to play incidental characters in the ghetto. Shooting began on 9 September, six days after the British and French had declared war on Hitler. Early shooting including scenes in the ghetto building the romance between the barber and Hannah, and occurred during a heat wave in Los Angeles that saw temperatures reach 114 degrees Fahrenheit. By December he had filmed preliminary scenes for the final speech with Garbitsch and Herring, but had not yet fully nailed down the content of the peroration itself. The final address would only be fully fleshed out in the week commencing 23 June 1940 – after, in other words, the French had surrendered to the advancing German Army and the war looked more or less won by Hitler. It was even braver than it looked (see Figure 7.1).

After editing and scoring the picture through the autumn, eventually the film received its New York premiere in October 1940. It

Figure 7.1 *The Great Dictator* was Chaplin's greatest artistic risk to date and would stand as his most profound achievement.

Courtesy of Bridgeman Images

stayed fifteen weeks there, playing two big theatres – the Astor and the Capitol – and proved Charlie's biggest gross to date. One invitee to the premiere who could not attend was President Roosevelt himself. An intriguing telegram has survived in his official archive in upstate New York, however. On 22 October Edwin M. Watson, Roosevelt's secretary, cabled to Chaplin that 'before November 5' – the Presidential election in which FDR would secure an unprecedented third term – the President was 'now faced with the necessity of preparing five major political addresses' and thus could not make it to Chaplin's premiere. Yet, evidently, Roosevelt had been moved by the film, for Watson continued noting that 'he asks that I explain the circumstances to you and say he had hoped so very much to see you this week and to attend the screening in the White House of your new picture'. FDR was 'sorry you must return to the West Coast so soon' and asked 'is there are any chance you will be east again and can be here when the picture is screened'.[66] This was not just perfunctory acknowledgement of a big cinematic name. Unable to get Roosevelt, Charlie was successful in convincing Harry Hopkins, FDR's Chief Advisor, to attend a preview for the film. Hopkins judged the film 'a great picture' and 'a very worthwhile thing to do'. But he believed 'it hasn't a chance. It will lose money.'[67] In this regard, as mentioned, he was proved comprehensively wrong.

The timing was also appropriate for Chaplin's homeland. Its British release (London Premiere: 16 December 1940; nationwide release March 1941) coincided with the Blitz – seventy-one German bombing raids on the British capital over 1940–1 that damaged in the region of one million homes and killed more than 40,000 civilians – and was thus a much-needed morale boost for Chaplin's countrymen. Just before its London Premiere the Duchess of Marlborough, Churchill's Secretary Jock Colville, Brendan Bracken and several other luminaries gathered at Chartwell to watch *The Great Dictator* with Winston Churchill. Colville's account records the group sitting down to watch the film that had 'not yet been released in this country and which everyone has been eagerly awaiting'. He continued: 'The film at which we all laughed a great deal, being over, Winston dictated to me a short telegram to Roosevelt, asking whether Lloyd George would be acceptable as Ambassador, and went to bed early.'[68] There remained a war to win, and whose outcome still remained in the balance.

As Winston Churchill saw, the film itself makes great use of the physical similarities between Charlie Chaplin and Adolf Hitler. Charlie plays two characters – a Jewish barber (notably, unlike Chaplin, a veteran of the Great War) and Adenoid Hynkel, leader of the Double Cross movement and Dictator of Tomania. As ever with Charlie's political films, it begins with a caption: 'This is a story of a period between two World Wars – an interim in which Insanity cut loose. Liberty took a nose dive, and Humanity was kicked around somewhat.' We move from some business on the Western Front in the Great War to a post-war world where newspaper headlines make clear that economic Depression had given way to mass rioting before bringing the 'Hynkel Party' to power. The film contains several notes of broad comedy such as (the Hermann Goering mocking) Marshall Herring attempting to 'tighten his belt' as per a Hynkel speech from Charlie, but being unable to do so due to his expansive stomach. It was not his funniest work, but the slapstick does on occasion neatly cut through.

Yet it is the politics that really shines throughout the film, and not just in the direct sense of portraying the Nazi regime in a negative light. Chaplin used his global fame to make some very specific points. First, his work suggested that the Western democracies were being fed a pack of lies about Hitler's intentions, and to some degree willingly swallowing them. In one speech, for example, Hynkel goes on an anti-Semitic tirade so vicious that even the microphones physically recoil in terror. The well-mannered German translator simply notes that 'his excellency has just referred to the Jewish people.' Second, for all the pomp of the Nazi state, the film suggests that Hitler was fundamentally driven by domestic public opinion – that to some degree the tail was wagging the dog. When dissent breaks out across Tomania in protest at working conditions, Propaganda Minister Garbitsch/Goebbels pushes his leader to invade the neighbouring country of Osterlich as a distraction. This concept of a *flucht nach vorn* – a flight to the front – has subsequently been applied to German aggression before both the two world wars by major historians. Fritz Fischer's thesis regarding Germany's grasp at world power before 1914 is probably the most well known, but Tim Mason and other scholars have pointed to working-class unrest as driving much of Hitler's aggressive actions from the invasion of the very real Austria in March 1938 onwards. In some sense, Chaplin got in there before such academics.

Third, there is also the issue as to how different nations and leaders are treated. Chaplin would be guilty by omission for some – indeed for a film about dictators it is odd that there is no reference, even obliquely, to a Stalinesque parody figure. If Dan James is to be believed, he and Bob Meltzer talked Charlie out of including a reference to Stalin in the climactic speech that ends the film. And, thus, if the next chapter will discuss Rep. Martin Dies's tunnel vision for anti-communism, so too would Chaplin be fixed on the Nazis. Yet, equally, the democracies do not appear in the 1940 film – save by implication through the English translation of Hynkel's speeches, and a journalist from 'the international press' who appears briefly. The film's ending (where Chaplin famously implored soldiers not to give themselves 'for brutes', but 'for liberty') we will get to, but for a film that presented the realities of the dictatorships – concentration camps, anti-Semitic pogroms and a police state – its main body was absent of any even comedic references to real-world America, Britain and France.

Such geopolitical analysis can be extended further. With Chaplin's sometime previous warmth towards Mussolini in mind, Jack Oakie's character of Benzino Napaloni remains very interesting. Put bluntly, is he even a villain at all? He attempts to thwart Hynkel's invasion of Osterlich, is one of the few non-Jewish people to mock the Tomanian dictator and, it is implied, has a far bigger army that could stop Tomania in its tracks. Napaloni's only major error, like the real-life Neville Chamberlain, was to believe that the 'scrap of paper' signed by Hynkel had any actual value. Whereas Hynkel's armband displays a double cross, the symbol of duplicitousness, Napaloni's contains two dice – he is a gambler, a chancer, but not of the same order of evil as Hynkel.

Generally, the film follows two story arcs. In one, Hynkel the Dictator is shown to be an absurd blunderer guided by the ridiculous Marshall Herring and the Machiavellian Garbitsch. His stormtroopers invade the ghetto to beat innocent Jews, although they withdraw when the Tomanian government needs a loan from a Jewish financier. They soon, however, go back in to terrorise the Jews and, subsequently, to invade the neighbouring nation of

Osterlich into which many have fled. In the second arc, Charlie plays a Jewish barber who looks exactly the same as der Phooey, Adenoid Hynkel. Initially shown on the front of the Great War and saving a German officer, Commander Schultz, the barber suffers amnesia after an aeroplane crash and is initially unaware of Hynkel's rise to power. Reacquainting himself with the ghetto, he meets Paulette Goddard's Hannah. As Hannah's father had been killed in the war and her mother had died the previous year, she is watched over by friendly neighbours Mr and Mrs Jaeckel. Hannah and the barber soon fall in love, but the moments of romance are mostly tempered by the political backdrop. The Jaeckels and Hannah eventually flee into Osterlich under the mistaken belief that 'that's still a free country'. They have good reason to do so. Stormtroopers are shown marching through the Tomanian ghetto, shouting, 'The Aryan-The Ary-Ary-Ary-Ary-Aryan, and Hynkel marches high!' They steal food, throw tomatoes and paint shops with the word 'Jew'. In a make-believe country where shop names are all written in Esperanto, Charlie made the point of having them daub 'Jew' rather than 'jude', again to shake his audience with the reality of such actions.

After some business involving Napaloni and Hynkel, Charlie's Jewish barber is thrown into a concentration camp from which he subsequently escapes – and with Commander Schultz (throughout the film presented as something of a 'good German') flees to the Osterlich border. Unbeknownst to them, and after Hynkel is mistakenly arrested by stormtroopers believing him to be the fleeing barber, Osterlich is about to fall to the Tomanian Army. It is Schultz and the barber, who the army command believe to be der Phooey Hynkel (due to their physical resemblance), who lead this invasion. Called to address the world in the aftermath of Hynkel's diplomatic success, Schultz whispers to the barber that he 'must speak – it's our only hope'. 'Hope?' mournfully asks the barber. And so begins the film's famous final peroration.

The final speech stands apart from the rest of the film. It is not delivered in the grandiose pomposity of Hynkel or the mumbling nervousness of the barber. Instead, we have Charlie Chaplin the man holding court, speaking in a passionate yet frenzied manner. Certainly the speech is a denunciation of those who have 'goose-stepped us into misery and bloodshed' and urges soldiers:

'Don't give yourselves to these unnatural men – machine men with machine minds and machine hearts! You are not machines! You are not cattle! You are men!' But it is not just a piece of anti-totalitarian rhetoric. When Chaplin tells the people that they have the power to create machines and the power to create happiness, he follows it up with:

> Then, in the name of democracy let us use that power! Let us all unite! Let us fight for a new world, a decent world that will give men a chance to work, that will give youth a future and old age a security. By the promise of these things, brutes have risen to power, but they lie! They do not fulfill their promise; they never will. Dictators free themselves, but they enslave the people! Now, let us fight to fulfill that promise!

Ridding the world of Hynkels or Hitlers was not enough. People in the democracies needed something positive to fight *for* – 'a chance to work . . . a future . . . a security'. Throughout the time Charlie was crafting this speech in late 1940 many Western democrats were waking up to the fact that they had not yet convinced their populations that they could deliver this 'new world'. On 11 October 1940, a few days before the New York premiere of *The Great Dictator*, Julian Huxley received a letter from Harold Nicolson then at the British Ministry of Information. Both had met Charlie previously and, as noted, Huxley had (unsuccessfully) urged Chaplin to help German Jewish academics in the mid-1930s. Huxley and Nicolson regularly corresponded on so-called 'War Aims' during this period, with the aim of shifting public opinion, and that of Prime Minister Churchill, into creating a more positive programme for reconstruction after any victory. On this occasion Nicolson told Huxley,

> I think that a definite governmental plan going into some detail of national . . . reconstruction would have an enormous effect. Little good will be gained if that plan merely speaks in amiable generalities about freedom and democracy unless it includes concrete details . . . We must take rather dramatic action here and now.[69]

Through the Beveridge Report of 1942 and its emphasis on problems such as unemployment and ill health Britain would eventually find some meaningful meat to put on these bones. One upshot of this would be the new National Health Service (NHS), introduced in 1948, which Charlie would later praise. But Charlie was part of this pre-Beveridge mindset, too – defeating *The Great Dictator* would have less meaning if it restored the world to that of *Modern Times*. Democracy needed to justify its existence once more.

A bad record for supporting the dispossessed was not the only contemporary democratic ill that Chaplin identified either. When his speech stated, 'let us fight to free the world, to do away with national barriers, to do away with greed, with hate and intolerance', this was hardly just an anti-fascist point. American policy towards African Americans, the innately unequal nature of the British and French Empires and the hyper-capitalism that had gripped the democratic world from Santiago to Sydney were all under the microscope, too. As the film critic Roger Ebert commented in 2007, '*The Great Dictator* ended with a long speech denouncing dictatorships, and extolling democracy and individual freedoms. This sounded to the left like bedrock American values, but to some on the right, it sounded pinko.'[70]

The left indeed swung behind the picture. In May 1941 Upton Sinclair wrote to tell Charlie of 'the great pleasure I got from seeing the Dictator . . . It seems to me the best thing you have ever done, and has as much fun as any other picture of yours, but underneath it is the undercurrent tragedy we all know about.'[71] Later, on the parliamentary benches of Charlie's homeland, the Labour MP (and later briefly Cabinet Minister) Richard Stokes remarked that he 'thought that most of [*The Great Dictator*] was awful nonsense, but the [final] peroration was one of the finest things that has ever been written'. He told the chamber that 'if we are to avoid a repetition of the awful conflicts which most of us have experienced twice in a lifetime we have to pay attention to what is said in that great speech'.[72]

Film critics were more mixed. In *The New York Times* Bosley Crowther noted that the film illustrated 'the courage and faith and surpassing love for mankind which are in the heart of Charlie Chaplin'. He did, however, argue that 'the speech with which it ends – the appeal for reason and kindness – is completely out of step with what has gone before'.[73] The *New York Post* was similar: 'Laughter and tears, long held to be closely akin, don't mingle quite so well on this political plane. The final speech demonstrates that it has even put Mr Chaplin momentarily off balance.'[74] Further afield, the *Sydney Morning Herald* told its Australian audience that the *Great Dictator* 'proves that he is unique as a satirist and as social critic'. As for the final speech: 'The intensity is almost embarrassingly sincere: but it emphasises Chaplin's burning hatred of Nazism.'[75] In Britain the picture sold out immediately, with some critics urging the government to acquire copies of the film and distribute them wherever possible on the continent to provide hope for those occupied by the Nazi jackboot.

After the frantic worry over what *The Great Dictator* would mean for the diplomatic picture in the summer of 1939, it is perhaps apt that we end this chapter on the note of this volte face undertaken by the British. Indeed, the month after its London premiere (which he did not attend) Charlie had visited New York and briefly met with the British Consulate General stationed there. There 'Mr Chaplin expressed a conviction that if he could make his next feature film in England, he would like to do so, as he felt that such a policy on his art would be beneficial to our interests'.[76] The initial London official charged with responding to the information from New York remarked that 'on the face of it [it was] a very good idea'.[77] As it moved further up the chain, however, the idea was nixed. This was not on political grounds, but because 'Chaplin is an eccentric and works under conditions which would be impossible in any commercial studio in peace time, and would certainly be impossible in this country in wartime'.[78] Still, if he could not work commercially in his homeland for the time being, he was at least in its good graces and the very idea of Chaplin making a film was no longer beset with worry. *The Great Dictator* had cemented his reputation to his countrymen. The question was: for how long would this still be true of America?

Notes

1 Foreign Office to Los Angeles Consulate, 28 April 1939, TNA/ FO/395/663.
2 Undated note written by Chaplin, *c.* 1945, CIN/CCA.
3 See, e.g., Lunts to Beaton, 3 April 1948, St John's College, Cambridge/Cecil Beaton Papers, uncatalogued.
4 Oelrichs (writing under her pseudonym Michael Strange) to Chaplin undated 1929, University of Birmingham Special Collections [UBSC], Oswald and Cynthia Mosley Papers [OMN]/2/12/15.

5 'A Comedian Sees the World' Unpublished Typescript, CIN/CCA.

6 John Strachey, *The Coming Struggle for Power* (London, 1932), 284.

7 Charlie Chaplin, *My Autobiography* (London, 2003), 351.

8 Cited in Wolfgang Schivelbusch, *Three New Deals: Reflections on Roosevelt's America, Mussolini's Italy, and Hitler's Germany, 1933–1939* (New York, 2006), 24.

9 Thomas Doherty, *Hollywood and Hitler 1933–1939*, (New York, 2013), 125.

10 *Pittsburgh Sun Telegraph*, 4 April 1929, COP/CCP/29.

11 *Los Angeles Examiner*, 6 March 1932, COP/CCP/39.

12 Charlie Chaplin (Lisa Stein Haven ed.), *A Comedian Sees the World* (Missouri, 2014), 124.

13 Harry Crocker's unpublished memoir, 'Charlie Chaplin: Man and Mime', MHL/HRC, XIII–8.

14 Schivelbusch, *Three New Deals*, 30–1.

15 Tantalisingly, the correspondence between the Chaplins and Vanderbilts is limited to an 18 January 1968 letter from Oona to Vanderbilt acknowledging receipt of a cake: Cornelius Vanderbilt IV Papers, Vanderbilt University, Nashville, TN.

16 Chaplin, *My Autobiography*, 316.

17 *The New York Times*, 1 May 1934.

18 Doherty, *Hollywood and Hitler*, 77.

19 *The New York Times*, 13 March 1933.

20 House of Lords Debates, 12 December 1956, vol. 200, col. 1,095.

21 Charles Chaplin, *My Trip Abroad* (London, 1922), 119.

22 Chaplin Interview Transcript, MHL/CCI, 33.f-302.

23 Chaplin Interview with the Immigration and Naturalization Service, 17 April 1948, within FBI/CCF File 8.

24 Montagu to Chaplin, 20 January 1934, BFI/IWM Item 320.

25 Adams to Wells, 29 October 1935, Bodleian Library, Oxford [BOD]/ Society for the Protection of Science and Learning [SPSL]/58/3.

26 Huxley to Adams, 27 November 1935, BOD/SPSL/58/3.

27 Huxley to Adams, 28 November 1935, BOD/SPSL/58/3.

28 Chaplin Interview with the Immigration and Naturalization Service, 17 April 1948, within FBI/CCF Files 7 and 8.

29 Wells's secretary to Adams, 23 December 1935, BOD/SPSL/58/3.

30 Adams to Wells, 24 December 1935, BOD/SPSL/58/3.

31 Cited in *The American Legion Magazine*, 53/6, December 1952, 50.

32 Reported widely, including *Chicago Sunday Tribune*, 30 July 1939.

33 Bercovici Trial Testimony, April 1947, Cornell University, Rare Books and Manuscripts Archives, Ithaca, New York [CURMA], Konrad Bercovici vs. Charles S. Chaplin Case [KBC], Part 1.

34 Bercovici Trial Testimony, April 1947, CURMA/KBC, Part 1.

35 Bercovici Pre-Trial Deposition, 5 March and 15 April 1942, CURMA/ KBC.

36 Bercovici Trial Testimony, April 1947, CURMA/KBC, Part 1.

37 Bercovici Trial Testimony, April 1947, CURMA/KBC, Part 1.

38 Joyce Milton, *Tramp: The Life of Charlie Chaplin* (London, 1996), 368.

39 Bercovici Trial Testimony, April 1947, CURMA/KBC, Part 2.

40 Michael Chaplin, *I Couldn't Smoke the Grass on My Father's Lawn* (London, 1966), 83.

41 Gallup Poll, 25–28 September 1938, USAIPO1938-0133.

42 Gallup Poll, 13–18 September 1939, USAIPO1939-0169.

43 Gallup Poll, 26 October 1939, USAIPO1939-0175.

44 Ben Urwand, *The Collaboration: Hollywood's Pact with Hitler* (Cambridge, MA, 2013), 178.

45 Will Hays open letter to Hollywood industry leaders, 15 September 1939, FIRTH/MPPDA, No. 3,015.

46 Ibid.

47 Memorandum on 'Propaganda' and 'Hate Pictures', 22 April 1940, FIRTH/MPPDA, No. 1,210.

48 All via survey appendix of 'A Study of the Effect of the Production Code and its Administration and Content of American Motion Pictures, and Certain Other Basic Industry Policies and Their Current Application', 22 June 1938, FIRTH/MPPDA No. 1,192.

49 *The Atlantic Monthly*, August 1939.

50 Warner to Hopkins, 6 March 1939, Franklin D. Roosevelt Presidential Library [FDRPL], Official Files [OF] 73.

51 Bercovici Pre-Trial Deposition, 5 March and 15 April 1942, CURMA/KBC.

52 Urwand, *Collaboration*, 203.

53 Urwand, *Collaboration*, 204.

54 Keeling to Butler, 22 February 1939, National Archives, Kew, London, UK [TNA], Foreign and Commonwealth Office Papers [FCO] 395/663.

55 Butler to Keeling, 20 June 1939, TNA/FCO/395/663.

56 Nicolson to Butler, 26 April 1941, Trinity College, Cambridge [TCC]/ Richard Austen Butler Papers [RAB]/F79/160.

57 Foreign Office newswire, 1 March 1939, TNA/FCO/395/663.

58 Urwand, *Collaboration*, 206.

59 Reprinted in Chaplin's later (unpaginated) book *My Life in Pictures* (London, 1974) .

60 Foreign Office News Department to Los Angeles Consulate, 28 April 1939, TNA/FCO/395/663.

61 Los Angeles Consulate to Foreign Office, 17 May 1939, TNA/ FCO/395/663.

62 Kenney to Brooke-Wilkinson, 16 June 1939, TNA/FCO/395/663.

63 Recounted in Brooke-Wilkinson to Kenney, 21 June 1939, TNA/ FCO/395/663.

64 *Liberty*, 2 June 1940.

65 Tully, 'King of Laughter', UCLA/JTL, 69.

66 Watson to Chaplin, 22 October 1940, FDRPL/OF/73.

67 Chaplin, *My Autobiography*, 393.

68 Martin Gilbert, *The Churchill Documents, Never Surrender, May 1940–December 1940, Volume 15* (London, 2011), 1,236 [14 Dec 1940].
69 Nicolson to Huxley, 11 October 1940, University of Houston [HOU], Julian Huxley Papers [JHX] Series 3 Box 14.
70 Ebert's review of *The Great Dictator* via www.rogerebert.com/reviews/great-movie-the-great-dictator-1940 (accessed 7 November 2016).
71 Sinclair to Chaplin, 2 May 1941, LLBI/UPS Box 47.
72 House of Commons Debates, 18 May 1943, vol. 389, col. 1,060.
73 *The New York Times*, 21 October 1940.
74 *New York Post*, October 1940 via BFI/IVM Item 324.
75 *Sydney Morning Herald*, 23 December 1940.
76 Ford to Cleugh, 28 April 1941, TNA/Central Office of Information [INF]/1/583.
77 Cypher, 17 May 1941, TNA/INF/1/583.
78 Bernstein to Beddington, 30 May 1941, TNA/INF/1/583.

8   Comrades and controversy

In March 1972 the White House received an invitation for the then President Nixon to attend 'A Salute to Charlie Chaplin' soon to be held in New York. Nixon's Deputy Director of Communications Ken Clawson was charged with responding, and his verdict said much about the shadow that Chaplin's earlier politics had cast by this point. For Clawson, it was 'inappropriate . . . to even consider the possibility of having Charlie Chaplin come and meet with the President'. Referring to Chaplin's decision never to become a US citizen, he went on to note that 'there was considerable discussion during the 1930s and 1940s about Chaplin's loyalty to our form of government, much less the government itself'. Besides, Clawson concluded, 'I don't think anyone in the country will be able to separate this gigantic artistic talent from Chaplin's decidedly un-American utterances and stances.'[1] Three months out from the Watergate burglary there was something of an irony here. But the persona non grata status afforded to Chaplin by the Nixon White House was, although fading by the early 1970s, merely reflective of what Chaplin's views over several decades had wrought. Although Clawson did not directly refer to it, this was largely caused by the widespread belief that Chaplin had been, to say the least, soft on communism.

This had a large degree of truth. Yet from Charlie's point of view kind words towards the Soviet Union were the product of wartime. If it was reasonable for Roosevelt and Churchill to meet with Stalin (and later help carve up the map of Europe with him), why was it unreasonable to praise the brave efforts of Soviet soldiers resisting Nazi invasion? And anyway, was he not just a mere filmmaker? As this chapter will note, providing answers to either of these questions was not sufficient for many in the American political establishment.

The House Un-American Activities Committee

Although the FBI had been tracking Chaplin's activities since 1922, it was only in the mid-1930s that the suspicion many had in Washington regarding Charlie's motives was publicly formalised. The first incarnation of this was the Special Committee on Un-American Activities chaired by two Democratic congressmen, John McCormack and Samuel Dickstein. As with Nixon's White House denouncing Chaplin's motives a few decades later, hypocrisy marked this committee from the outset. The remit of this committee was to search for subversive activities carried out by forces primarily sympathetic to either Russian communism or German Nazism – reasonable enough. Yet while Rep. Dickstein sought to root out America's enemies it subsequently transpired he was receiving $1,250 a month to pass on information to Soviet intelligence. Although the McCormack–Dickstein committee had comparatively little impact (beyond ascertaining, without much evidence, that a widespread fascist plot had tried to overthrow Roosevelt in 1933), its successor would create a good deal more controversy.

In May 1938 a more infamous and far-reaching Congressional body would be set up: the House Un-American Activities Committee (often referred to as HUAC), chaired by Rep. Martin Dies of Texas. Dies was a southern Democrat who had gradually become ever angrier and more disenchanted with the interventionist path taken by the Roosevelt administration in Washington. His papers survive in Liberty, Texas and are an under-utilised treasure trove of material related to 1930s and 1940s American anti-communism. Through this material we can certainly see how figures such as Dies became suspicious of Charlie. For Dies Rooseveltian schemes such as the National Recovery Administration that Charlie had viewed with much sympathy – and indeed endorsed on the radio in 1933 – were the thin end of a rather malign wedge. In a 1939 speech Dies told a huge Madison Square Garden audience that big government threatened to curtail American liberty:

> We are now witnessing the first stage of this campaign, namely, the attacks upon our economic system, the attempt to

convince people that the government ought to support them, and the proposals to regiment our economic life under cleverly devised schemes of planned economy.[2]

For Dies, Roosevelt was at best a meddling fool, and at worst someone looking to take America down the road of a totalitarian state of the left. Ironically, in fearing the big state Dies was not so far removed from some of Charlie's own views.

In an unsympathetic contemporary biography, the academic William Gellerman attempted to eviscerate Dies's reputation. Much of this concerned the work of HUAC, but Gellerman was also eager to point out the contradictions in Dies's early congressional career. Quoting one anonymous 'young woman', Gellerman suggests that 'in the course of his career, Martin Dies seems to have expressed almost every point of view at least once'.[3] In September 1931, for example, he called for 'an extended programme of public works' and 'conferences with industrialists to secure shorter working hours to offset the displacement of men by machines'. This was essentially political Chaplinism, even if Dies's desire to 'prohibit all immigration to the United States for five years' would hardly have chimed with an Englishman who had made *The Immigrant*.[4] Although he vehemently opposed the so-called 'Sit Down Strikes' of 1937 – where workers in Flint, Michigan physically occupied a General Motors factory to secure collective unionisation – as 'reprehensible . . . lawlessness' Dies maintained many left-of-centre views. These included making estate taxes as high as they were in England, blaming financial crises on bankers manipulating the credit system and providing a one-year moratorium on mortgage foreclosures.[5] He was a contradictory man.

Dislike for the President aside, Dies's view was that there was a far more dangerous hidden hand guiding Roosevelt and America per se in the wrong direction. In June 1932 he gave a speech listing fourteen means by which communists fostered class consciousness in America. Several of these criteria could have described Charlie Chaplin in the 1930s and 1940s, including the promotion of 'discontent and disregard for authority among the children' and the 'promotion among the intelligentsia of discontent with the existing order in the United States'. Dies argued that any opposition to 'the restriction of immigration', and perceived 'ridicule of the politics of the United States toward the present regime in Russia' would see one placed in this bracket, too.[6] These were fairly open-ended definitions, but that in a sense was the point. For, as Dies noted, 'not all the adherents of Marxism in America are card-holding members of the Communist Party. Some of them are distributed among scores of numerically inconsequential organisations, but the great majority of Marxists do not belong, as such, to any organisation. They masquerade under the name of liberals, and they deny, with technical accuracy, that they are Communists, but the truth is that they worship at the shrine of Marx and derive their political and economic conceptions from his writings.'[7] This quote said it all. Even if someone denied that they were a communist, and indeed Dies's committee could produce no evidence that they were a communist, it was still perfectly possible to claim 'they worship at the shrine of Marx'.

The rhetorical space for anti-communism was again in part created by wider questions of morality and decency. In June 1933 Dies's fellow Texan Democrat John Patman brought forward H.R.6097 with the express aim of creating a new Federal Motion Picture Commission (as well as banning so-called 'block booking').[8] The bill noted that 'no picture shall be produced which will lower the moral standards of those who see it' and that 'the history, institutions, prominent people and citizenry of other nations shall be represented fairly'. On both charges Charlie's 1930s and 1940s output could be said to be under the microscope. But in essence the role of H.R.6097 was to put the existing Hays Code onto the statute book and have a new Federal Commission police it. This was mostly accomplished, de facto, by the eventual creation of an industry-backed Production Code Administration (albeit not enjoying Patman's desired statutory underpinning).

The Patman Bill was interesting not just for the broad Texan Democrat anti-Hollywood measures it implied, but for the scores of letters that Dies received asking him to back the bill (which he was happy to do). For one, the Beaumont Motion Picture Council wrote to him decrying the 'large proportion of films which portray a small but lawless segment of American life' that was educating 'many of the younger generation in methods of committing crime and is a detriment to moral and social progress at home and a menace to America's good name and interests abroad'.[9] Similarly, the American Legion Auxiliary in Beaumont also felt 'the best way to insure the most desirable type of motion picture for the children of all ages is to demand federal supervision', a position with which more than one local parent–teacher association agreed.[10] Certainly Dies's committee was led by a charismatic figurehead, but that figurehead was always to some degree responding to his constituents. The voices demanding censorship were clearly louder than those more or less with the status quo, but a significant proportion of Dies's constituents were undoubtedly suspicious of the motives of liberal Hollywood. And as with Chaplin's own experience, it was easier to pin communism on Hollywood generally if people already felt Tinseltown to be immoral.

The perceived link between communism and the movies can be seen in the various reports produced by Dies's HUAC committee. First, there was the direct worry about Soviet-produced activities – and here Chaplin's previous associations with Sergei Eisenstein hardly helped. As the committee reported, 'the establishment in Hollywood in 1932 of a special American Proletkino [Soviet film studio] may be regarded as a first attempt to start in the United States of America the production of films to propagate Communist ideas through movies'.[11] In a sense this problem could be managed by pressurising theatres not to take on such films. The larger, more invidious problem was the American (or at least in Chaplin's case, Anglophone) fellow travellers who, in Dies's views, 'worshipped at the shrine of Marx' even if they could deny membership of the American Communist Party. As the committee noted in 1938,

> it has been the aim of leading film producers in America to produce pictures for amusement and not for propaganda, as is the chief purpose of Russian cinema and Communist cinema, although subtle efforts have been made at times to inject subversive propaganda into important films, and in Hollywood there are numerous players and other artists strongly sympathetic to communism.[12]

Doubtless this number, to Dies and the American right, included Charlie.

The spectre of HUAC cast a shadow wider than the movie industry and longer than Chaplin's own American residence. From the formation of the Dies committee in May 1938 to it being formally recognised as a Standing Committee of the House in 1945, its activities were only wound down as late as 1975. One of its most famous scalps would indeed be the famous 'Hollywood Ten' of communist sympathetic screenwriters and producers, with which we will deal later in this chapter. But its remit was always much wider – and the accusations of communism against state department official Alger Hiss in 1948, initially brought forward by HUAC and then continued into a subsequent perjury trial, rocked the American psyche. If the communists could be everywhere from the movie screen to the corridors to power, how was America to emerge victorious from the titanic struggles that awaited it?

The evidence brought before the committee varied in quality massively. Much like the FBI reports on Chaplin, which rested so much on news clippings and stories publicly reported but not necessarily verified, so too did HUAC encourage a variety of non-mainstream voices. But these remain interesting in and of themselves. For instance, on 19 November 1938 John Metcalfe, HUAC's chief investigator in Los Angeles, testified before the Committee. Handing Chairman Dies a copy of a pamphlet he had picked up from the American Nationalist Party on his travels, Dies read the following into the record. True patriots, the pamphlet noted, 'in every way, and wherever possible, [should] show an exclusive preference for gentile merchants, gentile professional men, and gentile working people . . . Your dime at the movies may endorse and support further Jewish attacks upon our Christian morality'.[13] The very type of 'hidden hand' agenda that some read into communism – Dies not least – dovetailed nicely with traditional notions of a Jewish conspiracy. With Chaplin allegedly denying his 'true' Jewish heritage and about to ridicule Adolf Hitler on screen, he was naturally drawn into this orbit.

In this vein, on 29 December 1938 General George Moseley spoke of his hope that America's Jews must 'disassociate themselves entirely from all communistic activities'. He proposed that they could

> stop communism in the United States in just 30 days . . . By using what power? The power that they now have so completely over the radio, the power that they have over the public press; the control they have over the "movies"; and, finally, the power they have now at home and internationally, in the money markets of the world.[14]

Six months later – his plea 'unanswered' – Moseley told the HUAC committee that a Jewish conspiracy was about to overthrow the American government and replace it with a Communist dictatorship. Even for HUAC some of his testimony was beyond the pale and subsequently deleted from the record. But the idea that the Jews were using Hollywood to ferment a communist plot was by no means a fringe view.

As such, the atmosphere in these committees was undeniably hostile. Witnesses would often begin on the defensive, and pre-emptively seek to exonerate those whom the committee had accused of communism by implication. Charlie himself would be called by the committee in the late 1940s but was in no hurry to attend – and one can see why. As Gellerman shows,

> while permitting witnesses to make unsubstantiated charges against persons or organizations, Dies insisted that those against whom charges were made must, if they were to appear before the committee, not only make denials under oath but produce books and records, "real evidence" to disprove such charges.[15]

Another irony was that Chaplin and Dies were both criticised for the same thing: neglecting the other side of the dictatorial coin. While Chaplin's *Great Dictator* took pot shots at fascist Italy and Nazi Germany, Soviet Russia was nowhere to be seen. But Dies's committee was also supposed to go after *both* communist and fascist forms of subversion, and yet seemed to lean heavily towards the former. Rep. Marcantonio of New York chided the committee for not having investigated the Silver Shirts, the Ku Klux Klan and other spokesmen of the 'native Nazi' section of America.[16] During its first five years the committee was said to have compiled an index of more than 1,000,000 subversive organisations and individuals – yet the list of individuals connected to Nazi activities that the committee handed to the Roosevelt White House contained just barely 17,000 names.[17] The majority of the committee's activities were therefore clearly aimed at Moscow rather than Berlin – indeed in Dies's 1940 book, *The Trojan Horse in America*, more than 300 pages outlined the threat of communism compared to the less than 50 on fascism.[18] Through 1940 Dies remained fixated on 'pre-mature anti-fascism' – that is to say, the idea that to have been overtly anti-fascist before America was forced into the Second World War was to invite suspicion of communist sympathy. In this light Chaplin's *The Great*

Dictator joined the Warner Brothers' *Confessions of a Nazi Spy* as somehow malevolent.[19] This was proven ipso facto misguided – in December 1941, after all, it would be Hitler and not Stalin who would declare war on America.

Praise for Dies's work, however, poured in from 'respectable Hollywood'. In late May 1940 Sam Goldwyn of MGM fame wrote to Dies to offer his 'congratulations for your splendid radio broadcast on Saturday. You have voiced the thoughts of millions of Americans who love this country dearly and who object strenuously to every type of "Fifth Column" activity'.[20] This was symptomatic of a growing divide between liberal and conservative Hollywood concerning the activities of Dies. In August 1938 HUAC investigator Edward F. Sullivan suggested that 'evidence tends to show that all phases of radical and communist activities are rampant amongst the studios of Hollywood and, although well known, is a matter which the movie moguls desire to keep from the public'.[21] He continued that he

> might say in passing that a very large number of motion pic-
> ture stars are strongly opposed to all this subversive activity
> but, as one very prominent star told me, if he spoke loud
> about the situation, he would soon be ditched by the studios
> and a campaign of vilification would be started against him.[22]

There was some irony in the right complaining about ill-treatment here. For one, on the liberal side of the movie industry stood the Hollywood Anti-Nazi League, formed in April 1936, that contained some 5,000 mostly left-leaning actors and motion-picture employees, including Edward G. Robinson and Melvyn Douglas. In investigator Sullivan's terms, this organisation was itself subject to a large degree of vilification. In the late 1930s Sullivan's HUAC colleague John Metcalfe brought another poster into the hearings that stated that 'the Jewish Hollywood Anti-Nazi League controls communism in the motion picture industry – stars, writers, and artists are compelled to pay for communistic activities'. Before reading out the poster, Dies icily commented to his audience that 'we find that many of those who are talking the loudest about racial and religious hatred are silent on the subject when it comes to class hatred'.[23] Jews and their allies not being able to take criticism of communism was the *real* problem to Dies, in short.

There was some sympathy from President Roosevelt and his administration towards those tarred with the Dies brush. In 1938, witness

J.B. Matthews, former chairman of the American League for Peace and Democracy, contended that communist organs were using celebrities as decoys for their propaganda. Among these, he claimed, was the ten-year-old Shirley Temple. Many in the administration had some fun with this – Secretary Harold Ickes for one guffawed that the committee had found 'dangerous communists in Hollywood, led by little Shirley Temple'.[24] By September 1941 Roosevelt himself was praising a cartoon in *The Washington Evening Star* that portrayed Charlie Chaplin holding a subpoena to testify before HUAC. In this amusing sketch, Charlie was depicted asking what he could teach these 'past masters' about comedy. Roosevelt also expressed amusement at a telegram he had received from an anonymous source in Connecticut that stated: 'Have just been reading book called Holy Bible. Has large circulation in this country. Written entirely by foreign born, mostly Jews. First part full of dangerous war mongering propaganda. Second condemns isolationists with fake story about Samaritan. Dangerous.'[25]

Charlie later gave his own explanation as to why he thought that HUAC had been after him. 'My prodigious sin,' he argued in 1964, 'was, and still is, being a non-conformist. Although I am not a Communist I refused to fall in line by hating them.' He found the description of the 'Committee on Un-American Activities – a dishonest phrase to begin with, elastic enough to wrap around the throat and strangle the voice of any American citizen whose honest opinion is a minority one'. Lastly, while he conceded he had 'never attempted to become an American citizen' he also pointed to the many Americans making a good living in Britain without becoming British subjects: 'The English have never bothered about it.' All in all, Charlie 'would say that in an atmosphere of powerful cliques and invisible governments I engendered a nation's antagonism and unfortunately lost the affection of the American public'.[26] With HUAC in full swing it was risky to be seen to be lionising the Soviet regime. That being said, during the Second World War Charlie certainly came perilously close to this.

Backing the Red Army

On 7 December 1941, 353 airplanes from Imperial Japan unleashed a surprise attack on the US naval base of Pearl Harbor, Hawaii. This resulted in the death of 2,403 Americans, with a further 1,178 wounded. After various declarations by the major powers, by 11 December America was at war with Germany, Italy and Japan. The US was now an ally of the Communist Soviet Union against the enemy that Charlie had so recently warned about on-screen – Nazi Germany. Whatever anti-leftist sentiment HUAC had been stirring up among the American public, for a time Charlie must have felt utterly vindicated. His most high-profile foreign policy analysis had been proven to be correct, and the world was now swinging behind this view. If he had left the propensity to make big political statements behind him at this point, all may have been well. But he did not.

On 18 May 1942, Chaplin gave a speech in aid of Russian War Relief in San Francisco. A last-minute addition to the bill after Joseph E. Davies, the American Ambassador to Moscow, had to pull out with laryngitis, Chaplin steadied his nerves with a couple of glasses of champagne. Listening to the previous speakers addressing the packed 10,000 crowd, Charlie had the general impression that 'our allies were strange bed fellows'. This, he felt, would not do. Taking to the stage wearing a rather incongruous black tie and dinner jacket, he began a speech with a single word: 'Comrades!' The audience erupted in laughter. When it subsided, Charlie added 'and I *mean* comrades'. More laughter followed, but then, applause. Later he claimed that he had merely used this address 'to clarify the air . . . I am naturally liberal', but it met with some scepticism.[27] Although billed to only speak for four minutes, Charlie launched into a forty-minute tirade. Addressing the 'many Russians here tonight', he told them that 'the way your countrymen are fighting and dying at this very moment, it is an honour and a privilege to call you comrades'. At the end of the speech, on the back of a very positive reception, he went all the way in: 'If I know Americans they like to do their *own* fighting. Stalin wants it, Roosevelt has called for it – so let's all call for it – let's open a second front now!'[28] At dinner after the speech, the actor John Garfield – later hauled before HUAC – told Charlie that he 'had a lot of courage'. 'This remark,' Charlie recalled, 'was disturbing.'[29]

Nonetheless, a few weeks later, on 22 July 1942, Chaplin gave a second speech over the telephone to Madison Square Park, New York. At this gathering of about 60,000 trade unionists and religious and civil society organisations, the audience heard speeches from Mayor La Guardia and Senator Mead backing American troops launching a second front in Europe. Charlie joined them in noting that 'on the battlefields of Russia democracy will live or die'. With 'the Germans . . . 35 miles from Caucasus, if the Caucasus is lost 95 per cent of the Russian oil is lost'. And then, Chaplin warned, 'the appeasers'll come out of their holes. They will want to make peace with a victorious Hitler.' For Charlie 'there is no safe strategy in war', and the time for American intervention was now.[30] Upton Sinclair wrote to congratulate him on this speech, but this was hardly a universal opinion.[31]

As the second front became delayed, Charlie stepped up the rhetoric even further. In October 1942 in a speech at Carnegie Hall, New York Charlie praised Roosevelt for having released the communist leader Earl Browder from prison. 'I want to thank the President of the United States. We the people, the artists, the bohemians and the great middle class are with you.' After 'bouquets were thrown at [labor leader] Harry Bridges' Charlie then went even further: as a result of the war 'they say communism must spread out all over the world. And I say, "so what?"' The extent to which this annoyed elements of the American right can be seen in the papers of Elizabeth Churchill Brown, a journalist later turned friend and political ally of Joseph McCarthy. Within her archive at Stanford is attached a pamphlet detailing Chaplin's Carnegie Hall address, with the phrase 'So what?' pointedly ringed in pen. Alongside this document stands a note criticising prominent publications for running the story: 'Charles Chaplin flew all the way from Hollywood to put on this bold display of scorn for our United States – why does *Life Magazine* persist in enhancing the career of people like this?' On another sheet of paper, she urged American business to pull out of backing any publications covering Charlie's controversial words, 'if Life continues to promote . . . "alien" Chaplin and food manufacturers still pay money to *Life* for advertising, can't retailers find other lines of merchandise to promote'.[32] The idea here was to make associating with Charlie politically toxic, an odd position to be in for a comedian.

In December 1942, an FBI source attended a dinner held 'in honor of Chaplin' at the Hotel Pennsylvania, New York City. The informant recorded that it was full of

> the typical fellow-traveller speeches: snide and would-be sub-tle cracks at our "capitalist" system, without however, any

outright subversive statements . . . plus the usual bleeding heart stuff about the valiant Soviet people and our own ill-housed, ill-clad and ill-nourished.

When Chaplin gave his own speech, he was reported as saying,

Thank God this war is sweeping away all this hypocrisy and nonsense about communism . . . The American people begin to understand the Russian purges and what a wonderful thing they were. Yes, in those purges the Communists did away with their Quislings and Lavals and if other nations had done the same there would not be the original Quislings and Lavals today.

This was strong stuff – even Martin Dies may have bristled at some of it. As for the climate that an allied victory should produce, Charlie declared,

I am not a Communist but I am proud to say that I feel pretty pro-Communist. I don't want any radical change – I want an evolutionary change. I don't want to go back to the days of rugged individualism . . . I don't want to go back to the days of 1929 . . . No, we must do better than that.[33]

This would eventually lead him in the progressive direction of Henry A. Wallace, then serving as Vice President under Roosevelt and his (very) unsuccessful 1948 campaign for the highest office in the land.

During the war, however, the Soviet–Chaplin bond of mutual appreciation remained suspiciously strong for some. On 25 August 1943, the Council of American–Soviet Friendship invited 500 guests for a screening of Kalatozov's film *The Unconquerable*, which told of the heroic efforts of the Red Army to defend Leningrad against the Nazi hordes. Chaplin made a speech there claiming that there was 'a good deal good in communism; we can use the good and segregate the bad'. Reassuring any watching FBI sources that 'I am just a clown, a retired humourist', he then jokingly enquired whether Rep. Martin Dies was in attendance. Ascertaining he was not, Chaplin then went on to note, 'I'm glad I'm not a ballet dancer – If I were, I might be banished from the country!' By April 1944 Charlie and his new wife Oona Chaplin were reported as learning Russian for a planned post-war visit.[34] And later that summer the Soviet Voks Agency – formed to promote cultural understanding between the Soviet Union and other nations – paid back Chaplin's previously kind words to the Russian people by praising him as a 'Militant Humanist' who 'Worships Love'. Solomon Mikhoels, Director of the Jewish Art Theater in Moscow, pointed to Chaplin's 'courage in taking an open anti-Fascist stand in his picture "The Great Dictator" and condemned the "mud-slinging, wholesale libel and slander" of the "Hearst-McCormick tabloid press"'.[35] If nothing else can be said for Chaplin, this was certainly not a man who sat on the political fence as the Second World War raged.

A by-product of all this was that the combination of his admiration for the Soviet war effort and the ire that this was increasingly garnering from American conservatives drew Charlie closer to American leftists as the conflict drew to a close. By 23 March 1945 *The Los Angeles Times* was reporting Charlie as on the guest list for a dinner at Dalton Trumbo's house that would pay tribute to Harry Bridges, the International Longshore and Warehouse Union leader.[36] Bridges was undeniably a divisive figure, and one who had been divorced even from the controversial Chaplin previously. Having split from supporting Roosevelt in the late 1930s, he had denounced the President as a warmonger prior to the American entry into the war. After the Nazi attack on the Soviet Union, however, Bridges demanded that America's employers increased productivity prior to America joining the effort against Hitler. Deportation proceedings against the Australian-born union leader began in 1939, and dragged on until 1955 – ten years after he had been naturalised as an American citizen. To attend a dinner held in honour of such a man, as the allies stood on the verge of victory and the Cold War seemed likely to become a lingering diplomatic issue into the period of peace, was undeniably a bold move from Charlie.

Joan Barry and the Cockney cad

As ever, the unhelpful backdrop to these political machinations were more tawdry revelations about Charlie's sex life. The specific difficulty here – as we will see with his political views and the Internal Security Act of 1950 (McCarran Act) – would stem from some pretty ambiguous legislation. In 1910, Congress had passed the White-Slave Traffic Act, known as the Mann Act after its sponsor the Republican Congressman James Robert Mann (of Illinois). This legislation prohibited the transportation across state lines of 'any woman or girl for the purpose of prostitution or debauchery, or for any other immoral purpose'. The last of these three descriptions was vague enough to capture almost any sexual act – consensual or otherwise – and certainly bad news for someone like Charlie. Although motivated by the Progressive era desire to tackle the existence of open red light districts in many American cities (and women being transported between states to work in them), there had been a distinctly racial dimension to this early twentieth-century crackdown. To give one example, the African American World Heavyweight boxing champion Jack Johnson would be successfully prosecuted under the Mann Act ostensibly for having sex with his Caucasian wife. In the era of 'separate but equal' such activities (and those with the other white women Johnson would sleep with after his fights) were given a directly criminal outlet. Vague notions of 'immorality' within Mann became a further recourse to crack down on miscegenation – illegal in the majority of American states in any case.

Crucially, for the caucasian Charlie Chaplin, the Mann Act also criminalised anyone 'who shall knowingly procure or obtain . . . any ticket or tickets, or any form of transportation or evidence of the right thereto, to be used by any woman or girl in interstate or foreign commerce'. It was here that the first legal problem with a woman named Joan Barry would begin. Charlie was involved with many volatile women, a product both of the youth he tended to favour and the cruelty of treatment he could meet out. Yet Joan Barry was exceptional even among Chaplin's partners. She had been born Mary Louise Gribble in 1920 to a former soldier father who had committed suicide while his daughter was still in the womb. Moving to Los Angeles and renaming herself, Barry took to shoplifting when she failed to make it as an actress. She began or attempted affairs with several wealthy men, including the oil magnate J. Paul Getty. During the Getty affair, his associate A.C. Blumenthal – who had witnessed Chaplin's iodine-coloured penis in a New York hotel room in 1925 – took to virtually pimping Barry around Hollywood. After Spencer Tracy proved uninterested, Joan was introduced to Charlie Chaplin.

As described by her later Attorney, the red-haired Joan was 'an attractive girl of limited intelligence' who had been on the

Chaplin payroll ($75 a week) since the summer of 1941.[37] Charlie had been attracted by what he called her 'upper regional domes immensely expansive', but discovered that her acting range and her nasal voice limited how far he could use her professionally. An affair began soon after and in the build-up to his Carnegie Hall speech of October 1942 Charlie paid for train tickets for Joan and her mother to come to watch. Later FBI files recorded that 'Chaplin took Barry to dinner in New York several times following his appearance in New York on October 16, 1942, at the Artists Front to Win the War Rally. Thereafter, Barry returned to the Waldorf Astoria apartment of Chaplin, where the alleged immoral acts took place.'[38] The deed done, Chaplin then gave Joan $300 to return to Los Angeles. For the remainder of 1942 the two had 'numerous trysts' – at least according to the FBI – although Charlie always asserted that their last encounter had been in the first half of that year. Throughout this time Joan was clearly mentally unstable (no doubt possibly exacerbated by Charlie's general treatment of women). On the night of 23 December 1942, she appeared at Charlie's house brandishing a gun, threatening to kill herself because Charlie had forsaken her for another, Oona O'Neill.

In February 1944, the Federal Grand Jury in Los Angeles indicted Chaplin under the terms of the Mann Act. This had largely been instigated at the behest of the FBI and Hoover's orders to 'expedite [the] investigation' of Chaplin's activities in this regard. In a trial lasting two weeks, Charlie was acquitted under all charges. He admitted supplying the tickets by which Joan had travelled between New York and Los Angeles, but the prosecution could not prove that there had been any immoral purpose behind the action. 'I believe in American justice,' exclaimed a jubilant Chaplin after the verdict. 'I have had a very fair trial.'[39]

Yet it would not be the last. In June 1943 Barry had also filed a civil suit against Chaplin, claiming he was the father of her baby Carol Ann, born four months later. For Charlie's eighteen-year-old new wife Oona it must have been a horrendous ordeal, albeit a fate she would have to get used to. Indeed, if Georgia Hale is to be believed this could have been an even more traumatic time for the young Oona. In the late 1970s Georgia wrote to Ivor Montagu telling him that 'the night before [Charlie] married Oona [in June 1943] he came to my house and begged me to leave the country with him. But I knew it wasn't right – not with him in his situation.

So at three in the morning he left and how sad it all was.'[40] True or not, the second Barry trial to settle the paternity of her daughter would rival Lita Grey's 1927 divorce papers in terms of public embarrassment and reputational damage for Charlie. In one sense, this was not actually his fault and more the product of a flimsy case. After all, Joan Barry's Attorney Joseph Scott had a fairly big problem: blood tests proved Chaplin was not the father of the baby in question. Carol Ann had been born blood type B while Joan was A and Charlie O. These tests were inadmissible under Californian state law, but they were undeniably an inconvenience to his case. And so unable to win on the science, Scott had to win on the theatrics.

To do so Scott wound back the clock to the same kind of tactics used by Lita's legal team. He declared that 'you [that is, the Jury] have promised me you would not hold it against her because she has fallen by the wayside and surrendered to this fellow's embraces'. After all, 'Chaplin is a master mechanic at his trade, a master mechanic at the art of seduction.' If Peter Ackroyd's estimate of more than 2,000 sexual partners for Chaplin is true, there may be something in this. According to Scott, 'He has violated this girl so many times he can't even remember himself – he talks about it as if he would about ham and eggs.' Really twisting the knife, Scott continued: 'This fellow is just a little runt of a Svengali . . . This fellow doesn't lie like a gentleman – he lies like a cheap cockney cad.' Certainly Joan and Chaplin were 'both equally guilty – only Chaplin is a man old enough to be her father. At his age you'd think he'd have something better to do.'[41] Tugging at the heartstrings of the seven women and five men on the jury, he declared that 'all Joan wanted was for this man to give the child a name'. Imitating his client, he shouted, 'Please [Scott banged the table], please [he pounded again] for my baby.'[42]

This was a trial of mutual mud-slinging. Joan had apparently begged Charlie to marry her at which point her intended beau had replied: 'How can you be so blatant and look me square in the face, and say such a thing, knowing the kind of life you have been living.'[43] 'That', the judge murmured disapprovingly, 'is a bit far from the swimming pool'. Yet the Getty affair and at least two others initially seemed to sway the jury's mind. After four and a half hours of deliberation on 4 January and then another day on 5 January 1945 the jury returned deadlocked – seven votes to five in Chaplin's favour. Barry's legal team insisted on a retrial that, after similar theatrics from Barry's team, cast its verdict on 17 April: this time nine votes to three against Charlie. This meant that Charlie had to pay $75 a week in support of Carol Ann (ironically the same 'salary' he had paid her mother). Whatever Charlie's involvement, the Barry case remains tragic. In 1953, *Time Magazine* reported that Joan had been 'admitted to Patton State Hospital . . . after she was found walking the streets barefoot, carrying a pair of baby sandals and a child's ring, and murmuring: "This is magic."'[44] As per the court's ruling, Charlie continued to pay maintenance for Carol Ann until her twenty-first birthday in 1964.

The financial penalty of $75 a week was neither here nor there to Chaplin.[45] But the reputational damage the two trials created was immense. As Chuck Maland points out, 'Chaplin's *legal* difficulties in the Barry affair, however much they soured him on the American legal system, had little effect on his star image.' On the other hand, 'the press coverage of those legal difficulties greatly effected his declining star image'.[46] This case brought Charlie the ire of two gossip columnists in particular – Florabel Muir of the *New York Daily News*, and Hedda Hopper of the *Los Angeles Times* who both ended up testifying against Charlie and passing on information to the FBI. While Muir seems to have been more motivated by an antipathy to Chaplin's supposed immorality, for Hedda Hopper the politics were vital. Hopper, a Republican, hated both Chaplin's progressive politics prior to 1939 and his desire to get American embroiled in the conflict about to break out in Europe. He also just was not terribly interested in feeding gossip columnists morsels of information for their columns, which made him eminently discardable without fear of losing a source. In early June 1943 Hopper published an article ostensibly about the Barry–Chaplin case, but that segued into various attacks on the man. Hopper wrote, 'It's been implied by many people here and elsewhere that a genius should have special privileges, [and] Chaplin's had many.' These included 'making his home, fortune and reputation in America, without ever making any attempt to become a citizen of our country'. When given the opportunity to contribute to the 'motion picture relief fund home, he didn't'. And, rolling out an old lie, while 'Jews should be proud of their heritage', apparently Chaplin was not.[47] As with America, it was rather difficult for Charlie to feel proud of an entity of which he was not a part.

All in all, by Chuck Maland's summary, 'the dominant press' came out against Chaplin 'strongly'. The *Chicago Tribune* gave front-page headlines to the case, and the moments of peak coverage were almost uniformly negative. Meanwhile, *Newsweek* headlines such as 'Chaplin as Villain' and *Time* magazine's assertion that the Barry case 'fitted into a familiar pattern' of 'unassailable arrogance and . . . affairs with a succession of pretty young protégés' did not help Charlie's declining image. The left-wing intelligentsia such as Rob Wagner's *Script* and the out-and-out communist-backing *Daily Worker* tried to re-frame Chaplin as a political victim rather than immoral leach, but this was an uphill battle by this point.[48] Crucially, his next film, a daring artistic experiment, would not serve to correct this.

Monsieur Verdoux

On 11 April 1947 Chaplin released *Monsieur Verdoux* – the first film since 1923 where he played no version of the Tramp character. Beginning with a shot of Verdoux's grave, the title character claimed in a voiceover that

> for thirty years I was an honest bank clerk until the Depression of 1930 – in which year I found myself unemployed. It was then I became occupied with liquidating members of the opposite sex. This I did as strictly a business enterprise to support a home and family.

If the *Great Dictator* had hinted at the type of non-tramp film Chaplin would make, *Verdoux* squarely smacked his audience across the face with the notion. Murdering widows and other financially independent women in order to steal their money was not something the cartoonish, ultimately sympathetic tramp would ever have countenanced, whatever petty crimes he occasionally engaged in.

The theme of the film, eventually played out in Verdoux's memorable courtroom speech at the end, is the similarity between one mass murderer's individually amoral decisions and those that capitalism per se encourages. As Verdoux said when in the dock, 'One murder makes a villain, millions a hero. Numbers sanctify.' In such an abysmal world, why not become a killer? Earlier in the movie Verdoux's wife reads the newspaper headlines to him: 'Depression worldwide, unemployment spreads to all nations.' 'Enough!' replies the killer Verdoux. 'It's too depressing.' Before being led to his execution at the end of the film, Verdoux is interviewed by a newspaper reporter eager to learn about his 'tragic example of a life of crime'. Verdoux simply replies that he did not 'see how anyone can be an example in these criminal times'. For some, this was something of a cop-out from an actor-director whose own personal sense of morality was skewed. The First World War, say, did not justify getting a barely sixteen-year-old Lita Grey pregnant; nor did the Depression justify associating with types who wanted the red flag flying over the White House. But the 1947 film was undeniably powerful even if it contained a central irony that Chaplin perhaps did not consider: Verdoux's victims were all ultimately undermined by not using that most capitalist of institution, keeping their money in a bank.

On 12 April 1947 Charlie entered the Grand Ballroom of the Gotham Hotel in New York – ostensibly to publicise the film. The atmosphere of this press conference can be gleaned from Chaplin's introductory remarks, and indeed the first question he was asked. After a brief smattering of welcoming applause, Charlie addressed journalists in a tense voice: 'Thank you, ladies and gentlemen of the press. I am not going to waste your time. I shall say, "Proceed with the butchery!"' The first voice sprung up, 'Could you answer a direct question: are you a communist?' Chaplin confirmed, 'I am not a communist.' The journalist shot back: 'A communist sympathiser?' Charlie hedged: 'A communist sympathiser . . . that has to be qualified again.' Charlie then proceeded to trot out his usual, and not in itself unreasonable, defence – that during the war he had sympathised with the Soviet Union because at the time they were America's ally.

In such a hostile atmosphere, the film met with a threefold disaster: organised protests outside theatres, poor reviews from many critics, and limited financial success at best on the American market. The first of these saw war veterans, particularly Catholic ex-servicemen, express widespread discontent at Charlie's recent activities. This would not prove an isolated incident. In February 1953, American Legion pickets would appear outside theatres showing Chaplin's nostalgic and utterly politically uncontroversial *Limelight*, too. In an open letter to Chaplin, one Legion district leader stated that his opposition was based on the fact that he had 'given aid and comfort to 11 organizations officially cited as Communist sympathizers'.

Placards were carried outside theatres, declaring that 'your box office dollar helps Charles Chaplin spread Red propaganda'. In 1953 a reluctant theatre manager interviewed by the press was able to at least comment that 'people like the picture'.[49] With *Monsieur Verdoux* back in 1947 it was not even clear that this was true.

As for the 1947 reviews, *The New York Times* found *Verdoux* 'slow – tediously slow – in many stretches and thus monotonous. The bursts of comic invention fit uncomfortably into the grim fabric and the clarity of the philosophy does not begin to emerge until the end.'[50] London was a little kinder, but many agreed that Charlie had gone too far with his latest piece of moralising. Still, ever the entrepreneur, Charlie sought to use the controversy surrounding the film to generate business. Adverts for the film called it 'the most controversial motion picture of our time', a claim given credence when its opening coincided with talk of Charlie being hauled before HUAC. Speaking to reporters, Charlie called it 'no ironical coincidence that my comedy also opens in the National Capital less than 24 hours after Rep. Thomas begins his probe into asserted Communistic film activities'. After writing to the committee and declaring that he was not a communist, Charlie did not have appear before it. But the suggestion that he may do so clearly harmed him artistically and financially.

Charlie had gone into *Verdoux* expecting to make at least $12 million gross. In truth, this was always ambitious, and would have more than doubled receipts seen from *The Great Dictator*. Given the box-office kicking that Charlie had taken in his last major artistic experiment – *A Woman of Paris* almost a quarter of a century earlier – taking a great leap forward financially while not playing the Little Tramp seemed a long-shot at best. After Joan Barry, perhaps the antics of a loveable underdog would have been given short shrift anyway. In the end, the film barely covered costs, pulling in less than $2 million worldwide.

Verdoux cemented Chaplin's political enemies against him. But it also bought him the loyalty of some new friends. The German-Jewish émigré novelist Lion Feuchtwanger (who had settled in Los Angeles in 1941) was one kind voice. Writing to Charlie, he told him that *Verdoux* would

> cause hundreds of thousands to think, it will improve many people and will make them more intelligent and better aware of

what is going on. Your film is a great ethical lecture, and makes the relationship between crime and the general economical situation clearer than a thousand essays. In your own way you have put into practice the principle that many a philosopher and writer adhered to: "By laughter may we improve the world."[51]

After Chaplin replied that he was 'happy to tell you that picture passed Hays office and New York censors without a cut', Feuchtwanger later told him that he was 'convinced that Monsieur Verdoux is not only the best picture of the year but of the whole decade'.[52]

Another similar case was the Austrian composer Hanns Eisler – who, like Feuchtwanger, had fled Nazi Germany on account of his Jewish background. Eisler would be hauled twice to face questioning under the HUAC hearings in the 1940s and eventually left America entirely in 1948. The two families were close. Oona Chaplin wrote to Eisler's wife Lou after the New York premiere of *Monsieur Verdoux* to report that the film had

got a lot of bad – really bad – reviews – even the good ones were not very good – this was a great blow to Charlie – and to me – naturally. Also there has been a lot of trash about Charlie's not being a citizen and being a communist and not helping 'our boys' in the war. He had a mass interview of about seventy five reporters this afternoon – It was broadcast all over the radio – And they really came to slaughter him. And I must tell you that one of the questions they asked was 'Are you a friend of Hanns Eisler?' Charlie said that you were close friends and then they asked if Hanns was a communist and Charlie said he didn't think so – that Hanns was a great musician and not in politics. Then of course they said – 'well if he were a communist would you still be friends with him?' And Charlie said 'of course.' Then they said 'Well if he were a spy would you be friends?' So Charlie said they were being absurd and that ended that.[53]

Unlike Chaplin, Eisler had indeed been a card-carrying communist. Prior to the Nazi seizure of power in Germany Eisler had taught at the Marxist Worker's School in Berlin, and thereby seen his musical compositions banned after Hitler became Chancellor in

1933. His brother Gerhart had been a liaison between the Comintern and communist parties in China (1929–31) and America (1933–6), and his sister Ruth a German communist turned HUAC informant (including on her brothers). Even with an acknowledged communist, however, the FBI still went to the trouble of recording Hanns's collection of books, which included *Das Kapital*, the Marx–Engels *Letters* and several works by Lenin.[54] According to a 1947 FBI report, Eisler had associated with 'many Communist sympathisers, including Charles Chaplin, Bertolt Brecht, Clifford Odets and others'.[55] This sympathy allegedly extended to Chaplin offering to throw a benefit party for Gerhart in 1946, and to lend Hanns money should he need to flee the country (although Hanns eventually found the funds elsewhere).[56] This was intended more to help out friends in need than to assert Chaplin's conversion to communism, and even the FBI spy reporting to Hoover noted

> the only conversation that he recalled concerned the projected appearance of Chaplin before the House Committee on un-American Activities. There was no political discussion at all and [redacted] stated that he had no information concerning any Communist connections on the part of Chaplin other than his association with Hanns Eisler and what he has read in the press.[57]

This would no doubt have included a January 1948 article in the Republic-leaning journal *The Argonaut*, which was also clipped by the HUAC committee keeping tabs on Chaplin. Pointing to a telegram Chaplin had sent Pablo Picasso trying to get him to speak out against Eisler's deportation, *The Argonaut* noted Charlie's 'conception of human morality is low, and almost, if not quite, everything else is low also'. They continued: 'Whether [Charlie] takes his orders from Moscow, as most of our Communists do, we do not profess to know. But he is evidently a partisan of Moscow, and sympathetically disposed towards all of the Politburo decrees.' Like Eisler therefore, 'Is it not time to deport Charlie Chaplin as an undesirable alien?'[58] The Eisler association clearly helped close the noose around Chaplin. Anti-Chaplin Senators in D.C. later latched on to Charlie's comments that he was 'proud' to be Eisler's friend, with Harry Cain reading out 'with the greatest feeling of revulsion' Charlie's telegram to Picasso.

This was a situation cemented by those willing to testify against him. During a meeting between the two in Malibu, Eisler told a man named Jack Bungay (who was also acquainted with Ayn Rand) about Chaplin's promise to help Eisler 'get him out of the country'. Also present at one of these gatherings was Edward Mosk, Attorney and active member of the Progressive Party under whose banner Henry A. Wallace ran for President in 1948, with Charlie's support. As an aside, Bungay certainly pressed the right buttons by mentioning Mosk, for the notion of a Hollywood cabal behind Wallace was fairly ingrained. In December 1946 HUAC Chief Counsel Ernie Adamson tried to subpoena Chaplin 'to hear more about reports that motion picture money is financing a third party, tentatively named "The People's Front" which has an eye running Henry Wallace for President'.[59] In any event, while Bungay admitted 'this information may be of little worth' he had previously turned a list of attendees at similar leftist meetings over to the journalist Hedda Hopper (with the understanding that she would inform Hoover at the FBI). Equally crucially, Bungay went to great efforts to note that although he had mixed with communists, 'I have never been a sympathiser or a member of the Communist party – merely a by-stander.'[60] It may have been for the Hoovers or McGranerys to frame Chaplin as a communist sympathiser in a top-down sense, but this approach always required bottom-up adherents.

In December 1947, Eric Johnston, President of the Motion Picture Association of America (the re-branded organisation formerly led by Will Hays), issued what became known as the Waldorf Statement after a meeting of forty-eight leading film executives, including Louis B. Mayer, Sam Goldwyn and Paramount's Barney Balaban. After the so-called 'Hollywood Ten' of leftist screenwriters (perhaps most famously, after a 2015 film covering his life, including Dalton Trumbo) and directors had refused to testify before HUAC, the Waldorf Statement attempted to distance such figures from the 'respectable' end of the movie industry. The Hollywood Ten were immediately discharged from their work at the signatories studios (without compensation) until 'such time as [the accused writer] is acquitted or purged himself of contempt and declares under oath that he is not a Communist'. The Waldorf Statement further committed each studio head to take 'positive action' to tackle the 'subversive and disloyal elements in Holly-wood', including not 'knowingly employ[ing] a Communist or a member of any party or group which advocates the overthrow of the government of the United States'. This policy, they claimed, would not 'be swayed by hysteria or intimidation from any source' and admitted that taking such steps involved 'dangers and risks'. But to preserve 'a free screen' change was needed. Finally, they requested 'Congress to enact legislation to assist American indus-try to rid itself of subversive, disloyal elements', not least to protect the '30,000 loyal Americans employed in Hollywood'. Chaplin's vagaries – the type of loose political talk he had been able to throw around in the 1920s and 1930s – would no longer do in this atmo-sphere. The question was, could he adjust?

The pressure intensifies

By this stage Chaplin had two options: denounce his friends and publicly renounce some of his apparent political views, or leave America – at least until the heat died down. Some suggested that he should go down the former route and apply for Ameri-can citizenship to show his 'loyalty'. Here communist leader Earl Browder had allegedly advised him not to do so 'since it would raise the whole question of his being an alien, attacks on his per-sonal life, and all sort of things that might lead to his deporta-tion'.[61] He was never much disposed to becoming an American in any case. By April 1948 he was therefore clearly exploring the latter option, and duly sat down for an interview with Inspec-tor John Boyd of the Immigration and Naturalization Service to determine his eligibility for a re-entry permit as a British subject should he travel abroad. Since many of the statements made dur-ing this interrogation were pertinent to the ongoing FBI inves-tigation into his politics, edited highlights of this meeting were passed over to the Bureau. Asked whether he had ever made any donations to front organisations of the Communist Party, Chaplin gave the reasonable explanation to Boyd, 'I don't know what con-stitutes a front organization of the Communist Party.'[62] Denying membership and direct financial contribution to the Communist Party, he did, however, make the odd tactical slip. Asked about his pro-Russian speeches in the early 1940s, he remarked that 'during the war, everybody was more or less a Communist sympathizer . . . I have always felt grateful because they helped us to get ready and prepare our own way of life.' When asked whether he had ever contributed to the Russia-American Society for Medical Aid to Russia, he replied, 'I might have done. I don't know. When I say that, I really shouldn't say that. To my knowledge, I don't think so.' Equally, 'he may have' made a donation to the National Council of American–Soviet Friendship. The explanation here was understandable, but not the type of thing likely to assuage his enemies: 'We get a million things here for all sort of donations. We don't carry a list of what is a Communist front or what isn't a Communist front.' By 1947, however, the FBI, HUAC and others had produced very clear lists along such lines.

During this interrogation, Chaplin was asked his impressions of both communism per se, and recent actions by the Soviet regime. After a Soviet-backed coup by the Communist Party of Czechoslovakia in February 1948, Chaplin stated he did not 'know much about the situation'. Yet, 'from what I read in the papers, I still maintain I don't think Russia has done a damn thing. That is my own personal belief.' Arguing 'no soldiers were there, [t]here was no bloodshed', he believed 'the press is trying to create a war . . . with Russia'. Among certain elements of the right, that may well have been true. Yet Russian co-ordination behind the Czechoslovak coup was clear: Andrei Zhdanov, Stalin's then heir apparent, had previously remarked that Soviet pressure had ensured 'the complete victory of the working class over the bourgeoisie in every East European land – except Czechoslovakia, where the power contest still remains undecided'.[63] The premeditation of the Soviet regime to ferment a takeover was therefore clear. In such a light, Chaplin's predilection to favour Stalin's government, particularly where he had no evidence either way, did not endear him to his American hosts.

Quite apart from his controversial personal life, politically Chaplin had been unable to move with the times. The American left had previously been divided between those progressives who refused to denounce Stalin (including Chaplin), and the anti-Stalinist left who very much did. During the war, as a result of the purges, the Nazi–Soviet Pact and a growing belief that the USSR was a militaristic power hell bent on expansionism, many

American liberals shifted their position from pro-Stalin progressivism to opposition to his leadership. While Harry Truman's combination of New Deal liberalism and an anti-Soviet foreign policy proved just about enough to win him the 1948 Presidential election, the former Vice-President Henry Wallace maintained the former more optimistic vision of what Stalin 'could' be, which informed his Progressive Party campaign that year, and earned Chaplin's support in doing so.

All this made the job for those in Congress who wanted action taken against this apparently 'red' foreigner much easier. Yet the electoral cycle also played its part. One moderate voice on the HUAC against the bombast of Chairman Martin Dies had been Jerry Voorhis, a Congressman from California's twelfth district since 1937. As Gellerman noted, 'There is a reasonable quality about Voorhis that has no place in a Dies report. Dies sees things in terms of black and white, whereas Voorhis insists that there are intermediate shades.'[64] For Voorhis – who published his own minority report opposing much of the tenor of the direction of HUAC – the Dies Committee was 'in danger of becoming an agency which abrogates to itself the right to censor people's ideas. That in itself is un-American.'[65] Once it became clear that his impact was ever diminishing, in 1943 Voorhis resigned from the Committee. Three years later Voorhis would lose his seat in Congress to an up-and-coming former naval officer then stationed in Baltimore, Richard Milhous Nixon. Nixon's campaign alleged that Voorhis's links to the labor federation of the Congress of Industrial Organizations (CIO) meant that he was pro-communist. This was a fudge at best – while it is true that the CIO Political Action Committee (CIO-PAC) was seen by some as a communist front, it had actually refused to back Voorhis. In fact, the National Citizen's Political Action Committee (NCPAC) that did back Voorhis was not only open to those outside the trade union movement, but included Ronald Reagan among its members. But blurring the CIO-PAC and NCPAC in people's minds certainly worked, and in November 1946 Richard Nixon won the seat for the Republicans by more than 15,000 votes (overturning a similar majority for Voorhis from 1944).

As a freshman, Congressman Nixon would launch his career on the back of the Alger Hiss case. After a *Time* magazine journalist had named more than half a dozen government officials including Hiss as communist spies, Nixon pressured Hiss to admit he was secretly working for the Soviet regime. This Hiss never conceded, although he would eventually be sent to prison for perjuring himself in a civil suit when he tried to clear his name. But the Hiss case showed that there was political capital and a national reputation to be gained for those able to identify the communists hiding in plain sight among America's elites.

In May 1952 Richard Nixon wrote a letter to Hedda Hopper. Six months away from being the Vice-Presidential candidate on Dwight Eisenhower's 1952 Republican ticket, Nixon told her, 'I agree with you that the way the Chaplin case has been handled has been a disgrace for years. Unfortunately, we aren't able to do too much about it when the top decisions are made by the likes of Acheson and McGranery. You can be sure, however, that I will keep my eye on the case and possibly after January we will be able to work with an administration which will apply the same rules to Chaplin as they do to ordinary citizens.'[66] Evidently, as we will see, he should have had more faith in McGranery.

This was something of a bug-bear for Hopper, who had not dropped her anger from the Joan Barry case. In April 1947, just as Chaplin was trying to launch *Monsieur Verdoux* to a sceptical public, Hopper had received an advance copy of *The Story of the FBI* from J. Edgar Hoover himself. Thanking him for the book and endorsing its red-baiting content, Hopper had replied,

> I'd like to run every one of those rats out of the country and start with Charlie Chaplin. In no other country in the world would he be allowed to do what he's done. And now that he's finished another picture, and Miss Pickford is back in NY helping him sell it, what are we doing about that? It's about time we stood up to be counted. You give me the material and I'll blast.[67]

This request for journalistic content went even further in August 1947 when, before a public event, Hopper wrote to Hoover asking him for

> some facts to hurl back at the angry mob in the audience who is going to ask me very embarrassing questions . . . Naturally I won't be able to accuse certain stars of being Communists, as

even those who are deny it, always have and always will . . . [But] I feel that I can call upon your friendship for help. I know you're just as anxious to rid the country of our enemies as I am.[68]

Even if Hoover did not always have legal proof of the wrongdoing of figures such as Chaplin, he was able to use sympathetic figures in the press to blacken their reputation in the public's mind. Other than $500 allegedly donated in 1934, the only 'evidence' of a financial contribution from Chaplin to the Communist Party was when 'Hedda Hopper, Hollywood columnist, wrote in her column of December 27 1943, as follows: "From things I have learned, Charlie Chaplin . . . contributed $25,000 to the Communist cause and $100 to the Red Cross.'[69] Feeding journalists information to put into the public record was a well-worn tactic by those wishing to discredit the left.

The third element necessary was to get politicians to use these newspaper columns to frame speeches that would add an official veneer to any accusations. By the late 1940s this was falling into place. For one, on 13 May 1949 the single-term Senator from Washington, Harry Cain, spoke in a debate on 'Communist Activities among Aliens and National Groups'. After Senator Pat McCarran had brought forward a bill on the subject of deporting 'subversives' – more on this in our next chapter – Cain 'presented the case of an alien who has been guilty of activities which are designed to injure the welfare and international position of the United States. He is, of course, Charles Chaplin.' For Cain, Chaplin's 'public utterances provide a series of eulogies for the Stalinist dictatorship but . . . I have never been able to find a single kind word for the United States.' The latter half of this claim was nonsense. Conversing with the very leftist Ivor Montagu, Charlie claimed, 'I'd never exchange one foot of my place here for all of England. I love it here. I love California, I love its climate and I admire the American people.' Even the communist-sympathetic Montagu conceded that 'the United States has opened its arms wide to you, loved you and enriched you. No wonder you feel the way you do.'[70] This was the general tenor of several of Charlie's public utterances. But claiming otherwise became standard fare in elements of the anti-Chaplin press, and this provided the political cover to go big for freshman politicians. Cain read Ed Sullivan in *The New York News* who had regularly been out for Chaplin: 'Don't tell us, Charlie, that you are reluctant to discuss politics. During the war, instead of entertaining the troops or our wounded, you delivered nothing but political speeches for Russia, demanding a second front.'[71] Cain springboarded from these comments to scornfully assert that he was 'sure that the men who gave their lives on the Normandy beaches . . . must be grateful to Charles Chaplin that he made speeches on behalf of a second front'.[72]

By the early 1950s Charlie's enemies were closing in on him. Before we deal with his bitter departure, it may be worth indulging in some alternative history, however. In October 1952 Edward G. Robinson published an article 'How the Reds Made a Sucker Out of Me' in *American Legion Magazine*.[73] If we want an indication of the alternative path that Chaplin could have travelled in the 1940s and 1950s then this serves a very useful purpose. Like Chaplin, Robinson had been through the wringer of public opinion. A pacifist and supporter of Socialist Party candidate Eugene Debs in 1920, Robinson experienced his big cinematic breakthrough in the Warner Brothers' film, *Little Caesar* (1931). As Hollywood steadily moved to the right, Robinson became a fan of Roosevelt's New Deal and was, according to Steven J. Ross, 'not a radical trying to replace capitalism with socialism', but rather a moderate 'left-liberal'.[74] Joining the Hollywood Anti-Nazi League and later the Hollywood Democratic Committee, Robinson's politics were not so dissimilar to Chaplin's. He certainly had a far more stereotypically 'patriotic' Second World War, selling war bonds, donating $100,000 to the USO, appearing at many US-government-sponsored rallies and becoming the first movie star to entertain the troops after D-Day.[75] Yet, as with Charlie, Robinson's other activities were viewed as innately suspicious. Being part of an open letter sent to Congress and the President calling for the boycott of all German products until the country ended its aggression towards the Jews and other countries, Robinson joined other signatories such as Harry and Jack Warner, Groucho Marx, Henry Fonda and James Cagney in falling under varying degrees of suspicion. Calls for universal health care did not endear Robinson to the right either, nor did his demanding equality for African Americans after the war. By the 1940s the FBI was keeping regular tabs on Robinson, and in May 1945 sent a memo to the White House naming Robinson as one of fifty movie stars accused of being a communist. In October and December 1950 Robinson appeared before HUAC to deny communist sympathy, but the accusation was enough to damage his career irreparably.

So, like Chaplin, what was to be done in such a bind? Extend the hand or extend the middle finger? In the aforementioned pages of the *American Legion Magazine*, Robinson repeated a statement from a previous HUAC interrogation: 'It is not easy for a man to admit to having been a dupe, but I've had to admit it.' The sum of Robinson's experiences told of 'how an honest liberal was tricked into keeping company with scoundrels with ulterior motives who masqueraded as supporters of decent causes'. Joining the Hollywood Anti-Nazi League had been 'grist to the communist mill', donating to the Committee to Aid Agricultural Workers in the late 1930s – the product of being moved 'by John Steinbeck's book *Grapes of Wrath*' – was unwittingly to have given to a body where 'the communists have control'. In retrospect, Robinson noted, 'I would still try to help any underprivileged group but I would be careful about the company I did it in.' Instead, the communists had been 'very successful in making "herd" thinkers out of a substantial section of Americans who wanted to be liberals. Given an idea that sounded sympathetic or tolerant, we were prone to accept it blindly. I did and so did many others.'

Robinson's charges against his former fellow travellers were not completely without foundation. His view that communist-sympathising Americans 'may worry about the deportation of a comrade from the United States, but they are unmoved by the forcible evacuation of tens of thousands in the [Soviet] satellite countries' arguably held some truth. The same people who 'scream for civil liberties in America' could indeed rarely be heard 'protest[ing] the absence of all legality, due process, judicial freedom in Russia'. But despite such charges, as Ross notes, neither this article nor his HUAC testimony managed to restore him to public favour. Robinson declared in 1952, 'I have one allegiance and one allegiance only; I am not a communist; I have not been; I never will be. *I am an American.*'[76] Chaplin would take a rather different course. In the end, both would see that their careers had been hit beyond the point of possible redemption.

Notes

1 Clawson to Parker, 24 March 1972, White House Central Files [WHCF], Richard Nixon Presidential Library [RNPL].
2 Madison Square Garden Speech, 29 November 1939, Sam Houston Research Centre, Liberty, Texas [SHRC]/Martin Dies Papers [DIES] Box 157 File 30.

3   William Gellerman, *Martin Dies* (New York, 1944), 33.

4   Ibid., 41.

5   Ibid., 40–1.

6   Ibid., 48.

7   Madison Square Garden Speech, 29 November 1939, SHRC/DIES, Box 157 File 30.

8   Block booking was the system whereby studios could sell multiple films to theatres, often unseen, in order to keep production and distribution costs down. Often hitting independent theatres hard, it was eventually outlawed in 1948.

9   Beaumont Motion Picture Council to Dies [undated], and L.G. Pounders to Dies, 20 March 1935, SHRC/DIES Box 4 File 25.

10 Mrs Harry Gordon to Dies, 11 March 1935, SHRC/DIES Box 4 File 25.

11 HUAC Hearings, 75th Congress on H. Res 242, 1938/vol. 1, 547.

12 Ibid., 1938/vol. 1, 540–1.

13 Ibid., 1938/vol. 3, 2,354.

14 Ibid., 1939/vol. 5, 3,581.

15 Gellerman, *Martin Dies*, 97.

16 Ibid., 177.

17 Ibid., 166.

18 Martin Dies, *The Trojan Horse in America* (Washington, D.C., 1940).

19 Kevin Starr, *Embattled Dreams: California in War and Peace, 1940–1950* (Oxford, 2003), 286. In a September 1938 speech, Harry Warner criticised 'certain bigots' – presumably Dies – who 'whisper that Hollywood is run by -isms'. See Warner to Roosevelt, 27 September 1938, FDRPL/OF/73.

20 Cited in Goldwyn to Dies, 29 May 1940, SHRC/DIES Box 89 File 53.

21 Thomas Doherty, *Hollywood and Hitler 1933–1939*, (New York, 2013), 231.

22 Ibid.

23 HUAC Hearings, 75th Congress on H. Res 242, 1938/vol. 3, 2,367–8.

24 *Milwaukee Journal*, 24 December 1939.

25 *Daytona Beach Morning Journal*, 17 September 1941.

26 Charlie Chaplin, *My Autobiography* (London, 2003), 458.

27 Chaplin Interview with the Immigration and Naturalization Service, 17 April 1948, within FBI/CCF File 8.

28 Chaplin, *My Autobiography*, 402–3; my emphasis.

29 Ibid., 404.

30 Ibid., 404–6.

31 Sinclair to Chaplin, 18 August 1942, LLBI/CCF Box 48.

32 Undated typescript within HOOV/ECB Box 18 Folder 13; emphasis in original.

33 'Communist Activities: Charlie Chaplin' Memorandum, 4 December 1942, FBI/CCF Part 7.

34 *Washington Times Herald*, 6 April 1944, FBI/CCF Part 6.

35 Memorandum for Mr Buckley, 18 May 1944, FBI/CCF Part 5.

36 Cited within McGranery's typescript simply titled 'Charles Spencer Chaplin', 14 July 1962, LOCDC/JMG Box 98 Folder 6.

37 *Milwaukee Journal*, 29 December 1944.

38 Charles Spencer Chaplin typescript, 14 July 1962, FBI/CCF Part 10.

39 *Evening Independent*, 5 April 1944.

40 Georgia Hale to Ivor Montagu, 6 January 1978, BFI/IVM Item 326.

41 All quotes above via *Milwaukee Journal*, 29 December 1944.

42 *Pittsburgh Press*, 30 December 1944.

43 *Spokane Daily Chronicle*, 21 December 1944.

44 *Time Magazine*, 17 August 1953.

45 Joseph Scott later considered the opportunity of using Chaplin's visa problems in 1952 to increase this fee. James O'Callaghan to James McGranery, 17 October 1952, LOCDC/JMG Box 79 Folder 1.

46 Charles J. Maland, *Chaplin and American Culture: The Evolution of a Star Image* (London, 1989), 207; my emphasis.

47 *Los Angeles Times*, 3 June 1943 and syndicated widely thereafter.

48 Maland, *Star Image*, 213–20.

49 *Evening Star,* 20 February 1953.

50 Within BFI/IVM Item 324.

51 Feuchtwanger to Chaplin, 11 March 1947, University of Southern California [USC], Lion and Martha Feuchtwanger Papers [FEU] Box C1-b, c. 16–19.

52 Feuchtwanger–Chaplin letters, 25 March and 27 December 1947, USC/FEU, Box C1-b, c.16–19.

53 Oona Chaplin to Lou Eisler, undated 1947 letter, USC/Hanns and Lou Eisler Papers [EIS] box 2.

54 L.B. Nichols Memorandum, 12 May 1947, FBI/Hanns Eisler file [HEF] Part 8.

55 Ibid.

56 SAC to J. Edgar Hoover, 20 November 1946 and 26 September 1952, FBI/HEF Parts 4 and 9.

57 SAC to J. Edgar Hoover, 26 September 1952, FBI/FEU Part 9.

58 *The Argonaut*, 2 January 1948 clipping within NADC/HUAC/2/23/1.

59 *Washington Post*, 7 December 1946, within FBI/CCF Part 7.

60 Bungay to McGranery, 23 September 1952, Library of Congress, Washington, D.C. [LOCDC], Joseph McGranery Papers [JMG] Box 79 Folder 1.

61 Louis F. Bundenz memorandum, 21 June 1950, FBI/CCF File 9.

62 Chaplin Interview with the Immigration and Naturalization Service, 17 April 1948, within FBI/CCF File 8.

63 Robert C. Grogin, *Natural Enemies: The United States and the Soviet Union in the Cold War, 1917–1991*, (Lexington, 2001), 134.

64 Cited in Gellerman, *Martin Dies*, 155.

65 Ibid., 163–4.

66 Nixon to Hopper, 29 May 1952, MHL/Hedda Hopper Papers [HEH] f.2,522.

67 Hopper to Hoover, 7 April 1947, MHL/HEH, f.1,713.
68 Hopper to Hoover, 7 August 1947, MHL/HEH, f.1,713.
69 Cited in Charlie Spencer Chaplin typescript, 14 July 1962, FBI/CCF Part 10.
70 Georgia Hale, *Charlie Chaplin: Intimate Close-Ups* (New Jersey, 1995), 129–30.
71 *The New York News*, 12 April 1947.
72 Ibid.
73 All subsequent quotes from Robinson via this source, *American Legion Magazine*, 53/4, October 1952, from 11.
74 Steven J. Ross, *Hollywood Left and Right: How Movie Stars Shaped American Politics* (Oxford, 2011), 99.
75 Ibid., 107.
76 Original italics.

9 A citizen of the world

In 1960 Charlie's long-time enemy J. Edgar Hoover received a letter from an anonymous source suggesting that the 'TV Entertainer Groucho Marks [*sic*] be investigated as a Communist'. The evidence here was apparently clear-cut: a couple had been watching the television and a dutiful wife had recorded that 'both my husband and I understood him to pronounce "The United States" as the "The United Snakes"'. To seal the deal this concerned citizen noted that 'in his book "Groucho and Me" he speaks quite affectionately of Charlie Chaplin, who is a well known communist'.[1] Sitting in Vevey, Chaplin would probably not have known whether to laugh or cry. But the point was that Chaplin would no longer be in America to face such hysteria. As this chapter lays out, a man who spent so long shaping Hollywood would spend only a few days of the last quarter century of his life in Tinseltown, or indeed the entirety of an America that had propelled him to global stardom.

Despite, or indeed *because* of, his exile these final years were not without political engagement and Charlie would go on to make his views on the Cold War known both on- and off-screen. He would become (rather understandably) bitter at an American establishment that had cast him asunder, before, with the passage of time, old wounds could begin to be treated if not healed. For the filmmaker Jean Renoir, writing in 1953, Charlie was 'certainly the victim of an unconsidered campaign and one day the American people will discover that there may be smoke without fire'.[2] This was not quite true, but there would eventually be something of a détente between the English director and his long-time homeland.

Indeed, although they began with such controversies, these final years would see Chaplin eventually reach peace with much of the world, and it with him.

Even Lita Grey, who had much to be bitter about, conceded in an interview towards the end of her life that Charlie 'was never a Communist as they accused him of being. He just liked to talk about the things that were good for every individual, all the people of the world.' If America did not want it, she declared, there were others who would: 'His talent was too big to be confined to one nation or one culture. He called himself a citizen of the world – and of humanity. And he was.'[3] In a sense this had always been Chaplin's theoretical position: internationalism trumped patriotism. Yet it now had a very practical dimension. This chapter, therefore, begins by outlining the circumstances in which his physical exile from America, and his leap into 'the world', began.

The Tramp leaves America

As someone who never assumed American citizenship, Chaplin was always on shaky ground when uttering his controversial political opinions. As early as 1917 Section 3 of the US Immigration Act allowed 'the following class of aliens [to] be excluded from admission to the United States'. A long list of potential exclusionary conditions followed, ranging from medical reasons to various acts of criminality. But also on the list were those 'who teach disbelief in or opposition to organized government' or who were 'affiliated with in any way' organisations that did similar. Few could genuinely have argued that Charlie Chaplin was advocating the violent overthrow of the American government but on the above – open-ended – definitions of illegal activity he had more cause for concern. As with the Mann Act on so-called White Slavery, there was enough room to go after Chaplin.

In 1950 Congress passed the McCarran Act, enacted over the attempted veto of President Truman who felt it made 'a mockery of the Bill of Rights and of our claims to stand for freedom in the world'.[4] Harry Truman himself, by way of context, held the reasonable position of being a fan of Charlie the comedian but not Chaplin the man. Writing to his wife Bess in June 1950, he told her 'we had a very old Charlie Chaplin [film] which is just

as funny and just as pathetic as it was in the early days. Wish
I knew nothing about him.'[5] Thanks to the McCarran Bill that
Truman had attempted to block, people were about to rake over
Chaplin's personal life and his politics once more, however. The
chief innovation of the new legislation was to require the registration of all communist and communist-sympathetic organisations in the United States with the Attorney General. Its tone was
harsh, as was the climate of the time. The Act stated that 'those
individuals who knowingly and willfully participate in the world
Communist movement . . . in effect repudiate their allegiance to
the United States'. Clarifying and extending previous Immigration Acts, it backed the exclusion of those 'aliens who write or
publish . . . or who knowingly circulate, distribute, print or display . . . any written or printed matter, advocating or teaching
opposition to all organized government'. Crucially, for Chaplin's
purposes, McCarran stated that 'no visa or other documentation
shall be issued to any alien who seeks to enter the United States
either as an immigrant or as a nonimmigrant if the consular officer knows or has reason to believe that such alien is inadmissible
to the United States under this Act'.[6] The passage of McCarran
meant that Chaplin's exile from the United States likely required
two components, therefore: the man himself to leave the country,
and for an Attorney General to state they had 'reason to believe'
he had or may break the terms of Act.

This all involved a heavy degree of double-speak and misno-
mer. First, contrary to later myth, Chaplin would not be 'kicked
out' of America. He would leave voluntarily and then be denied a
re-entry visa until his eligibility under McCarran could be determined. Yet like Kafka's Joseph K, it was unclear what crime he
was guilty of, and therefore what this ineligibility actually constituted. For one, the Act itself included instances of potential
repentance. Had Chaplin admitted to being a member of a communist front organisation it is possible that this would have satis-
fied the legal difficulties (his technical 'crime' under McCarran
arguably being not registering as a communist sympathiser, not
the alleged sympathies themselves). This would, of course, have
had the not inconsiderable by-product of ruining his career. But
President Truman perhaps put it best in his September 1950 letter
attempting to veto the bill. Under McCarran, a determination of a

'communist-front organization' could be 'based solely upon "the extent to which the positions taken or advanced by it from time to time on matters of policy do not deviate from those" of the communist movement'. As Truman noted, this led to the extraordinary situation whereby 'an organization which advocates low-cost housing for sincere humanitarian reasons might be classified as a communist-front organization because the communists regularly exploit slum conditions as one of their fifth-column techniques'.[7] This was no mere technical point. Included in a 1965 HUAC list proving Chaplin's involvement with 'Communist Front' organisations was the 'un-American' activity of being a 'signer of a letter to President Roosevelt "expressing appreciation of his position against discrimination and attacks upon Negroes and others".'[8] Edward G. Robinson, as we saw at the end of the previous chapter, was in this general bracket, too – although he took a distinctly different course to Charlie.

In any event, when Charlie boarded the *Queen Elizabeth* in New York on 17 September 1952 to sail to London to promote *Limelight*, he was taking a considerable risk. Three months prior he had made an application for a re-entry permit for his return, but had received no reply. With Oona wishing the children to be educated in Europe, Chaplin wrote to D.C. informing the immigration authorities that 'if they did not wish to give me a re-entry permit I intended leaving in any case'.[9] Eventually, they contacted him, asking to come by his house and question him. The inquiries included whether he had been born with 'a very foreign name' and came 'from Galicia'.[10] More difficult to parry was the question as to whether he had ever committed adultery. 'Listen,' Charlie answered, 'it you're looking for a technicality to keep me out of the country, tell me and I'll arrange my affairs accordingly.' Apparently, this was a 'question on every re-entry permit', although Chaplin's request to look up the definition of 'adultery' in the dictionary probably did not inspire the most confidence. Eventually, he settled on the legalistic reply, 'not to my knowledge'. Overall, Chaplin recalled that he 'should have had my lawyer present' but that he had 'nothing to hide'.[11]

The day after setting sail a telegram was brought to Charlie's attention by Harry Crocker. He waited until Charlie had finished his lunch with the musicians Adolphe Green and Artur Rubinstein before delivering the bad news. Charlie was to be banned from re-entering the United States unless he go before 'an Immigration Board of Enquiry to answer charges of a political nature and of moral turpitude'.[12] Understandably, he was furious. Chaplin issued a 'pompous statement to the effect that I would return and answer their charges', but swiftly resolved to liquidate his American assets as soon as possible. Arriving in London, Charlie found his old garret at 3 Pownall Terrace empty and ready to be demolished, while the centre of town was all 'American gimcracks, lunch counters, hot-dog stands and milk-bars'. 'Time,' he later noted wistfully, 'marches on.'[13] Oona soon flew home to extract from America what wealth she could from the Chaplin empire, and found that the FBI had twice interrogated Chaplin's butler Henry, 'wanting to know what kind of man I was, if he knew of any wild parties with nude girls that had gone on in the house etc'. When the loyal Henry defended his boss, 'they began to bully him and asked what nationality he was and how long he had been in the country, and demanded to see his passport'.[14]

Beyond Henry the butler, Charlie's former political allies swiftly came under officialdom's microscope. On 22 October 1952 Max Eastman was interrogated by the Immigration and Naturalization Service. The first questions, predictably enough, concerned whether Charlie had ever been a member of the Communist Party or any front organisations. Answering 'no', Eastman did, however, volunteer the information that Charlie had given him $1,000 to help with his magazine *The Liberator* – however 'this act was prompted more by personal sympathy', and neither the publication 'nor I had any affiliations with any Communist Party'. The only political remark Chaplin had made during their last meeting soon after the premiere of *Monsieur Verdoux* five years earlier was that, after the treatment of his friend Hanns Eisler, '[Charlie] thought the country was drifting towards fascism.' Women – and therefore the issue of 'moral turpitude' – was, however, a different matter. If Charlie had been reticent in their conversations to go beyond the odd outlandish political comment, Eastman reported that Chaplin had 'related to me intimately and apparently with great candor, the inside story of some of his relations with girls'. These tales had 'left me with a distinct impression that while he is romantic and impressionable and easily swayed by emotions, a great deal of the scandal about him is due to efforts to participate in his fame, or get hold of his money, on the part of girls or mothers'. Gold diggers or not, it seems unlikely that these dalliances helped Charlie's case.[15]

Viewed from the office of Attorney General James McGranery this heavy-handed approach was all perfectly logical. Within McGranery's papers at the Library of Congress, Washington are contained several letters from prominent sources expressing unfettered joy at Chaplin's exclusion. Thomas M. Madden, District Judge in New Jersey, wrote to tell him that 'if I ever had a desire to hug a man it was when the news broke about your actions regarding Charlie Chaplin'.[16] Walter Annenberg, the publisher (of *TV Guide*) turned American Ambassador to London (1969–74), wrote to 'personally congratulate' McGranery and noted that '[Chaplin] has hardly earned the continued hospitality of this country'.[17] Many of the letters endorsing McGranery's position emerged from Chaplin's adopted state of California.[18] For example, a J.K. McDonald, a Drive-In owner in Stockton, told McGranery that 'if and when you are masterfully able to keep him out good and all, your name will be honored by those many loyal American actors who have long doubted Chaplin's loyalty'. Such animosity he claimed on account of personal experience. In 'about 1933' Charlie and Paulette Goddard had patronised McDonald's previous Los Angeles establishment called None-Such Foods. Passing by the two in animated discussion at one of his restaurant tables, 'I heard Chaplin mention the name: "The United States." There was an intermission of perhaps a minute when I did not hear the intervening remarks, but as I then moved closer behind them, I heard him distinctly say this (coupled with his usual skeptical smirk): . . ."They have never learned how to run this country".'[19] For McDonald, this was 'further proof that Chaplin never did have any respect for Citizenship in America'.[20] All in all, McGranery's evidence base certainly varied in its quality.

Once Charlie was back in the UK, one kind letter came from his old friend Winston Churchill – once again back in Downing Street in his final spell as British Prime Minister. Having watched *Limelight* in his private cinema at Chartwell, he wrote to 'congratulate you cordially on this masterpiece which we all watched with mingled emotion and amusement'. Noting Charlie's recent troubles, the Prime Minister stated he was 'glad you have had such a cordial welcome home in your hard pressed land'.[21] For whatever reason – arrogance, forgetfulness, or the simple passage of time – Charlie never bothered to reply. Perhaps he was too embarrassed to tell Churchill he soon planned to leave England. Believing the Swiss climate to be more 'suitable for the children' than dreary English rain, the Chaplins soon purchased the Manoir de Ban in the village of Corsier, about sixteen miles from Lausanne. It was in the beautiful scenery and low-tax environment of the Swiss Alps that Charlie would live out his final days.

The latter factor was probably as important as the former. As we saw in Chapter 3, Chaplin had always been a reluctant US taxpayer at best. This no doubt emerged from his general antipathy to the type of 1920s Republican who had got to spend much of his contribution to Uncle Sam. With the halcyon days of Roosevelt's New Deal receding into memory, by January 1953 the White House was again in Republican hands in the shape of President Dwight D. Eisenhower. Exiling Chaplin may or may not have been good politics, but it was hardly good economics for the United States. In 1959, Charlie's fortune was estimated to be in the region of one hundred million dollars. The previous year his tax contribution to the Swiss authorities had been just $25,000 – it would have been about half a million dollars in the US.[22]

Tax aside, Switzerland was clearly something of a relaxing change from the turmoil of his final years in America. Writing to the leftist screenwriter Clifford Odets in September 1953, Charlie told him 'what a luxury it is, after living 40 years in that God forsaken country of yours – it's like just being out of prison'. Compared to America, 'Europe is taking on a new look, both politically and culturally . . . Living here gives one a perspective on the body politics of the world and America stands out like a large ugly boil.' In Europe, Chaplin could still 'rub elbows with illustrious' people but, most importantly, 'politically one can agree to disagree with all of them – so different from the master minded Americans that want to castrate you for having an opinion that differs from theirs'.[23] He would later refer to America as a 'police state', and in April 1953 he announced that he had given up his residence status in the States.[24] It seemed like there would be no going back.

Charlie and the Cold War

If the world could not start getting along a little better, it seemed like there may not be an America he could go back to. As friends such as Upton Sinclair knew, the prospect of nuclear warfare haunted Chaplin for decades.[25] For Charlie, 'the scientists are more irresponsible even than the politicians. They have created this Frankenstein and placed it in the hands of third rate men.'[26] These third-rate men would initially be the Americans, and Chaplin never could 'forgive mankind for [both] the Nazi atrocities and for the atom bomb'.[27] Making such moral equivalence between the orchestrated planning of the Holocaust and the undoubted horrors of Hiroshima and Nagasaki rather typified the type of comment that often landed Chaplin in trouble. While Chaplin 'did not assume to know the answers to the problems that threaten peace', he did 'know that nations will never solve them in an atmosphere of hate and suspicion, nor will the threat of hydrogen bombs solve them'.[28]

This filtered through to his later cinematic work. In *Monsieur Verdoux* (1947), the mass-murdering title character had used his final courtroom peroration to compare his 'amateur' killings with those achieved through the professionalisation of warfare seen in recent years. Later, in *A King in New York* (1957), a recurring theme would be the evil of using nuclear technology for making and dropping bombs instead of generating energy for domestic usage. On the latter film, the *Daily Mail* reported that 'Chaplin the matchless clown' was 'fighting a losing battle against Chaplin the pompous pamphleteer'.[29] But, as Charlie noted, 'if we are to survive this atomic age, we must have the bigness to criticize the folly of our ways'.[30] It was because of this that Chaplin declared he was never a Communist, but rather a 'peace monger'.

In practical terms this meant continuing to encourage détente between West and East, even when unpopular. In 1956, during a trip to London (see Figure 9.1), Charlie and Oona were invited to a party hosted by the Soviet Embassy at Claridge's Hotel. Seeing Soviet leader Nikita Khrushchev from a distance when guiding the Chaplins inside, a furtive bell-hop cried, 'Khrushchev! Charlie Chaplin!' At which point Khrushchev and Bulganin turned around, faces lit up. Through an interpreter pleasantries were exchanged,

Figure 9.1 After his exile from America, Charlie returned to his home-land and re-visited the impoverished sights of his youth. Here he is, pic-tured with fourth wife Oona, looking over 1950s London. Big Ben and the Houses of Parliament can be seen in the background.

Courtesy of Bridgeman Images

and the Chaplins were offered some vodka: Charlie 'thought the pepper-box had spilled into it, but Oona loved it'. Khrushchev's visit had so far proved an astonishing success and Chaplin told him 'it had come like a ray of sunshine . . . [and] given hope for peace to millions throughout the world'. The following evening, dining at the Savoy, the Chaplins happened to meet the Churchills. Winston, retired as Prime Minister the previous year, told Charlie that he too had 'always got along well with Khrushchev'.[31]

Just as Khrushchev could bring greater sympathy towards the Soviet Union among some Western power brokers, Charlie's views on capitalism also became tempered. There was the odd moment of social awkwardness here, as Harry Crocker witnessed first-hand. In one public speech, Charlie noted 'the great improve-ment in England since his previous visit in the 1930s. [Yet] as the Tories were now in power, there was a slight rustle in the room when Charlie spoke of the obvious health of the children and their dental care.' Charlie claimed that 'if socialized medicine is responsible [for such improvements], there is something to be said for it!' Since 'socialized medicine had been introduced by the Labour Party' in the form of Britain's new National Health Service (NHS), Crocker recalled that 'it was a touchy subject'.[32] As Winston Churchill had previously remarked, however, in British political terms Charlie was essentially a Labour man. Yet even during the 1950s he was able to muster positive words for the now Conservative-run Britain. In 1954, Charlie thought back to his London trip of 1921 when he

> saw the shops and they weren't filled – a lack of goods and so forth – and I saw the children, their little pasty faces, and there was a certain sort of melancholy about the place. It was after the war . . . But coming back I look at the children now and they have rosy cheeks and they have confidence and they are full of vitality and virility, and it is very heartening. And I feel this in the gait and tempo of the town. I feel there is a resurgence, something has happened to England. You've suffered and tightened your belt . . . But there has been a resurgence.[33]

This was perfectly logical (quite aside from Chaplin's positive social connections to previous British Conservatives, such as the Astors). The era of Chaplin's exile from America in 1952 until his death in 1977 would almost precisely mirror the period of Britain's 'post-war consensus'. This would see a period where the two major British parties would differ on the pace of travel towards more interventionist government with greater social spending, but broadly agree on the overall trajectory. As such, even with the Conservatives in Downing Street, it was easy for Chaplin to drop in frequent references to 'my country' and the 'gratitude' he felt towards the British people for having not abandoned him. After the turmoil of Washington politics, Westminster certainly seemed more sedate.

Yet if his homeland's politics were beginning to converge, global diplomacy could be a more divisive affair. Having seen his removal from the States and his obvious bitterness towards the country in the years that followed, the Soviet Union was keen to award the man several plaudits. In a sense this helped fulfil the prophecy the American right had previously been making – not only was Chaplin soft on Russia, it was soft on him, too. In June 1954 Moscow broadcast a lengthy eulogy to Chaplin that decried the 'dark forces in America who are preparing for a new war' that were waged against him. On the other hand, they claimed, 'All the champions of peace accepted the undesirable alien as their son.'[34] A year earlier the Soviet-sponsored World Council of Peace had awarded Charlie Chaplin its International Peace Prize. Accepting the prize in a simple ceremony in the garden of his home at Vevey, Chaplin released a statement proclaiming that 'the desire for peace is universal. To promulgate a demand for peace, whether from east or west, I firmly believe is a step in the right direction.'[35] As the French publication *Défense de la Paix* put it, 'Chaplin's struggle has no other goal than the reconciliation with men and the world.'[36]

It took time for this world view to incorporate America, however. When Jerry Epstein flew into Geneva to see the Chaplins on 20 June 1953 he found Charlie livid at the news that the Americans had executed the Rosenbergs the previous day. Convicted of passing atomic secrets to the Soviets, husband and wife Julius and Ethel had been sentenced to the electric chair. Epstein recalled that 'Charlie wept when he talked about it. Then he would explode: "Those bastards: how could they murder these people?" Whether the Rosenbergs were guilty or not did not enter into the argument. It was the humanity of the thing.'[37] As to his own exile, late at night he ranted to Epstein that 'he wasn't going to be blackmailed by fascist gang, or bend down on his knees to anyone when he'd done nothing wrong'.[38] Slowly but surely he began to craft an artistic answer to his critics – the last time he would attempt to make a political picture.

The result was 1957's *A King in New York*, which saw Chaplin take various pot shots at America. Certainly, this film incorporated many jokes that said more about Chaplin's age than his political leanings – in one scene Charlie's King Shahdov is unable to hold a conversation because of the noise of a nearby band and reacts in a grumpy manner. The political content of the film was even less subtle. For one early reviewer of the film, 'nearly all craftsmanship has been thrown away. It's a raw pamphlet indicting the American way of life . . . All the bile of Chaplin's estrangement from the States gushes out.'[39]

The plot sees King Shahdov of some non-specific land flee the bloody coup that is taking place in his own country to seek refuge in America – 'one of the minor annoyances of modern life is a revolution'. Along the way Shahdov acquaints himself with 1950s reality television, rock and roll and sensationalist cinema (the coming attractions Shahdov sees include one entitled 'Man or Woman?'). Yet it is Shahdov's visit to a progressive school where the children are encouraged to develop their individuality that really saw Chaplin lay the politics on thick. There Shahdov encounters a young boy named Rupert (played by his son Michael). Hearing that Rupert is reading Karl Marx, Shahdov asks him, 'Are you a communist?' 'Do I have to be a communist to read Karl Marx?' says the indignant boy. 'That's a valid answer,' replies the King. Rupert then goes on to launch something of a Chaplinesque manifesto, 'I dislike all forms of government . . . leadership and government is political power and political power is an official form of antagonising the people.' It was not all the 'bile' the critical press asserted, but it could be something of a bore.

Later it transpires that Rupert's parents are to be hauled before the House Un-American Activities Committee as potential communists. Shahdov himself faces the same accusation, although forwards the line that 'royal communist? The expression is a reductio ad absurdum.' The real-life Charlie said much the same thing about his own wealth when it came to charges of being a Bolshevik sympathiser. Eventually, Rupert is tricked into indicting his own parents, with a HUAC interrogator commenting that 'we consider Rupert a hero and a real patriot'. As David Robinson points out, whereas 1921's *The Kid* had seen Charlie unite with a young actor to deliver a tale of physical deprivation, *A King in New York* meditates on personal morality, and the consequence of individual decisions. On one level this is certainly true, but while *The Great Dictator* and *Monsieur Verdoux* had just about been able to get away (artistically) with their rampant moralising, the views of 1957 Charlie bled too overtly on to the screen. *A King in New York* just was not a good enough film.

Later plaudits and a final reconciliation with America

Other than making one truly terrible film, *A Countess of Hong Kong* (1967), Charlie's final years were full of plaudits, composing music to overlay some of his silent films and, ultimately, something of a reconciliation with America. *A Countess of Hong Kong* is barely worth re-telling. It had lain in Charlie's scrapbook of ideas since the 1930s and had originally been intended for Paulette Goddard. The film concerns a stateless Russian countess being assisted by an American Ambassador to flee Hong Kong and attempt to start a new life. A dreadful farce, it marked the last film Charlie would make (and briefly appear in, as a seasick steward). Two vignettes remain of some interest, however.

The first concerns Chaplin's inability to get on with Marlon Brando, his star. Brando had won his first Oscar in 1954's *The Waterfront* and was only five years away from his most iconic role as Don Vito Corleone in *The Godfather*. He was, in short, a big star who expected to be treated accordingly. Brando and Chaplin thus clashed as to who should receive greater promotion on material advertising the film. Chaplin recalled this argument in the late 1960s: 'God, in the billing, I never knew there was so much importance attached to whose name comes first [in the] title or so forth. I should think that a star that's already established wouldn't care much about that.'[40] Yet, this had not always been his position. As far back as 1919, with the foundation of United Artists, his own contract had put in writing that 'the name of Charles Chaplin shall receive "chief prominence" (and by "chief prominence" is meant that his name shall be in larger letters than, at least twice the size of, any other part of the subject matter in which his name appears)'.[41] Charlie Chaplin could be bigger than the film itself, but evidently not Marlon Brando. In the end, however, Charlie did eventually cave, and the contract specified that 'Mr Brando would receive first star billing above the title in the same size, color and prominence as the title'.[42]

Sophia Loren was different. Chaplin clearly adored her, not least because she was so stunning. In one scene Sophia asked Charlie if she could be excused from wearing her character's high heels from a dancing scene and wear flats instead. A cameraman murmured to his director his concerns about a potential break in continuity: what would the audience think if Sophia's footwear suddenly changed between shots? Despite being such a perfectionist on set, Chaplin told him, 'Don't worry. When Sophia's on screen no one looks at her feet.' This was followed by a comedic sigh. 'If only I were sixty again.'[43] Given that Oona would give birth to the couple's last child, Christopher, as late as 1962 (when Charlie was seventy-three) evidently his libido had not yet waned.

Before his final film he worked for many years on what became the oddly titled *My Autobiography*. Reviews for this work, when it finally arrived in 1964, were mixed. In Britain, the left-leaning *New Statesman* noted that his tone was 'less Dickensian than Chekhovian; reality is seen in a clear and tender light'.[44] Bosley Crowther in *The New York Times* was less positive, and noted that the book 'tells so little about him in certain areas that only he could reveal . . . It is too bad that Mr Chaplin doesn't tell us more about his ideas and experiences as a film-maker and how he happened to make certain films, especially "Modern Times," "The Great Dictator," and the fatal "Monsieur Verdoux."'[45] The *New Republic* pointed to the style being 'at its best . . . attractively simple. Sometimes it is coy, and occasionally it is impressively literary, presumably to prove his intellectual status.'[46] For *The Times*, it was 'fascinating if in certain respects disingenuous'.[47]

Some, like Charlie's literary agent Max Reinhardt, urged him 'to consider the possibility of publishing the book in more than one volume'. In March 1958, he noted that 'the accounts you read us from your early childhood and your life in Lambeth are absolutely first-rate and there is obviously enough material there to constitute the first volume, say up to your arrival in the United States'.[48] Reinhardt enlisted the novelist Graham Greene, also a friend of Charlie's, to try to persuade his client to re-shape the book's content, too. Greene had told Reinhardt that 'when Chaplin's feelings are personally engaged he writes admirably, and the first hundred and fifty or so pages containing his early life, his mother's insanity and his departure from England are excellent'. The problem came 'when the story shifts from Chaplin himself or concerns rather unimportant episodes of his life'. For example, 'on pages 304 and 305 we are interested in Upton Sinclair but we could hardly be less interested in the rather bad novelist Rupert Hughes'.[49] Still, in the end, sales did well enough. In its first three months more than half a million copies of *My Autobiography* had been sold.

As the years went by, the honours rolled in. Despite the relatively mundane nature of all this, Hoover and the FBI continued to monitor such awards, as subsequently revealed in FBI papers.[50] In June 1962, Charlie received an honorary Doctor of Letters from the University of Oxford. Hearing this news Chaplin's old adversary former Attorney General James McGranery caustically noted that although 'good old Charlie' may be 'more of a crowd pleaser than Dean Rusk [also honoured by Oxford the same day] . . . all of this should not add up to re-entry for the Little Tramp.' Even in the early 1960s 'an official change of heart toward Charlie might look like an official softening of our position against flagrantly immoral conduct and pro-Communist sentiment'.[51] Forgiveness took time.

Three years later Charlie was awarded the prestigious Erasmus Prize in Amsterdam. When explaining why Charlie had been awarded this latter accolade, the press release for the event noted that it was 'because he has succeeded in wrapping sorrow, disappointment and injustice so poetically in jokes and comical situations, that a message of warm human compassion has emerged which has been understood by everyone'. He 'remained the interpreter of the characteristically European hesitation between collectivism and individualism, between the absolute and the relative, between the preaching of a message and the enjoyment of laughter'. He was, in short, 'a great European and world citizen'.[52]

Many English people wanted to honour one of their most famous sons, too. In fact, the question of a knighthood for Charlie Chaplin first arose as early as his promotional tour for *City Lights* in 1931. Despite a Labour government then in office, and Chaplin spending several hours with the then Prime Minister Ramsay MacDonald (both as Labour PM, and later upon the formation of the National Government) in the course of his visit, no knighthood was as yet forthcoming for the left-leaning thinker. Given his various political problems for the next thirty years it rather looked like Charlie may miss the boat altogether.

In 1956 the British Foreign Office gave serious consideration to the question again. This resulted in a flurry of paperwork indicative both of attitudes to Chaplin and the wider atmosphere of the Cold War (certainly pre-American hostility to the Anglo-French incursion into the Suez Canal, later to topple Prime Minister Eden). One civil servant, A.N. McCleary, noted that the Americans had three specific grievances that would make a knighthood for Chaplin difficult to countenance. The first was that 'they regard him as a Left-Winger and a fellow-traveller'. Although McCleary noted that Chaplin had always denied being a communist, and

> the messages [of support] which he has sent to some of these organisations may have been in the nature of liberal gestures, he has done it so consistently over the years that he would probably have some difficulty in re-entering the U.S. on political grounds alone.

Second, there was 'the grounds of morals'. Since Chaplin 'has been married to two 16 year olds' and 'his marriage to Paulette Goddard has been criticised on the grounds that they never went through a proper marriage ceremony at all', there was a potential question mark here, too. Lastly, there was the issue of 'his income tax obligation to the U.S.' On the latter two, McCleary respectively commented, 'It is possible that he may be forgiven for the wild oats he has sown in the past' and any tax owed to the Americans 'does not concern us'. He doubted very much, however, that the Queen 'could overlook the moral charges since they are of concern to the British public [too]'.[53]

The 1956 claim saw the Foreign Office generally take a balanced view on Chaplin. Elsewhere in the extensive paper trail debating the merits of a 'Sir' Charles Chaplin, it was noted that 'the American Legion and other right wing organisations have at times been almost hysterical both [in] their opposition to the showing of his films and in their agitation to have him declared an undesirable alien'. That said, Chaplin's refusal to show 'much sense of gratitude for the material prosperity which his forty-two years in America bestowed on him' and his regular associations with the 'Communist Orbit' – including accepting the 'Communist sponsored World Peace Council [prize] in June 1954, his dinner with Chou En-lai in Geneva in July 1954 and meeting with Premier Bulganin in London in April 1956' – had not helped his cause.[54] Then US Ambassador Sir Roger Makins intervened to note that 'there was considerable danger of a British award causing unfavourable comment and even bringing disrepute in the United States on our honours system'.[55] With Chaplin only having left the US in 1952, the 1950s was not a period where the climate had yet softened sufficiently. The matter was quietly dropped.

In the wake of the more liberal sentiment of the 1960s, however, a knighthood for Charlie was back on the agenda. If The Beatles could get an MBE, why not a KBE for Chaplin. In 1969 the question was again seriously revisited, and was 'not without support' among the honours committee, even if it did not yet gain full approval. By August 1971 the British view was that 'an honour for Mr Chaplin would do no harm to our relations with the US and could indeed do some good, in liberal circles'. Since 'neither his communist affiliation nor his colourful romantic past would be seen in the same light now as in 1956', the FCO felt a revisiting of the matter was entirely possible. One official was, however, keen to stress that 'we must rely on Washington's comments', and 'if Washington thinks otherwise, I would not venture to disagree'.[56] With the general feeling that it was time to let 'bygones be bygones' politically (and morally), the only major questions were artistic.[57] Certainly, the British Ambassador to Washington Lord Cromer believed 'a lot of water has flowed under the bridge'.[58] Yet he also questioned 'whether such tardy recognition of Mr Chaplin's talents displayed so very long ago would really be desirable now'. 'As good a claim', Cromer argued, could be made for the English-born Bob Hope – whose charity work and promotion of 'friendship between the US and the UK' presented a strong case. In the event, both Hope (1998) and Chaplin (1975) would go on to become Knights of the Realm.

On 2 December 1974 Chaplin accepted 'the honor with great pleasure' and, after a bout of influenza delayed matters, eventually travelled to Buckingham Palace to receive it in person.[59] The Queen apparently told him 'that she had seen many of my films and that they had helped her a great deal'.[60] As Principal Private Secretary to Prime Minister Harold Wilson, it had fallen to Robert (now Lord) Armstrong to sign the letters conveying the Prime Minister's proposal to recommend Charlie for the honour. In the same set of New Year's honours another long-time British exile, the author P.G. Wodehouse, received his own knighthood. Today, Armstrong recalls that he was 'glad to sign the letters to Chaplin and Wodehouse . . . I was one of very many people, in other countries as well as in the UK, who had greatly enjoyed and admired their work.' As to 'the impediments that had until then stood in the way of recognition by means of a public honour, the time had come when they could and should be set aside, so that they could receive the public recognition that their achievements deserved'.[61] This seems broadly indicative, and the British honoured their countrymen with palpable relish. *The Times* called it a 'pleasure to hear of their knighthoods, which they both richly deserve'.[62]

Britain was usually loyal to her own son, but America had been a different matter. Yet even here, a couple of years earlier, Charlie had managed to make a form of peace with the nation that had so shunned him. Although billed as such, this was actually not the first time he had set foot back on American soil since boarding the *Queen Elizabeth* in 1952. In the early 1960s Charlie had taken Oona and the children on a global tour through Bali, Singapore, Hong Kong and Japan. Flying back to Europe, Charlie suddenly recoiled in horror when he saw where the plane was touching down to refuel: Anchorage, Alaska. As Michael Chaplin remembered, 'No sooner had he set foot on the tarmac than it struck him that Alaska had recently become America's forty-ninth state. He was standing on US territory!' At this point, almost like one of his films, 'he did a quick about face and tried to scuttle back into the aircraft and sweat out the two hours' wait inside the cabin'. There was no such luck – Charlie had to go through customs and immigration to the airport lounge itself. In the event, 'the duty officers' of Anchorage 'could not have been nicer'. All the same, Charlie was glad to be back in the air – 'terrified lest they take away his passport, money, socks and braces'.[63]

Charlie's gripe was always with American officialdom and not the American people. As he remarked in 1962, 'Some of my best friends are Americans. I like them . . . There are many admirable things about America and about their system too. I have no ill feeling.'[64] This was not quite true and, certainly, there was the odd flash of anger. For one, the assassination of President Kennedy in November 1963 shocked him deeply – as it did so many. Convinced both the killing of Kennedy and the subsequent murder of Lee Harvey Oswald had been engineered by 'haters', he bitterly stated, 'Thank God I am not American.'[65] This type of comment provided fodder for those continuing to monitor his activities – which still included HUAC and the FBI.

In January 1972 J. Edgar Hoover received an anonymous letter noting that 'Chaplin is to return to the United States to receive some kind of award from the American motion picture industry'. Rather confusingly, given that the American right took such pleasure at having hounded Charlie out of the country, this writer noted that 'this communist bastard turned his back on this land of ours and took millions of dollars out of this country when he went to live in Switzerland'. They concluded that 'as a red-blooded American, I want you to make every effort to keep this son-of-a-bitch out of our country'.[66] Hoover replied that this correspondent's 'concern . . . is understandable' and forwarded the comments on to the Immigration and Naturalization Service.[67]

Yet overall policy had already shifted. As Hoover's angry correspondent knew, the cinematic community was planning to invite Chaplin back into the fold. The previous March the American Ambassador to Switzerland (Davis) had 'recommended swift waiving of Chaplin's ineligibility [to enter the States] to avoid unfavourable publicity for U.S.'[68] This was eventually granted, and at the 44th Academy Awards in April 1972 Charlie received a twelve-minute round of applause prior to his receiving an honorary award for 'incalculable effect he has had in making motion pictures the art form of this century'. To some sceptics this 'honorary Oscar' merely 'help[ed] salve Hollywood's conscience'.[69] But the award presented to the 'white haired and frail looking Chaplin' proved a sweet moment indeed. 'Oh, thank you so much,' he gushed, 'words are so feeble and futile. Thank you for the honor of inviting me here.'[70] After all the glad handing and not keen to stay very long in an America he no longer recognised, Charlie returned to Switzerland as soon as practicable. Less than a month later, with Charlie's triumph fresh in his mind, J. Edgar Hoover died of a heart attack. For a man whose life had been mired in controversy and who attracted such powerful opponents, Charlie had gone on to outlive most of his enemies and see the Cold War thaw. On Christmas Day 1977, with the presents under the tree and seven of his eight children by Oona around him, the now elderly Tramp took his last breath. A great twentieth-century life reached its conclusion.

Notes

1 Redacted to Hoover, 20 June 1960, FBI/Groucho Marx File [GMF] Part 1.
2 Renoir to Vogel, 25 March 1953, UCLA/Jean Renoir Papers Box 12 Folder 3.
3 *Reading Eagle*, 20 December 1992.
4 Truman to House of Representatives, 22 September 1950, Harry S. Truman Presidential Library, Independence, Missouri [HSTPL]/ Harry S. Truman Papers [TRU].
5 Harry to Bess Truman, 3 June 1950, HSTPL/TRU.
6 Statutes at Large, 81st Congress, 2nd Session, 23 September 1950, 987.
7 Truman to House of Representatives, 22 September 1950, HSTPL/ TRU.
8 Document prepared for HUAC on Chaplin's Communist Affiliations, 25 January 1965, NADC/HUAC/RG 233 Box 42.
9 Charlie Chaplin, *My Autobiography* (London, 2003), 449.
10 Ibid., 450.
11 Ibid.
12 Ibid., 455.
13 Ibid., 457.
14 Ibid., 457–8.
15 Interrogation of Max Eastman, 22 October 1952, LLBI/Max Eastman Papers [MEP] Box 2.
16 Madden to McGranery, 22 September 1952, LOCDC/JMG/Box 79 Folder 1.
17 Annenberg to McGranery, 22 September 1952, LOCDC/JMG Box 79 Folder 1.
18 See also Steckler to McGranery, 22 September 1952, LOCDC/JMG Box 79 Folder 1.
19 Underlining in original.
20 J.K. MacDonald to McGranery, 20 September 1952, LOC/JMG/Box 79 Folder 1.
21 Churchill to Chaplin, 29 November 1952, CIN/CCA.
22 HUAC clipping, 21 July 1959, NADC/HUAC/RG 233/2/23/1.
23 Chaplin to Odets, 2 September 1953, LLBI/Clifford Odets Papers [COD] Box 4.
24 Clipped within HUAC, 29 November 1955, NADC/HUAC/RG 233/ Box 42.
25 See Sinclair to Chaplin, 20 October 1964, LLBI/UPS Box 63.
26 *The New York Times*, 6 June 1962.
27 *Los Angeles Times*, 20 September 1964.
28 Chaplin statement in *Bulletin of the World Council of Peace*, June 1954, TCC/Richard Laurence Milton Synge Papers [SYNG]/A.410.
29 *Daily Mail*, 11 September 1957.
30 1947 Press Conference note within CIN/CCA.

31 Chaplin, *My Autobiography*, 467–9.
32 Harry Crocker's unpublished memoir, 'Charlie Chaplin: Man and Mime', MHL/HRC, XV–14.
33 BBC Radio Interview, 8 December 1954.
34 *Evening Star*, 22 June 1954, clipped by NADC/HUAC/RG 233/ Box 42.
35 Chaplin statement in *Bulletin of the World Council of Peace*, June 1954, TCC/SYNG/A.410.
36 Le discours de Chaplin in *Défense de la Paix*, July 1954, TCC/ SYNG/A.411.
37 Jerry Epstein, *Remembering Charlie: The Story of a Friendship* (London, 1988), 106.
38 Ibid., 109.
39 *Washington* Post, 13 August 1957.
40 Chaplin Interview Transcript, MHL/CCI, 33.f-302.
41 Charles Chaplin's Contracts, Folder 29, MHL.
42 Marvin Meyer (Brando's solicitor) to Keith Allinson, 3 September 1965, BFI/Jerome Epstein Papers [JLE] 3/2.
43 Unidentified clipping within UCLA/George Johnson Papers [GRJ]/ Box 56 Folder 5.
44 *New Statesman*, 2 October 1964.
45 *New York Times Book Review*, 4 October 1964.
46 *New Republic*, 3 October 1964.
47 *The Times*, 28 December 1978.
48 Reinhardt to Chaplin, 21 March 1958, British Library, St Pancras, London [BL]/Max Reinhardt papers within Add MS.88987/2/15.
49 Reinhardt (quoting Greene) to Chaplin, 29 December 1960, BL/Add MS.88987/2/15.
50 E.g., 12 July 1962 memorandum FBI/CCF Part 10.
51 McGranery comments in attachment to Byron to McGranery, 18 July 1962, LOCDC/JMG Box 98 Folder 6.
52 Erasmus Prize press release, 24 June 1965, BL/Add MS.88987/2/16.
53 A.N. McCleary note, 1 October 1956, TNA/FCO/57/291.
54 FCO Research Department note, 24 September 1956, TNA/FCO/ 57/291.
55 See Morgan note, 11 August 1971, TNA/FCO/57/291.
56 R.A. Vining note, 12 August 1971, TNA/FCO/57/291.
57 As Lord Armstrong recalls to the present author (26 April 2016), 'Opinions were divided, of course, but I think that most people thought that [Prime Minister] Wilson's decision [to recommend Chaplin for a knighthood] was a reasonable one.'
58 Cromer to Stow, 16 September 1971, TNA/FCO/57/291.
59 Chaplin to J.R. Wright, 2 December 1974, CIN/CCA.
60 *The Times*, 5 March 1975.
61 Lord Armstrong to the present author, 26 April 2016.
62 *The Times*, 2 January 1975.

63 Michael Chaplin, *I Couldn't Smoke the Grass on My Father's Lawn* (London, 1966), 72.
64 *The New York Times*, 6 June 1962 via NADC/HUAC/RG233/ Box 42.
65 *Baltimore Sun*, 13 April 1964 via NADC/HUAC/RG233/Box 42.
66 Name redacted to Hoover, 26 January 1972, FBI/CCF Part 10.
67 Hoover to redacted, 3 February 1972, FBI/CCF Part 10.
68 Swiss embassy to Hoover, 3 August 1971, FBI/CCF Part 10.
69 *Montreal Gazette*, 27 January 1972.
70 *Lodi News-Sentinel*, 12 April 1972.

Conclusion

Even in death everyone wanted a piece of Charlie. The obituaries poured in, column inches were unfurled and people generally sought to lay claim to his legacy. But our conclusion's first sentence was also true in a very direct and grisly sense. In March 1978, Charlie's corpse was stolen from its burial site in Corsier, Geneva, Switzerland, by two motor mechanics. They tried to pressure Oona into paying a 600,000 Swiss franc ransom for its return, which she robustly refused. Eventually, the coffin, still in-tact, was found buried in a cornfield. Although more macabre than even *Monsieur Verdoux* may have contemplated, this bizarre episode remained oddly Chaplinesque in its sheer absurdity.

As the grave-robbers were presumably hatching their plot, they may well have caught the numerous tributes extended to Charlie across the globe. For one, Charlie's old friend Ivor Montagu would take to the pages of *Marxism Today* to urge the construction of a statue in London in honour of the Tramp. As he noted, 'the little man really was a giant', but he also reflected on the controversies that had passed. For Montagu, Charlie had never 'sold out' to the trappings of stardom: 'VIPs buzzed round him like flies as urgent to get into the picture as the tramp was in one of Chaplin's earliest films, *Kid Auto Races* . . . Could they know that his main interest in them was that of a zoologist studying animals in a game reserve?' Montagu found the final years of reconciliation, 'the Special Oscar and the "Sir"' rather nauseating – a way for the establishment to get 'the public to forgive their past behaviour' towards Charlie. There had been a standard interpretation reached of Charlie: 'He was all right once. Poor chap – starting to preach.'

Still, as Montagu knew, 'he was no Communist – for all that he had kind words to say to a *Daily Worker* seller he met in the street. He had no politics. He had no party.' Charlie's son Sydney wrote to Montagu to thank him 'for sending me your most amusing contribution to that most serious publication MARXISM TODAY'.[1]

Unsurprisingly, the mainstream press was less fawning. For the *Pittsburgh Post-Gazette* 'his private life was controversial. Criticized as egocentric, Chaplin had as many enemies as he had friends.'[2] Equally, according to the *Spokane Daily Chronicle*, the 'bitter estrangement from the United States' had been engendered by 'allegedly dangerous political affiliations'.[3] These were both no doubt accurate. All in all, most of the American press paid a good deal more attention to Chaplin's political problems than did that of his homeland, however. *The Times* in London played down such controversies and noted that 'even his later contretemps with the American authorities over his flirtations with Marxism and his staunchly preserved British nationality . . . was essentially resolved to the complete satisfaction of both sides'. In a slight barb, they declared that Buster Keaton had been a 'more subtle and imaginative filmmaker than Chaplin could ever claim to be', but also noted that 'his greatness as a clown and his crucial role in the history and serious acceptance of the cinema as an art form are certain to stand the tests of time'.[4]

It is his politics rather than his art that has concerned us, however, and certainly Chaplin's politics evolved over the gamut of that long life. In the years before the First World War he had undoubtedly taken on board something of a suspicion of 'the establishment'. The war itself then gained him his first major political enemies from the British right but also lent him a greater appreciation of the implicit contract and mutual interdependence between government and the private sector. As he came to believe more and more in his own cinematic abilities, the corollary was a fervent belief in the power of technological innovation and, in short, commercial entrepreneurialism. Henry Ford could erroneously attack him as a Jew in disguise, but this did not preclude Chaplin admiring Ford's efforts. As a pioneer of a new genre of film splitting comedy and pathos, and later the man who took on the big film companies through United Artists, Charlie was a capitalist, no question. As such, his politics took on board both leftist antipathy to 'the man' and right-leaning bug-bears concerning statist bureaucracy. He flouted the law through both ignoring prohibition and the statutory age of sexual consent. He did not pay his taxes until the threat of jail or deportation brought him scurrying to the negotiating table with the IRS. Clearly, his films portrayed a sympathetic figure from the dispossessed classes. He occasionally murmured about the Russian revolution, and no doubt admired its adventurism. But the idea that Chaplin was a communist in the 1920s was frankly ludicrous. He was either a hypocrite, a businessman or both. He wanted a Square Deal for the American worker, but not the red flag flying over the White House.

What changed him from a Teddy Roosevelt to a Franklin Roosevelt was the Depression and his particularly international perspective on it. Just as FDR drew on the best, pro-big-government brains America had mustered in the Great War to populate his 1930s administrations, so too did Chaplin reconfigure his world view. Crucially, the Wall Street Crash occurred just as Chaplin's art seemed severely under threat from the march of sound. A lurid divorce case, accusations of tax evasion and now *The Jazz Singer* had conspired to rather jolt Charlie's confidence. If he had lost his Midas touch, perhaps 'the business of America' should not be 'business itself'. And if a new broom could sweep the Republicans out of office in either Sacramento or Washington – preferably both – what should come next?

Clearly, Charlie retained a life-long antipathy for an amorphous 'establishment' – the type of invisible forces that had condemned him to the workhouse or separated him from his mother, Hannah. But what of a William McAdoo who had been so kind to him on the Liberty Bonds tour, or an Upton Sinclair whose book *The Jungle* had so moved him. What of the British consensus of seemingly reasonable men – Keynes, Lloyd George, even Oswald Mosley – who were arguing for greater state intervention? Should the state step in and apply a jolt to an economy that looked like collapsing, even if this meant bigger government in the short term? The world was changing in ways he did not fully understand – few did – but it was not time to stand on the sidelines. Most of his programme was no more radical than, for example, the British Labour Party and, in some senses, he fell victim to being an Englishman abroad. He never quite 'got' America for all the many years he lived there. His political compass and sense of the Overton Window – the range of politically acceptable options and how to shift them through reasonable discourse – was always lost somewhere over the Mid-Atlantic.

Yet for all he was 'just' a movie star and occasionally was a little politically naive, who can say that his solutions of the 1930s were particularly wrong? Germany was undoubtedly the key problem facing the global economy and, were extremism to triumph, the diplomatic scene, too. Sketching out his June 1932 memorandum on writing-off their war debt took courage from Charlie (particularly given his past reputation as a wartime 'shirker'), and no little brains to diagnose the urgency of the moment. Likewise, the exploitation of low-paid workers was indeed a massive problem across the globe – and thus the concept of C.H. Douglas's Social Credit Movement to re-capitalise the poor via state-sponsored transfer payment was hardly a ludicrous notion. And in 1933 and 1934, albeit semi-reluctantly, he did get off the fence to back the mainstream versions of limited intervention propagated by Upton Sinclair and Franklin Roosevelt. Chaplin always hated Hitler, but during the 1930s he likely preferred the capitalist-statism of Mussolini to the dead hand of Stalin. Like Keynes, Chaplin came to save capitalism not to bury it and, in this regard, he trod an interesting artistic path. In 1940 George Orwell wrote of Dickens's *Hard Times* that 'there is not a line in the book that can properly be called Socialistic; indeed, its tendency if anything is pro-capitalist, because its whole moral is that capitalists ought to be kind, not that workers ought to be rebellious'.[5] He could well have written the same about much of Chaplin's output, and indeed his personal leanings.

Any political vices, such as they were, may never have caused such controversy had it not been for the other areas of his life. It is difficult to defend Chaplin's private life: he was not someone who just liked the odd drink or even had the 'odd' affair. He was consistently an autocrat in the studio, a cad in his relationships and a sometime sexual predator of teenage girls. To do all this, and *then* elect to sleep with press baron William Randolph Hearst's mistress on the one hand and mock key figures such as film-censor Will Hays on the other took a staggering degree of disregard for any consequences. This may well have emanated from a childhood where predicting the next five minutes due to an absent father and mentally unstable mother was difficult in the extreme. But it meant that, in a sense, meeting with various communists such as William Z. Foster and Ivor Montagu and making the odd pro-Bolshevik comment was only the tip of an adventurous iceberg. Charlie lacked both a sense of consequences and a sense of grounding. He hoarded money and erected walls emotionally – as those who tried to get close to him, such as Georgia Hale, found out to their cost.

But here comes the twist. Given the shifting diplomatic picture in the late 1930s, for a brief moment, the window for such gamblers and loose cannons swung wide open. Years earlier, when Charlie Chaplin invited Winston Churchill to the set of *City Lights*, the two men were at something of a crossroads. Charlie was wrestling with the issues vis-à-vis sound already discussed, but Churchill had just been turfed out of power in Britain (he had served as Chancellor of the Exchequer from 1924 to 1929) and increasingly looked like a political irrelevance. In the years to come he and Charlie would diverge over their views on Gandhi, as the two would jovially discuss at Chartwell in 1931, and by this point Churchill seemed to have made one controversial comment too many to ever bring him back to mainstream prominence. Ironically, however, it was Hitler who resurrected both Chaplin and Churchill. And, in this regard, for all the self-regarding historiographical interpretation of a 1930s *Gathering Storm* that Winston would help entrench, it was Charlie who took the greater risk in adopting an overtly anti-appeasement stance. For all the problems that Charlie's personal anarchism and devil-may-care attitude may have brought, *The Great Dictator* was a massive historical achievement. If 1940 saw much of the world governed by maverick gamblers – Churchill, Hitler, Mussolini and Stalin – then Chaplin can certainly be added to that list in cinematic terms.

When Prime Minister Churchill and guests sat down at Chartwell to watch Chaplin's satire on 14 December 1940 few may have dwelt on the long odds of this event occurring just two years earlier. While Churchill placed what few chips he had on Chamberlain's policy of appeasing Hitler proving a failure, Chaplin had risked financial disaster, being completely cut off from 'respectable' Hollywood, and drawing the further ire of Martin Dies's HUAC or the FBI, which already found his personal life and leftist politics suspicious. In a sense the Nazis had made the fight – erroneously calling Chaplin a Jew and thereby actually going after his brother Sydney and partner Paulette Goddard. But he could have ducked the Hitler issue and made, for example, the Napoleon film he had scripted with John Strachey. But he did not. Ignoring the interventions of the British government, the tenor of his own industry (or certainly the major studios as defined by Hays's MPPDA), much of the American establishment (if not its President) and indeed the potentially aggressive actions of the Nazi regime itself, he ploughed ahead with the film regardless. In this regard, history would utterly vindicate Chaplin.

Having met with both moral triumph and disaster, Charlie henceforth resolved to treat these imposters the same. In making *The Great Dictator* Charlie had been proven right and those behind movements such as America First wrong. But they were not about to let him forget this. Risking a career was all very well, but where was the satire of Stalin? Temporary allies or not, why was Chaplin praising the Soviet regime in later years? Why was this Englishman who refused to take American citizenship pontificating on the ills of democracy at a time when America was facing such a cataclysmic struggle? And to some degree – why indeed?

As the arc of what it meant to be 'an American' changed, Chaplin did not change with it. The pragmatic thing to have done would have been to have adopted American citizenship, made a few donations to the war effort and otherwise stayed out of politics altogether. But Chaplin was no pragmatist. This was his gift and his curse. When pragmatists were signing the Munich Agreement or joining America First, he was urging the allies to fight a war that looked like it may be unwinnable. When pragmatists had told him to make sound cinema, he had produced two back-to-back classics in *City Lights* and *Modern Times*. He had beaten monumentally long odds to have risen from his humble circumstances to become one of the most famous men in the world. What were Martin Dies or James McGranery against all that?

The issue was that the power possessed by such types was very concrete – while Chaplin's political power was charismatic and essentially ephemeral. He was assuming the risk of political endeavour without holding the offices to back it up. The accusation that somehow Chaplin was playing at politics is therefore unfair. He was taking on board huge questions of importance to millions – how to conquer unemployment, what to do about Hitler, what the balance between citizen and state should be, among others – but without the direct power to do much about them. The odd leftist comment was hardly the end of the world. Indeed, even J. Edgar Hoover had to sift through reports from agents that did 'not believe [Chaplin] to be communistically inclined . . . he became interested in the Second Front movement and went overboard in advocating it, all without knowing anything about communism or having any desire to see it in America'.[6]

When it came to his eventual fall from grace and exile from the United States, however, Charlie clearly made a rod for his own back. Praising Stalin's purges was a ludicrous position for someone already accused of Bolshevik sympathies to take in wartime America. Equally, Chaplin's personal life may well have been his own business had he stayed the right side of Californian law regarding the age of consent. The American right may have been pompous, self-regarding and indulging in a good degree of muck raking, but the point was that with Charlie they did not have far to look. With Hoover and McGranery both keeping tabs on Chaplin virtually to the day they died (in McGranery's case a good ten years after he left the job from which he had pursued Charlie), this was not about to be dropped.

As interesting a question, however, and one, given the lack of actual polling on the politics of Chaplin's films, which involves some supposition from the author, is whether Chaplin actually managed to achieve anything politically. With the great exception of playing a role – albeit limited – in helping shift American public opinion on the prospect of entering the Second World War, Chaplin's filmic output could only have a limited effect. After all, to borrow from our earlier reference to Edward VIII, the implicit lesson from Chaplin's pictures was that 'something must be done' about the poverty he depicted. In a sense this was fine, but 'what' exactly should be 'done'? What was the actual take-home message for the average American viewer? It was here that we must begin to leave Charlie's films behind and look again at the political realities in which he dealt, and the concrete solutions – vague or not – that he advocated. Charlie Chaplin was a man we may well describe as theatrical, emotional or mercurial, but to these well-worn epitaphs it is time to add a fourth, for he was equally political.

Notes

1 *Marxism Today*, March 1978 and Sydney Chaplin to Ivor Montagu, 20 March 1978 via BFI/IVM Item 323.
2 *Pittsburgh Post-Gazette*, 26 December 1977.
3 *Spokane Daily Chronicle*, 26 December 1977.
4 *The Times*, 28 December 1977.
5 Orwell's work is readily available for free online, including via the Project Gutenberg site: http://gutenberg.net.au/ebooks03/0300011h.html#part10 (accessed 7 November 2016).
6 Memorandum for the Director, 24 June 1943, FBI/CCF Part 1.

Select bibliography

Archival collections

NB: Archival collections are listed in full during their first usage in a note in the main body of this work, and then where necessary abbreviated using the following acronyms.

Australia

Flinders Institute for Research in the Humanities, Flinders University, South Australia (FIRTH)
Motion Picture Producers and Distributors of America (MPPDA)

France

Chaplin Office, Paris (COP)
Charlie Chaplin press clippings (CCP)

Italy

Cineteca di Bologna (CIN)
Charlie Chaplin Archive (CCA)

Switzerland

Municipal Archives, Montreux (MAM)
Charlie Chaplin press clippings (CCP)

United Kingdom

As well as the privately held papers of John Strachey (**PRIV/STCH**) this
    study utilises:
Bodleian Library, Oxford (BOD)
The Society for the Protection of Science and Learning (SPSL)
British Film Institute, London (BFI)
Jerome Epstein (JLE)
Ivor Montagu (IVM)
British Library, London (BLL)
Max Reinhardt (Add MS.88987)
Cambridge University Library (CUL)
Additional Manuscripts (Add.)
Churchill College, Cambridge (CAC)
Randolph Churchill (RDCH)
Winston Churchill (CHAR)
Imperial War Museum, London
Ministry of Information First World War Official Collection (Q)
London Metropolitan Archives (LMA)
Greater London Council (GLC)
Microfilm related to Lambeth Workhouses (X113)
Minet Library, Lambeth Archives (MLA)
South London Press (FPP3) and other local newspapers
National Archives, Kew, London (TNA)
Foreign and Commonwealth Office (FCO)
Central Office of Information (INF)
Security Service (KV)
Parliamentary Archives, House of Lords, London (HOL)
William Jowitt (JOW)
People's History Museum, Manchester (PHM)
Communist Party of Great Britain (CP)
St John's College, Cambridge (SJC)
Cecil Beaton (BEA)
Trinity College, Cambridge (TCC)
Richard Austen ('Rab') Butler (RAB)
Richard Laurence Milton Synge (SYNG)
University of Reading Archive (UOR)
Nancy and Waldorf Astor (AST)
Elinor Glyn (EGN)
University of Birmingham Special Collections (UBSC)
Oswald and Cynthia Mosley (OMN)

United States of America

Charles E. Young Research Library, University of California, Los Angeles (UCLA)
George Johnson (GRJ)
Jean Renoir (JRN)
Jim Tully (JTL)
Rob Wagner (RBW)
Cornell University, Rare Books and Manuscripts Archives, Ithaca, New York (CURMA)
Konrad Bercovici vs. Charles S. Chaplin Case (KBC)
Federal Bureau of Investigation, Washington, D.C. (FBI)
Charlie Chaplin file (CCF)
Hanns Eisler file (HEF)
Groucho Marx file (GMF)
Franklin D. Roosevelt Presidential Library, Hyde Park, New York (FDRPL)
Franklin D. Roosevelt Official Files (OF)
Harry S. Truman Presidential Library, Independence, Missouri (HSTPL)
Harry S. Truman (TRU)
Hoover Institute, Stanford University, California (HOOV)
Elizabeth Churchill Brown (ECB)
News Research Service (NRS)
George Sokolsky (SOK)
Library of Congress, Washington, D.C. (LOCDC)
James McGranery (JMG)
Lilly Library, Bloomington, Indiana (LLBI)
Clifford Odets (COD)
Upton Sinclair (UPS)
Los Angeles County Superior Court (LACSC)
Lita Grey-Charlie Chaplin Legal Papers (LGLP)
Margaret Herrick Library, Academy of Motion Pictures Library, Los Angeles, California (MHL)
Valeria Belletti (VLB)
Louise Brooks (LBP)
Charlie Chaplin Scrapbooks (CCS)
Charlie Chaplin Interview (CCI)
Harry Crocker (HRC)
Hedda Hopper (HEH)
National Archives, Washington, D.C. (NADC)
House Un-American Activities Committee material (HUAC)
Richard Nixon Presidential Library, Yorba Linda, California (RNPL)
White House Central Files (WHCF)

Sam Houston Research Centre, Liberty, Texas (SHRC)
Martin Dies (DIES)
University of Houston, Texas (HOU)
Julian Huxley (JHX)
University of Southern California, Los Angeles, California (USC)
Lion and Marta Feuchtwanger (FEU)
Hanns and Lou Eisler (EIS)
Vanderbilt University, Nashville, Tennessee
Cornelius Vanderbilt IV
Wesleyan University, Middletown, Connecticut (WES)
Gorham Munson (GMN)

Correspondence

Lord Robert Armstrong (Principal Private Secretary to Prime Ministers Heath and Wilson) kindly provided thoughts on Chaplin's 1975 Knighthood to the present author.

Published sources

The bible of Chaplin studies remains the biography written by David Robinson, *Chaplin: His Life and Art* (London, 1992). That said, in the decades since Robinson published his volume (originally in the mid-1980s) Chaplin's 'Life' and 'Art' have seen significant engagement from historians. Two more recent works that anyone seeking to analyse Chaplin must consult are Kenneth S. Lynn, *Charlie Chaplin and His Times* (London, 1998) and Charles J. Maland, *Chaplin and American Culture: The Evolution of a Star Image* (London, 1989), both of which consider the man outside the film studio. Elsewhere, Joyce Milton, *Tramp: The Life of Charlie Chaplin* (London, 1996) remains a controversial (and mostly negative) account, but a worthwhile read. For those interested in the intersection of movies and politics generally, Steven J. Ross, *Hollywood Left and Right: How Movie Stars Shaped American Politics* (Oxford, 2011) is a modern classic.

For Charlie the man, the relevant chapter in Alistair Cooke's *Six Men* (London, 2008 edn) is crucial, although perhaps overly sycophantic. Max Eastman, *Great Companions: Critical Memoirs of Some Famous Friends* (Toronto, 1959) does not pull as many punches. The testimony of Lita Grey (Jeffrey Vance ed.), *Wife of the Life of the Party* (London, 1998), understandably does not cast Chaplin in the best light. Ivor Montagu, *With Eisenstein in Hollywood* (Berlin, 1967) gives an interesting narrative of Chaplin and the broader atmosphere of early 1930s Hollywood.

Meanwhile, Chaplin's own writings display his political and artistic lean-ings often enough. Perhaps regrettably, we must be fairly reliant on *My Autobiography* (London, 2003) for the early years. It is a good read – but one wonders about the veracity in some areas (partly due to difficulties of memory). *My Trip Abroad* (London, 1922) sees Chaplin dabble in politi-cal commentary but as something of a starry-eyed observer. By the original 1930s publication of *A Comedian Sees the World* (Missouri, 2014) (edited by Lisa Stein Haven), we are dealing with a different, more serious operator.

Finally, this study rests heavily on original archival material, but some interesting samples of the Chaplin collection have recently been published in Paul Duncan (ed.), *The Charlie Chaplin Archives* (London, 2015). This is an exceptionally well-presented, if pricey, volume.

Other cited published works

Peter Ackroyd, *Charlie Chaplin* (London, 2014).

Theodor W. Adorno and Max Horkheimer, *Dialectic of Enlightenment* (London, 2010).

Peter Bailey, 'Conspiracies of Meaning: Music-Hall and the Knowingness of Popular Culture', *Past and Present*, 144 (1994), 138–70.

Tino Balio, *United Artists, Volume 1, 1919–1950: The Company Built by the Stars* (Wisconsin, 1976).

Michael Ball and David Sunderland, *An Economic History of London, 1800–1914* (London, 2001).

Gregory D. Black, *Hollywood Censored: Morality Codes, Catholics and the Movies* (Cambridge, 1996).

Charles Booth, *Life and Labour of the People in London*, Volume 1 (London, 1902).

Marc Brodie, 'Free Trade and Cheap Theatre: Sources of Politics for the Nineteenth-Century London Poor', *Social History*, 28 (2003), 346–60.

Louise Brooks, 'Charlie Chaplin Remembered', *Film Culture*, 40 (Spring, 1966), 5–6.

Richard Carr and Bradley W. Hart, *The Global 1920s: Politics, Econom-ics and Society* (London, 2016).

Larry Ceplair and Steven Englund, *The Inquisition in Hollywood: Politics in the Film Community, 1930–1960* (Berkeley, 1983).

Colin Chambers, *Here We Stand: Politics, Performers and Performance – Paul Robeson, Charlie Chaplin and Isadora Duncan* (London, 2006).

Charlie Chaplin, *My Life in Pictures* (London, 1974).

Michael Chaplin, *I Couldn't Smoke the Grass on My Father's Lawn* (London, 1966).

Christian Delage, *Chaplin: Facing History* (Paris, 2005).

James Denman and Paul MacDonald, 'Unemployment Statistics from 1881 to the Present Day', *Labour Market Trends* (January 1996), 5–18.

Martin Dies, *The Trojan Horse in America* (Washington, D.C., 1940).

Thomas Doherty, *Hollywood and Hitler 1933–1939* (New York, 2013).

Jerry Epstein, *Remembering Charlie: The Story of a Friendship* (London, 1988).

Alan Fischler, 'Dialectics of Social Class in the Gilbert and Sullivan Collaboration', *Studies in English Literature, 1500–1900*, 48/4, The Nineteenth Century (Autumn, 2008), 829–37.

Eric L. Flom, *Chaplin in the Sound Era: An Analysis of the Seven Talkies* (London, 1997).

Waldo Frank, 'Will Fascism Come to America?' *Modern Monthly*, 8 (1934), 465–6.

Ian Gazeley and Andrew Newell, 'Poverty in Edwardian Britain', *Economic History Review*, 64/1 (2011), 52–71

William Gellerman, *Martin Dies*, (New York, 1944).

Martin Gilbert, *The Churchill Documents, Never Surrender, May 1940–December 1940, Volume 15* (London, 2011).

Alan G. Green, Mary Mackinnon and Chris Minns, 'Dominion or Republic? Migrants to North America from the United Kingdom, 1870–1910', *Economic History Review*, 55/4 (2002), 666–96.

James Greenwood, *A Night in the Workhouse* (London, 1866).

Adrian Gregory, *The Last Great War* (Cambridge, 2008).

Robert C. Grogin, *Natural Enemies: The United States and the Soviet Union in the Cold War, 1917–1991* (Lexington, 2001).

Georgia Hale, *Charlie Chaplin: Intimate Close-Ups* (New Jersey, 1995).

Kyp Harness, *The Art of Charlie Chaplin: A Film-By-Film Analysis* (London, 2007).

Owen Hatherley, *The Chaplin Revue: Slapstick, Fordism and the Communist Avant-Garde* (London, 2016).

Theodore Huff, *Charlie Chaplin: A Biography* (London, 1952).

Patrick Joyce, *Visions of the People: Industrial England and the Question of Class 1848–1914* (Cambridge, 1990).

Buster Keaton, *My Wonderful World of Slapstick* (New York, 1960).

Walter Kerr, *The Silent Clowns* (London, 1975).

Stanley Lebergott, *The Measurement and Behaviour of Unemployment* (Washington, D.C., 1957).

Mary McKinnon, 'Poverty and Policy: The English Poor Law, 1860–1910', *Journal of Economic History*, 46/2 (1986), 500–2.

Adolphe Menjou, *It Took Nine Tailors* (New York, 1948).

Libby Murphy, *The Art of Survival: France and the Great War Picaresque* (New Haven, CT, 2016).

James L. Neibaur, 'Chaplin at Essanay: Artist in Transition', *Film Quarterly*, 54/1 (2000), 23–5.

Max Pemberton, *Lord Northcliffe: A Memoir* (London, 1922).

David Robinson, *Chaplin: The Mirror of Opinion* (London, 1983).

Steven J. Ross, *Working-Class Hollywood: Silent Film and the Shaping of Class in America* (Princeton, 1998).

Wolfgang Schivelbusch, *Three New Deals: Reflections on Roosevelt's America, Mussolini's Italy, and Hitler's Germany, 1933–1939* (New York, 2006).

Arthur M. Schlesinger Jr, *The Coming of the New Deal*, (Boston, 1958).

Miranda Seymour, *Chaplin's Girl: The Life and Loves of Virginia Cherrill* (London, 2009).

Upton Sinclair, *I, Governor, And How I Ended Poverty* (Los Angeles, 1934).

Henry M. Stanley, *Through the Dark Continent* (Dover, 1988).

Kevin Starr, *Embattled Dreams: California in War and Peace, 1940–1950* (Oxford, 2003).

Gareth Stedman Jones, 'Working-Class Culture and Working-Class Politics in London, 1870–1900; Notes on the Remaking of a Working Class', *Journal of Social History*, 7/4 (Summer, 1974), 460–508.

John Strachey, *The Coming Struggle for Power* (London, 1932).

John Street, 'Celebrity Politicians: Popular Culture and Political Representation', *British Journal of Politics and International Relations*, 6 (2004), 435–52.

J. Lee Thompson, *Politicians, the Press and Propaganda: Lord Northcliffe and the Great War* (Kent, OH, 1999).

Parker Tyler, 'Kafka's and Chaplin's "Amerika"', *The Sewanee Review*, 58/2 (1950), 299–311.

Ben Urwand, *The Collaboration: Hollywood's Pact with Hitler* (Cambridge, MA, 2013).

Doctoral theses

Suzanne W. Collins, *Calling All Stars: Emerging Political Authority and Cultural Policy in the Propaganda Campaign of World War I* (PhD thesis, New York University, 2008).

Jack D. Meeks, *From the Belly of the HUAC: The Red Probes of Hollywood, 1947–1952* (PhD thesis, University of Maryland, 2009).

Jack Rundell, *The Chaplin Craze: Charlie Chaplin and the Emergence of Mass-Amusement Culture*, (DPhil thesis, University of York, 2014).

Sarah C.J. Street, *Financial and Political Aspects of State Intervention in the British Film Industry, 1925–1939* (DPhil thesis, University of Oxford, 1985).

Michael R. Weatherburn, *Scientific Management at Work: The Bedaux System, Management Consulting, and Worker Efficiency in British Industry, 1914–48* (PhD thesis, Imperial College London, 2014).

Other important works

Although not directly cited in this volume, the following works also deserve due acknowledgment. Kathryn Cramer Brownell's Showbiz Politics: Hollywood in American Political Life (Chapel Hill, NC, 2014) provides an excellent sweeping overview of the relationship between celebrity and the politics of Washington DC. Likewise, Donald Critchlow's When Hollywood Was Right: How Movie Stars, Studio Moguls and Big Business Remade American Politics, (Cambridge, 2013) takes the story into the Reagan era and beyond. Nahuel Ribke's A Genre Approach to Celebrity Politics Global Patterns of Passage from Media to Politics, (Basingstoke, 2015) takes the story worldwide, from Argentina to Israel. Doubtless the election in 2016 of a celebrity as President of the United States will invite further considerations in the years ahead.

Index